A BLACKMAILER AT FROGMORE

A BLACKMAILER AT FROGMORE

The Adventures of Queen Caroline's Ghost

James Travers

AMBERLEY

In gratitude to Dr Amanda Bevan, for leading me to
The Claustral Palace;
a suitable subject for lockdown.

First published 2022

Amberley Publishing
The Hill, Stroud
Gloucestershire, GL5 4EP

www.amberley-books.com

British Library Cataloguing in Publication Data.
A catalogue record for this book is available from the British Library.

ISBN 978 1 3981 0658 1 (hardback)
ISBN 978 1 3981 0659 8 (ebook)

1 2 3 4 5 6 7 8 9 10

Typesetting by SJmagic DESIGN SERVICES, India.
Printed in the UK.

Contents

17 July 1830

For the New Police it was an exercise in what they had just begun to call 'the prevention of crime'. Thomas Quick of J Division followed the suspect – a tall, handsome Irishman of most respectable appearance – from his low lodging house in King Street, Kensington Square, until he reached the new bridge at Hammersmith. He seemed to pause for reflection. Here at Hammersmith his exalted patron, Queen Caroline, had received those hundreds of loyal addresses at the time of her 'trial'; here she had died surrounded by her few remaining friends, some less loyal and enduring than he had been; surrounded too by charred manuscripts, the inspiration for some of his own most successful works.

Already memories of the queen were fading. Her vengeful husband had ordered her house to be torn down, to erase all trace of her should he ever pass along the river that way as King George IV. Now he too was dead, and the succession had fallen on his unsuitable brothers, hastily cajoled after years with accommodating mistresses outside the scope of the Royal Marriages Act into rigid, respectable unions firmly within its bounds.

The pace of the suspect quickened, tired as he was, given that he had walked to London from Carlisle the week before, tailed all the way by the Home Secretary's agents. He hastened along the tow path by the river into Barnes, avoiding Barn Elms – though the delicious possibility of stopping there to murder his rival as Caroline's ghostwriter, William Cobbett, that hypocritical sergeant of the 54th Regiment, may have occurred to him. Then on through Mortlake to Kew Green, where Thomas Quick's superiors knew a murder was likely to be committed. The victim was to be Ernest, Duke of Cumberland. Many people wanted the duke dead, but this man had his own particular literary and financial motivations.

The suspect, as the nation would soon learn at his Old Bailey trial, was the author of letters threatening the life of the duke, and of the blackmailing manuscript *Osphia, Or the Victim of Unnatural Affections*,[1] which he sent to the duke and which had not been returned. Its contents were so terrible that they could not be discussed openly, though they were the cause of long discussions at the Duke of Wellington's cabinet meetings. Wellington described the manuscript as 'an atrocious libel upon the King and upon the whole royal family, in particular Princess Sophia and the Duke of Cumberland', which gave the game away a little. Europe was convulsed with revolutionary fervour that summer. Could this incendiary manuscript supply the spark that would set Britain ablaze? Could the author be tried without the contents of the manuscript becoming known?

Thomas Quick watched as his quarry moved across the green to the duke's house. After some conversation with a figure in the doorway whom Thomas Quick could not identify, he walked briskly towards the residence of the duke's *aide-de-camp*, Colonel Poten. After a long conversation, the suspect, whistling merrily, with coins in his hand and a spring in his step, strolled towards the Coach and Horses hotel.

Thomas Quick waited, feeling a thirst come upon him, but did not follow. His orders were to observe and only to confront the suspect if he seemed intent on committing an offence. Still, the officer of the law watched with some admiration. For a penniless outsider who had just spent his sixtieth birthday alone and in obscurity, the suspect seemed oddly confident and well connected.

Introduction

As is all too well known, Harry and Meghan, Duke and Duchess of Sussex, felt they had to make a choice between their relationship and their official role. They are not the first royals to face that dilemma. In the press, parallels were quickly drawn between their sudden announcement that they were 'stepping down as senior royals' and the abdication crisis involving King Edward VIII and Wallis Simpson, but the issue goes much further back. The memorable headline 'King's Moll Reno'd in Wolsey's Home Town' reminds us that Wallis Simpson obtained her divorce in Ipswich, birthplace of Cardinal Wolsey, and through him came the parallel with Henry VIII's 'Great Matter', his divorce from Catherine of Aragon and the religious cataclysms that followed. It is quite impressive, looking back, that readers of the popular press in New York in 1936 were expected to be able to recognise these subtle connections with events four hundred years earlier; newspaper vendors in the United States might struggle to find many new customers on the back of that kind of headline today.

To the relief of American journalists, in the case of the Sussexes, the most striking historical parallels with their predicament are more recent, much more direct and just as intimately bound up with North America, in fact with the creation of the United States itself. The couple's chosen marital home, at least when they were in Britain, was at Frogmore Cottage, on the royal estate near Windsor. Given the history of the place, it was a very odd choice for them to have made. Princess Eugenie, to whom the cottage has now passed, described it as an ideal place to bring up a family. That might be the view of an estate agent, but it is not the verdict of history. Frogmore has been at the centre of the tension between love and royal duty since the royal family first acquired property there in the 1790s. Then it was a semi-rural retreat for King George III's daughters, supervised by their mother, Queen Charlotte, a place to escape the temptations of court and the attentions of suitors. It was a sanctuary, or perhaps a prison, in which to preserve the princesses in a state of celibacy until suitable matches could be made for them within the terms of the Royal Marriages Act, which since 1772 had placed legal restrictions on royal matches. Frogmore soon became known as 'the Nunnery'.

Frogmore at least offered the Sussexes safety from media intrusion, which they have found difficult to bear – when it was not wanted, anyway. In the time of Queen Charlotte and her daughters there were no photographers with long lenses, but there was definitely a flourishing press. Indeed, perhaps what brings the royals of two hundred years ago closest to those of today is the way they attempted to manipulate opinion through the media and the way in which the media, in turn, used them. Perhaps the biggest difference between the Hanoverians and the Windsors is the perceived political importance of the monarchy and the royal children themselves. Then, the great and the good of both government and opposition were often to be found camped in formation, divided between the princesses' beloved brother George, Prince of Wales (later George IV) and his deeply unloved wife, Caroline of Brunswick. There was widespread agreement among both loyalists and radicals that, for better or worse, the fate of the family was inextricably linked to the fate of the nation, and that the power to make and unmake governments still lay with them. At that time, with the French Revolution fresh in public memory, any royal bedroom farce seemed to threaten real tragedy. A serious scandal might provide the spark to topple the established political order. Alongside the factional fighting around the royal couple was a battle in print. This was conducted by an army of pamphleteers, caricaturists and even novelists, who blackmailed the government with threats of revelations about the royal marital circus, and who were alternately bribed, threatened, turned and suppressed with stupendous sums routinely promised and sometimes actually paid, through the Treasury Solicitor and Privy Purse.

Caroline had arrived from Brunswick in 1795 as part of a theoretically ideal match under the terms of the Royal Marriages Act. She was Protestant and impeccably royal, being her prospective husband's first cousin. The rapid failure of her relationship with Prince George made her a natural focus for the political opponents of her spouse. Her cause was championed by many of the leading figures of the day, at various times. She suspected, rightly in most cases, that they found her politically useful rather than a just cause in her own right. Her growing sense of powerlessness and of being used, by her supposed friends as much as by her enemies, made even Caroline herself resort to the threat of blackmail. George III's favourite daughter, Princess Amelia, later confirmed that Caroline had threatened to 'blow the roof off the Nunnery' when she discovered that she herself was being investigated. She would expose the strange goings-on of the lovers, suitors and guards of Amelia and her sisters at Frogmore if she were not exonerated by the investigation's report. Could the blackmailer at Frogmore really be the woman destined to be queen herself?

Queen Caroline's Ghost

Two hundred years ago, on 7 August 1821, Caroline Amelia Elizabeth of Brunswick-Wolfenbuettel, the estranged wife of King George IV, died at Brandenburg House in Hammersmith. Though it was summer, the fireplaces had blazed with incriminating letters and manuscripts that she had thought it wise to deny to posterity. Among the papers smouldering in the grate were said to be her memoirs, detailing her adventures since her arrival in England and giving her impressions of the royal family and its members. These no doubt came with her excellent, if not very regal, powers of mimicry, which enabled her to give hilarious renderings of the eccentricities of the family in her own inimitable style at dinner parties.

Her last will and testament desired that her coffin should bear the legend 'Caroline, the injured Queen of England'. Some wags were so unkind as to attach significance to the fact that she had not taken the opportunity to proclaim herself 'the innocent queen of England', since her moral conduct had been the subject of public debate as well as official investigation for much of her married life. Perhaps hers was a more honest assessment, for while she might not have been entirely innocent, she had certainly been injured by the behaviour of her husband, who was was very far from guiltless. Characteristically, though, her wording was slightly clumsy, as if the 'injured' queen were not dead at all, but simply resting after an accident and that after a well-earned lie down she might emerge to take revenge on her husband at last. In one important sense, she has done so; Queen Caroline's ghost haunts the monarchy.

After years of being bribed to stay away, Caroline turned up uninvited to her husband's coronation in July 1821. Motivated by a sense of personal injustice, she threatened to wreck the pomp and circumstance of the occasion and claim her rights as queen. How many times since have failed royal relationships and the friction between love and duty threatened to upset the ceremony of monarchy at some crucial time? We have only to go a generation back from Prince Harry to find parallels between his parents, Charles and Diana, Prince and Princess of Wales, and the disastrous couple who held those titles two hundred years earlier. The parallels are not exact – not least because Prince George seems to have had another wife as well as a mistress when he acquired his princess – but with Caroline, the precedent was set.

Caroline's memoirs and readily bestowed confidences were a shadowy but constant threat. Her mocking letters, intended to be seen only by her mother, were read by those to whom she entrusted them and were used against her by her enemies. She, in turn, could use the vulnerability of correspondence to her advantage and allow her letters, or letters much like them, to appear in epistolary novels written by her friends, to give her side of the story. The Royal Marriages Act was designed to prevent 'misalliances' with outsiders of low rank who risked bringing the monarchy into disrepute, and its opponents argued that it prevented royals from marrying for love and instead encouraged loveless political marriages with a narrow group of Protestant royal families to whom the Hanoverians were already related. The chances of an unhappy marriage in these circumstances were high, and an unhappy insider was arguably more dangerous to the family than an outsider who had married for love. Caroline, it was feared, was the unsuitable match who knew the family all too well. She knew things that could bring her husband down.

The Adventures of Captain Thomas Ashe

Thanks to the bonfires at Brandenburg House, we do not have Caroline's story as she was reputed to have written it herself. She did not circulate it, but instead left it to a real specialist in that art, the handsome Irishman we left in the Coach and Horses on Kew Green in 1830. He was her favourite author and one of her favourite Irishmen, and he was known as Captain Thomas Ashe.

Ashe was Queen Caroline's ghostwriter, and not just in works designed to advance her cause in the corridors of power and make some tidy hush money on the side. He was the author, more or less authorised, of her defence of her conduct following the 'Delicate Investigation' of 1806, the official account of whose proceedings were so incendiary and sinister it became known simply as *The Book*. Ashe's apologia in the form of letters from Caroline to her daughter Charlotte, called *The Spirit of the Book*, took advantage of the delay in publication of *The Book* and the public appetite for its sordid details, and ran to several editions in 1811. In fact, it was so successful it spawned an abridgement, *The Spirit of the Sprit*. In *The Spirit of the Book*, we learn the extent of Caroline's relationship with the handsome Irish officer Captain Browne, who is only hinted at in other sources but who was well known to his comrade Thomas Ashe. After the phenomenally successful *Spirit of the Book*, Ashe was known to be working on a scandalous and revelatory work about the princesses at Frogmore: *The Claustral Palace*.

The adventures of Captain Thomas Ashe will take us through his relationship with Caroline at the court of Brunswick. There is also her affair with Captain Browne and their proposed elopement to Ireland, an act of rebellion against the constraints of political marriage engineered by their mutual friend Lord Edward Fitzgerald. Debt and a series of seductions then oblige Ashe to embark on a career in North America first as a fur trapper, then as a fossil hunter and finally as a political journalist just as Washington establishes itself as the capital city of a new nation state. Ashe had travelled in hope of finding a freer, more democratic society, but he soon returned. He claimed this was a result of disillusionment with what he found across the Atlantic – not to mention a personal falling-out with Thomas Jefferson – but perhaps he needed the foibles of British society, in particular its indiscreet royalty and aristocrats, to feed his peculiar literary career. His relationship with Caroline continued and intensified after her disastrous marriage to the Prince of Wales, culminating in the humiliation and farce of the Delicate Investigation. Our story will continue to follow Ashe's career during Caroline's exile and return, all the way up to her death. His campaign of blackmailing novels and satirical journalism had a terrifying effect on later governments, causing panic in the corridors of power.

The Claustral Palace

The haunting theme of the royal role being incompatible with a normal relationship, the Gothic spectre of the Frogmore nunnery and the threat of scandal and blackmail, when love and power are in conflict, are brought together by Ashe's *The Claustral Palace*. This is the book that would have 'blown the roof off the Nunnery', as Caroline had threatened, if it had not been acquired by government agents and supressed. In a neat irony, the Treasury Solicitor, the government's chief agent in suppressing seditious literature, has preserved the novel among his papers. Once thought to be a myth, it has languished for the two centuries since Caroline's death, alongside a host of papers relating to the suppression of works. In its full title, it is *The Claustral Palace, or Memoirs of the Family: A Political Romance upon the Royal Marriage Act of Denmark*. Despite this Danish pretence – a slightly feeble attempt to protect the author from charges of a direct attack on 'the family' – *The Claustral Palace* is set at 'Toadmore'.

The three packed volumes of *The Claustral Palace* detail the secret lives and loves of the children of George III and the youthful indiscretions of the king himself, taking the form of letters from George's third daughter, Princess Elizabeth, to her cousin and sister-in-law Caroline. The novel details the frustrations and melodrama of the Nunnery and the Gothic horror of daily life for the princesses, guarded by savage dogs and victims of their mother's constant suspicions. It reveals the identities of their secret lovers and the predations of their unsuitable tutors and official suitors. What harm could this book have done if it had not been suppressed? How important and how vulnerable was the monarchy? What powers did the state have to combat seditious literature, and how did it use them and why? Thomas Ashe, for his part, always seemed confident his work would meet with commercial success or an official bribe rather than court action.

Kew, Madness and Manuscripts

In another neat irony, the manuscript of *The Claustral Palace* along with the associated papers of the Treasury Solicitor and the law officers of the Home Department are now to be found in The National Archives at Kew. A researcher there is only a ten-minute walk from the palace and gardens that were a favourite home of the Royal Family, and from Kew Green, where George III was walked by his minders in his madness. The green was also to be the scene, so the prosecution at the Old Bailey alleged, for the intended murder of Ernest, Duke of Cumberland by Captain Thomas Ashe for failing to return his blackmailing manuscript *Osphia, or the Victim of Unnatural Affections.*

The government sadly appears not to have preserved that manuscript after it was suppressed, but it still left screeds of panicked official correspondence in its wake, also now at The National Archives. *Osphia,* and Ashe's threatening letters, occupied long cabinet meetings during the Duke of Wellington's ill-fated government as revolution spread across Europe in the summer of 1830, but its location is a mystery after it found its way to the duke's 'strong closet' at Downing Street. Like Caroline's letters, Ashe's manuscripts might be fragile, but they had a lasting and terrible power. By 1830, Ashe was up against new forces beyond even his ability to control or even manipulate. Sir Robert Peel and the New Police were now in a position to soothe the panic of the royal family and senior law officers. There was no need to negotiate with Ashe as a gentleman blackmailer to be bribed and threatened; they could move Ashe on or detain him in a corrections house as the vagrant and beggar he admitted he had become.

Ashe was perhaps the most prolific and adaptable of a brigade of prolific and adaptable writers brought into the conflict between the Prince Regent and his wife, but he did not stop once Caroline was dead. Unlike most blackmailers, he was a genuine confidant of the royal and noble women about whose lives he wrote, and who generally provided him with his information. He had a knack of winning people over and earned the confidences, friendly advice, encouragement and gentle admonishments not just of his scandalous sources but also of prominent figures who might have been thought too busy or too superior to deal with him, from Lord Edward Fitzgerald to Lord Byron. The mostly unlikely range of men (they were nearly always men) sought to give him moral advice. Even at his Old Bailey trial, aged sixty, he was a tall, dapper Irishman 'of most respectable appearance' despite his war wounds plaguing him and with his spirit broken by years of grinding poverty. Though he had a prose style and social skills beyond those of a jobbing hack, he lived by his own confession 'a life of literary prostitution perhaps unparalleled in the history of letters'. It is this disreputable scribe, and in particular his role as the blackmailer at Frogmore and the author of *The Claustral Palace,* the cause of so much official panic, who is the subject of this book.

Dramatis Personae

The Royal Family

George III (1738–1820)
Framer of the Royal Marriages Act

Caroline (1768–1821)
'The lovely, suffering Princess of Wales'

George, Prince of Wales (1762–1830)
'George was ever in pursuit of adventures, to bring Virgins into distress and violate women of condition'

Frederick, Duke of York (1763–1827)
'A soldier, changeable and arrogant and unaffected by any gentle ideas'

William, Duke of Clarence (1765–1837)

Princess Charlotte (1796–1817)
The Patriot Princess

Charlotte, Princess Royal (1766–1828)
Later Queen of Wurttemberg, 'the senior recluse'

Edward, Duke of Kent (1767–1820)
'Abject insignificance'

Augusta (1768–1840)
'She was in an undress composed of Carnation-Taffety stained with Indian figures'

Elizabeth (1770–1840) — Narrator of *The Claustral Palace*

Ernest, Duke of Cumberland (1771–1851) — Later King of Hanover; 'a tea table general'

Augustus, Duke of Sussex (1773–1843)

Adolphus, Duke of Cambridge (1774–1850)

Mary, Duchess of Gloucester (1776–1857)

Sophia (1777–1848) — 'The victim of unnatural affections'

Amelia (1783–1811)

William Frederick, Duke of Gloucester (1776–1834)

Nobility

The Duke of Northumberland — Patron of Captain Thomas Ashe

The Duke of Wellington — Prime Minister

Lord Edward Fitzgerald (1763–1798) — Friend and patron of Captain Thomas Ashe

Lord Byron (1788–1822) — Correspondent and patron of Captain Thomas Ashe

Mary Cole, Countess of Berkeley (1767–1840) — *The Persecuted Peeress*

Sylvester Douglas, Baron Glenbervie (1743–1823)

Judith Noel, Lady Milbanke (1751–1822) — Byron's mother-in-law (from 2 January 1815)

John Perceval — Viscount Perceval, later 4th Earl of Egmont

Lady Brigit Perceval (d.1826)

Frances Villiers, Countess of Jersey (1753–1821)

Prime Ministers, Blackmailers, Law Officers, Authors and Others

William Adam (1751–1839)	Politician and advocate
Captain Thomas Ashe (1770–1835)	Late ensign of the 83rd Regiment, tutor in languages to the ladies of the court of Brunswick, author
William Draper Best, 1st Baron Wynford	
Sir Richard Birnie (*c.* 1760–1832)	Police magistrate
Francis William Blagdon (1778–1819)	Newspaper editor and author
Sir Nathaniel Conant (1745–1822)	Bookseller and magistrate
John Edward Conant (1777–1848)	Magistrate
John Singleton Copley	1st Baron Lyndhurst, Lord Chancellor
Edward Drummond	Civil servant, victim of assassination
Richard Edwards	Printer of Paternoster Row and author
Sir Francis Freeling Bt (1764–1836)	Secretary of the Post Office
Timothy Joseph Haydn	Author and agent
JC Herries	Private secretary to Spencer Perceval
Edward Law, Baron Ellenborough (1750–1818)	Judge
Edward Law, Earl of Ellenborough (1790–1871)	Politician
H. C. Litchfield	Treasury solicitor

W. Lindsell	Bookseller of Wimpole Street
George Maule (1776–1851)	Litchfield's assistant as solicitor to the Treasury, later Treasury Solicitor himself
Spencer Perceval (1762–1812)	Chancellor, Prime Minister and blackmailer
William Playfair (1759–1823)	Statistician and pamphleteer, inventor of the pie chart and bar graph, victim of Spencer Perceval and *The Book*, blackmailer
James Scarlett, Baron Abinger	Attorney General
Davenport Sedley	Author and blackmailer
William Vizard (1774–1859)	Caroline's solicitor
Walter Honeyford Yate	JP, MP, Parliamentary reformer, blackmailer

BOOK I

'Stupid German Tragedies'

1

The Making of
The Claustral Palace

Three major factors inspired writer and blackmailer Thomas Ashe to turn his attentions to the princesses at Frogmore. First was the peculiarity of their social situation and the constraints on their marriage choices; second was the way their story lent itself to one of the popular novel forms of the day, along with the impossibility of their being allowed to tell or even record that story themselves; third, and perhaps most important, was the way the government chose to deal with literature that threatened to reveal the private lives of the royal family, and the financial opportunities the system presented.

Life at Frogmore: Inside the Claustral Palace
The princesses' early lives passed in relative happiness before the king's first attack of mental illness in 1788–9. They were taught the standard accomplishments under a well-regarded governess, Lady Charlotte Finch, and lived in close proximity to their beloved brothers. The fragile state of the king's health became apparent just as the elder sisters – Charlotte, Augusta and Elizabeth – might have expected negotiations for their marriages to begin. Instead, on top of the legal restraints of the Royal Marriages Act, the potential effect of any alliance or relationship on the balance of the king's mental and physical wellbeing became a perpetual restraint on their movement and prospects. Marriages, particularly private ones but even dynastic matches that would take the girls away from him, might send him into a decline. Indeed, the relationship between the sedate soldier Charles Fitzroy and Princess Amelia, the king's youngest and most cherished daughter, is often said to

have precipitated the bout of illness from which George III never recovered.

The need to raise the children close to their father but not in his immediate proximity saw the queen purchase a rambling farmhouse with eleven rooms to a floor at Frogmore, which was variously known as Frogmore Farm, Amelia Lodge and, from 1792, the Great Frogmore Estate. Life in the Nunnery began in quiet if sterile happiness, but the king's health clouded their mother's moods and judgement, making their confinement more irksome than it would otherwise have been. As time passed, with the king's more frequent and sustained bouts of madness, both regime and atmosphere underwent a shift. The new circumstances darkened the queen's humour. The memory of the king's lewd remarks and aversion to her in his illness stayed with her after his recovery, and her attitude to her daughters became harsher and less forgiving. The prospect of a relapse was ever-present and lent a fragility to their happiness.

The girls' growing frustration at the limits of their lives and their inability to express and record that frustration brought outbreaks of daring and defiance in their relationships and their writing, and with this came the whiff of scandal in their letters. Thomas Ashe gives the impression of sisters whose warmth and vivacity is gradually overcome by claustral sloth. They all had youthful relationships that threatened alliances outside the scope of the Royal Marriages Act, but they were worn down until they accepted dull dynastic marriages, or no marriage at all, despite their own inclinations.

Fourth daughter Mary, considered the beauty among her sisters, and who remained remarkably free from scandal despite this advantage, is credited by Ashe with a love affair that ended when the man in question was implicated in a military disaster only two years before *The Claustral Palace* was written.

The eldest daughter, Charlotte, Princess Royal, styled by Ashe as 'the senior recluse', was set by their mother to supervise the others and was therefore considered by them to be her spy. On her side, she thought herself less free and less favoured than the other sisters were. As revealed by Ashe, her secret love was politically unacceptable to her brothers and her marriage was the stuff of caricature and gothic horror.

The second daughter, Augusta, is credited by Ashe with fierce youthful attachments that led to violent disagreements with her family and attempts to bypass the Royal Marriages Act. She remained unmarried, finally inheriting and remaining at Frogmore, taking on the spirit of the Claustral Palace. Her charitable works and benevolence were mixed with an increasing resistance to change.

Elizabeth, the third daughter, was the nearest in age to Ashe and provides his most sympathetic portrait. She had a genuine talent in art and an interest in books. With slightly more conviction than Ashe, she espoused the virtues of the rustic life. She was the most articulate of the sisters, and the most conscious and expressive chronicler of their predicament. She was probably the most determined of the sisters to find contentment in their regime, as there was for her a measure of intellectual and creative fulfilment in botany, poetry and drawing, and even in publication. She was Ashe's obvious choice as the voice of the Nunnery, and she wrote the letters to Caroline that form the basis of *The Claustral Palace*.

Sophia, the fifth daughter, was the sister who occupied Ashe's thoughts and books for the longest. Lord Melbourne thought her 'very like a gypsy' in youth; she was considered by her niece, Caroline's daughter Charlotte, to be unlike her other aunts and more likeable. She seemed to exert a rather fatal attraction for a certain kind of older man. She merits a long section in *The Claustral Palace* which goes into great detail about her love of the hideous equerry General Garth, but that book gives no hint of the relationship with her brother, which eighteen years later made her the titular Osphia, 'Victim of Unnatural Affections'.

Amelia, the youngest of the sisters and the king's favourite daughter, having supposedly contracted a venereal disease from an unqualified assistant surgeon, battled for much of her short life against a sea of ailments. Towards its end, she fostered a secret longing for General Charles Fitzroy, an even duller and more sedate soldier than Augusta's most enduring attachment.

Scandal and rumour dogged the sisters despite the restraints under which they laboured. Journals and formal record-keeping were discouraged by the queen as being potentially damaging if they fell into the wrong hands. They attempted to chronicle their lives in commonplace books called 'Memorabilia', which, Ashe says, were discovered by their mother and 'stopped at the third volume'. But their feelings had to come out somehow.

Among the princesses themselves, exacerbated no doubt by their incarceration at Frogmore and their careful preservation from usefulness, there was a frustrated confusion as to their purpose. In the fictional Frogmore which is at the heart of

The Claustral Palace, Princess Elizabeth describes herself and her fellow royal children, particularly her 'seven illustrious brothers', as 'great state puppets only to be employed for the amusement of the public',[1] a lament that has a disconcertingly modern ring to it. Their marriages should have offered alliances in Europe against Republican France and protected against the weakness inherent in a royal house settled by Parliament rather than right of inheritance. By the time the marriages came, if they came at all, they did neither.

The regency eventually allowed the sisters' beloved brother George to alleviate their plight and loosen their bonds a little, and this is the background to *The Claustral Palace*. What was the political fallout of their revelations likely to be? With the ailing king out of the picture, did it matter so much? The state certainly seemed very keen that the revelations contained in *The Claustral Palace* stayed under wraps.

In 1808, Elizabeth recorded herself and her sisters 'vegetating as we have been for 20 years', dating the period from the king's first illness. It was not a flattering description, nor was it a fruitful period. After the Nunnery finally broke up, Frogmore was pronounced 'a remarkably dull place'. It had retained the essential character – 'a frog infested swamp' – that it had held before the family had acquired it; despite all the botanical efforts of the queen and princesses, and Augusta's years of careful stewardship when the others had left, it appeared old-fashioned and overgrown. Were it not for the air of scandal hanging about the place, it was as if they had never been there.

The Royal Marriages Act: The Theme of The Claustral Palace

The injustices of the Royal Marriages Act gave Ashe the theme and moral justification for *The Claustral Palace*. Despite the evasions of the book's subtitle, 'A Political Romance framed upon the basis of the Royal Marriage Act of Denmark', the legislation that lay behind the novel and the confinement of the princesses at Frogmore was British, and still relatively new and controversial when Ashe was writing in the summer of 1811. The Act, which passed under pressure from the king and against considerable opposition in 1772, made it necessary for the descendants of George II (except those deriving from princesses married into foreign royal houses) to seek the approval of the king before marrying. Lord North, then Prime Minister, foresaw trouble with Parliament around this extension of royal prerogative and added the proviso that at the age of twenty-five someone refused permission in this way could seek to marry with the consent of Parliament instead. The passage of the bill, with the aid of bribes and threats, was immediately taken by some as encouraging adultery and fornication. There is also some question about the usefulness of the Act, since it could not help in a real constitutional crisis as the king himself was not restrained by it. Did it work? Well, only four of the king's many children had legitimate offspring.

What was an improper marriage within the terms of the Act? It does not seem to have been defined clearly, but it could include marriage to an English person, since even an aristocratic English spouse would frustrate the dynastic purpose of royal marriages and risk creating factions and splitting patronage at home. The Act followed the 'misalliances' of George III's youngest brother, Prince Henry, Duke of Cumberland, who was caught cavorting with Lady Grosvenor and was then sued for adultery by her husband. The court awarded £10,000 and £3,000 costs to Lord Grosvenor, and Henry expected the king to pay. The case, before the Court of King's Bench, attracted lots of ribald comment and, crucially for the subsequent literature on the subject, the evidence came in the form of comically amorous and badly written letters. The celebrated case furnished writers with the model and raw materials they needed; royal letters could be incriminating and highly entertaining, but they were also potentially lucrative. Despite using the 'invisible ink' of the conspirator – lemon juice or even milk – Prince Henry's letters to Lady Grosvenor betrayed him and their exhibition in court revealed the terror and impotence of the state when faced with public revelations about the errant behaviour of members of the family.

Henry's stern lecture from the king on the consequences of his actions for the prestige, not to mention the finances, of the Crown were to no avail. The following year came his alliance with Mrs Anne Horton and their disappearance to France. This second relationship was viewed by the king as being especially dangerous, not only because it was a repeat offence but because the difference in their rank was greater still. For a prince to marry a commoner in England would, the king believed, lead directly to social disorder: 'Here where the crown is but too little respected it must be big with the greatest mischiefs – civil wars would by such measures again be common in this country, those of the Yorks and

Lancasters were greatly given to intermarriages with the Nobility.'[2] Could this be true? It may seem unlikely to us, but if the king believed it then perhaps it did not need to be true to be significant. In *The Claustral Palace*, Thomas Ashe took his readers back to the Wars of the Roses, which could be argued to have led eventually to the Hanoverian monarchy: 'foreigners brought in to govern a people who could not govern themselves'.

Ironically, the king's fear of the country descending into civil war after ill-considered royal marriages was expressed in a letter to his brother William Henry, Duke of Gloucester, who, unbeknown to the king, had already married for love. His eventual confession of his marriage to Lady Waldegrave immediately challenged the terms of the Act and made 'Prince William Henry' the obvious candidate to be the dedicatee of *The Claustral Palace*. He was also a safe dedicatee as he died in 1805, six years before the book was written. William Henry 'of Denmark', as he appears in the book, was also the brother of Caroline Matilda, whose own failed marriage to Denmark's Christian VII and politically convenient death in 1775 following an affair with one of his ministers gave *The Claustral Palace* and its pretended Danish setting an added air of gothic horror. Denmark, then, was not just a convenient if rather transparent cover for Ashe's descriptions of the love affairs of the British royal family; it was a reminder of the family's connections with that royal house and the scandals attached to it.

The Royal Marriages Act was a symptom of the fragility of the succession in Britain. The Georges came from Hanover with plenty of family and the right shade of religious belief but little deep-seated loyalty and without the powers and patronage of an absolute monarchy. The king believed that scandal and 'misalliances' could destabilise the family and undermine its hold on the throne, and the French Revolution and the king's own madness intensified this sense of fragility. James Gillray's 1792 caricature *Taking Physick or The News of Shooting The King of Sweden* shows Prime Minister William Pitt bringing the news of 'another monarch done over' to a startled George III and Queen Charlotte. They are side by side on a commode, the king's bared bottom in the foreground while above him the lion of the royal arms demonstrates that he shares their terror in the traditional cartoon fashion. The vulnerability of the monarch is emphasised by his sputtered 'What! Shot! What! What! What!' in reaction to Pitt's news. These were habits of speech associated with his high emotion and bouts of madness, fits of expostulation that had begun close enough to the French Revolution for the association to work for a satirist's purposes.

The initial public reaction to the Royal Marriages Act shows that Ashe's moral objections to it were nothing new in principle, but what was powerful was the way he showed in detail its effect on the lives of the royal family through recent and hitherto secret examples in *The Claustral Palace*. The Act rendered the princesses less free and more vulnerable to blackmail than other aristocrats. They met few men save for household servants, equerries and the occasional eligible titled young British man who was nevertheless debarred to them by the terms of the Act. Their legitimate husbands – older, uglier, madder and less interested in them – sat heavily on their German thrones, waiting for international diplomacy to bring their bride to them. However, even this escape was denied to the princesses in the short term as their mother's possessiveness and their father's increasingly fragile state ensured they remained in celibate seclusion, lest their departure upset the delicate equilibrium of the royal household. In practice, this left the sisters with nothing to do but to be conventionally accomplished and unnaturally good.

Thomas Ashe's attitude to the family sets him apart from the caricaturists and writers of broadsheet verses. He shows genuine sympathy for Caroline of Brunswick and her daughter Charlotte, for Princess Elizabeth and her sisters and even for her brothers as victims of the Royal Marriages Act themselves, albeit to a lesser extent. Ashe was the insider satirist, attacking the causes of the miseries of the family, not the family or its members themselves. The establishment and its tentacles of patronage – the Thing, as William Cobbett called it – did not concern him, at least as long as he felt he might benefit from it.

How important was the monarchy to the political sphere at that time? Contemporary books of court gossip and biographies of the princesses since are prone to a continual bathos, since they juxtapose the princesses' indispositions, their drawing lessons and fan painting and the events of the French Revolution and Napoleonic Wars: 'The Queen had two things to worry about that morning, French forces had taken Holland and Princess Sophia's chilblains had worsened.' Serious socio-economic histories of the period can happily be written without the Prince Regent, or his wife and sisters, appearing in the index.

Ashe and others dealt with the reality of a royal power in decline but still perceived by the political class as very great. Caroline's lawyer Henry Brougham dismissed his client and her husband as 'Mad Mother P' and 'Prinny', which seems to a modern readership to be no more than a clear-headed view of figures who have become caricatures, but his attitude was incendiary at the time, earning him the nickname 'Guy Fawkes'. Even Brougham felt the royals were important tools in his political game, though. They were vital to politicians precisely because the real power and durability of the old order was in question. Even among the opposition, few doubted the Prince Regent's power to make and break governments, though his theoretical powers and his practical will to exercise them seemed very limited. If the monarchy had no significance, then why attack it?

Ashe ended as a relic of a previous age, dependant on the royalty he plagued. He needed the monarchy to be important for his type of literature to be lucrative. He needed it to be open and responsive to personal attack in ways a modern state is not. He also needed the Privy Purse he despised so much. Most of all, he needed the funds of the Treasury Solicitor.

Letters and Blackmail: The Form and Function of The Claustral Palace

Sylvester Douglas, Baron Glenbervie, himself a scandalous figure, considered the use of letters for blackmail almost a standard procedure in high society. On 26 October 1796, he reported the Prince of Wales giving his mistress Lady Jersey letters written by Queen Charlotte as a kind of insurance policy. This led him in turn to recall Robert Harley, Earl of Oxford, blackmailing the Duke of Marlborough with letters written to the Old Pretender. Glenbervie, in diaries that were not to be published for another century, illustrated the two sides of this aristocratic life of manuscripts: the daylight and the shadows. They were the currency of high society and the nemesis of reputation, a joy to write and a terror to lose. This was mirrored by the monarchy itself, theoretically the zenith of social aspiration and respectability but hovering precariously over the threat of scandal.

Glenbervie took immense pride in his wife's connection to Caroline as her lady-in-waiting, but he was also clear-eyed as to her faults and the potential scandal attached to a place in the royal household: 'The situation in times less revolutionary is highly respectable.' Was it the revolutionary times that made being a lady-in-waiting less respectable, or were the 'times' simply a way of looking at Caroline's personality, which had made her position what it was? Lady Glenbervie was approached in December 1807, beginning her duties in March 1808. According to his diary, Glenbervie had been pretending to be out when Caroline called on him since 1801.

Caroline's letters to her mother were betrayed to Lady Jersey and then to the Prince Regent himself; her confidences to Sir John and Lady Douglas formed the basis of *The Book*; and her confessions to Ashe and his circle became *The Spirit of the Book*. In return, Princess Elizabeth's confidences to Caroline form *The Claustral Palace*. By writing these works and others – including *The Persecuted Peeress* about the Countess of Berkeley and *The Patriot Princess* about Caroline's daughter Charlotte – Ashe was somehow controlling or at least directing the lives of his subjects. His own riotous *Memoirs and Confessions*, published in 1815 when his adventures were still very much ongoing, provides a rollercoaster ride through his own life, his powers as a writer redeeming him from the misery and disgrace of his character. Against all the odds, he managed to place a pattern and a purpose on the mischances and mistakes that littered his biography. Towards the end of his life, he lost his connections and control. With the deaths of Charlotte and Caroline and the gradual marrying off and moving abroad of the Frogmore princesses, Ashe's royal sources left him behind. Only Sophia remained, unmarried and still malleable, the subject of his final major work, *Osphia, or the Victim of Unnatural Affections*.

The marital travails of the royal family were quickly seized upon as drama for the entertainment of the public, but were they comedy or tragedy? Today it is difficult to see the individual struggles of George III's daughters as being important to anyone but themselves, but they were clearly significant enough for their treatment to be a political issue in Parliament and in the press. The gap between reputation and conduct was the space in which Ashe operated, a gap particularly wide in the case of Spencer Perceval and the next Duke of Cumberland, George III's son Ernest Augustus.

'Stupid German tragedies': The Literary World of The Claustral Palace

The poet William Wordsworth was in no doubt about the degrading effect of the kind of books Thomas Ashe wrote. In the preface to *Lyrical Ballads*, his collaboration with Samuel Taylor Coleridge, he delivered a public and magisterial denouncement of the whole genre of popular prose romances. The reasons for the explosion of sensational literature were, Wordsworth said, rooted in major social changes, the effects of which he hoped could be counteracted but which have an oddly familiar ring two hundred years later:

> For a multitude of causes, unknown to former times, are now acting with a combined force to blunt the discriminating powers of the mind, and unfitting it for all voluntary exertion, to reduce it to a state of almost savage torpor. The most effective of these causes are the great national events, which are daily taking place, and the increasing accumulation of men in cities, where the uniformity of their occupations produces a craving for extraordinary incident, which the rapid communication of intelligence hourly gratifies. To this tendency of life and manners, the literature and theatrical exhibitions of the country have conformed themselves. The invaluable works of our elder writers, I had almost said the works of Shakespeare and Milton are driven into neglect by frantic novels, sickly and stupid German tragedies, and deluges of idle and extravagant stories in verse. When I think upon this degrading thirst after outrageous stimulation, I am almost ashamed to have spoken of the feeble effort with which I have endeavoured to counteract it; and, reflecting upon the magnitude of the general evil, I should be oppressed with no dishonourable melancholy, had I not a deep impression of certain inherent and indestructible qualities of the human mind, and likewise of certain powers in the great and permanent objects that act upon it, which are equally inherent and indestructible; and did I not further add to this impression a belief, that the time is approaching when the evil will be systematically opposed, by men of greater powers, and with far more distinguished success.[3]

By the time *Lyrical Ballads* was published, Wordsworth and Coleridge had been harried out of Somerset by the attentions of Home Office agents, who were alarmed at the reputed radicalism of their circle. They toured Germany together, presumably with the opportunity to confront some of these sickly and stupid authors in person. There is an odd feel of modernity about these complaints – mass communication, the craving for sensation, and the repetitious occupations of urban life. With hindsight, it seems a rather reactionary or at least very conservative view to find in the proclamation of a radical new poetic movement. The sudden appearance of 'great national events', as if such turmoil had not occurred in previous ages, is possibly an oblique reference to the expansion of press coverage. By the 'rapid communication of intelligence', world events were becoming a mass shared experience for an ever larger literate population through the efforts of journalists like Thomas Ashe and William Cobbett, whose works were distributed nationally. It is interesting that Wordsworth felt that writers like these two, who satisfied the hourly craving for 'extraordinary incident', were dictating the form of literature and drama.

Wordsworth pointed to the degradation of the public sensibility and the prevailing style and morality of literature by 'frantic novels' and 'sickly and stupid German tragedies'. The latter refers to a popular verse form of the period, but it serves as a good description of any narrative of the events surrounding the love lives of the royal family at this time. The horror and the melodrama of these works was all too well suited to the court of Mad King George, the gothic confinement of the passionate princesses, and the punishments and callousness of their mother and governesses. Sickly and stupid German tragedies indeed, for the horror was in large part self-inflicted, played out against a background of poorly defined and understood maladies. The Germanic origin of the family was a standing joke in popular satire, which loved to depict unpopular members of it setting sail for Hanover to escape the attentions of their hostile British subjects.

We might be tempted to think that the great Wordsworth must have carried this argument and that the sickly and stupid authors began to question themselves, but this was not so. And what of the legions of writers and thinkers of 'greater powers' who would follow his lead and reform the public sensibility? Perhaps it could be argued that a less frenzied period followed in the reign of Victoria, but the lasting effect on public morals and the cultural aspirations of popular entertainments seem to have followed what Wordsworth would have regarded as a downward curve.

Wordsworth's great plea was not even accepted as accurate by a literate aristocrat like Baron Glenbervie, who agreed with his friends about the undesirable 'indignation and arrogance of the Wordsworth–Coleridge School'. Wordsworth's view was not necessarily shared by fashionable society; there was an appetite for such literature in aristocratic circles as well as among the army of bored clerks. The tide in favour of this kind of literature was unstoppable.

Which market did Thomas Ashe target? How many subgenres were there, and who patronised them? Byron wrote for pleasure and refused money for his poetry despite his debts and perpetual money troubles. Wordsworth wrote the kind of serious poetry he advocated, free from the need for aristocratic patrons and the tired poetic diction that wooed them, but he came to depend on a government sinecure for regular income, much to Byron's disgust and later, Browning:

> Just for a handful of silver he left us
> Just for a riband to stick in his coat...
> Shakespeare was of us, Milton was for us,
> Burns, Shelley, were with us,—they watch from their graves!
> He alone breaks from the van and the freemen,
> —He alone sinks to the rear and the slaves!

Ashe claimed his serious books like his *History of the Azores* and *Henry Percy or The Liberal Critic* did not repay the effort expended in compiling them; there were much more lucrative forms of writing, either through takings for a limited run or as a bribe for not publishing at all. *The Spirit of the Book* was spread by circulating libraries as well as private readers. Wordsworth's hopes on this front conspicuously failed to materialise. Indeed, there was little immediate effect as far as Thomas Ashe was concerned. Even the poet's revised preface, published in 1805, came before the beginning of the Delicate Investigation and the real frenzy about Caroline, which Ashe would find so profitable.

The epistolary gothic structure adopted by Ashe in *The Claustral Palace* was not just a conceit; it was suggested by the events and milieu he described, inspired by the love notes left in bushes at Frogmore only to be discovered by their mother rather than their lovers. The sheer repression of the Nunnery also brought such novels to mind, as did the straight gothic horror of the king's birthday, when George's erratic behaviour would make the great occasion unbearable. Letters of scandal were analogous to the children of dubious legitimacy those scandals produced. How, in the absence of modern scientific method, could their origins be proved? They were traced to their fathers by style. How else could they tell? Sophia was at the height of her affair with Thomas Garth when she supposedly conceived a child by her brother Cumberland. Such allegations were largely unprovable but likely to damage reputations regardless.

This was the environment that produced Thomas Ashe. Many of the characters we will meet lived a double life in and out of the limelight. The figures in the gilded ballrooms kept secret diaries in their darkened studies, with compromising letters in locked desk drawers as insurance. Ashe had many contacts in high society and moved among the powerful but often wrote in seclusion, in a cottage outside Bath, on the Isle of Man, or in rural Cumberland, putting the confidences of his sources to some literary purpose, usually with their consent.

Government as a Dealer in Literature: The Finances of the Claustral Palace

To many of us Spencer Perceval is a footnote Prime Minister, famous only for having been assassinated. To a good number of contemporaries, however, he was a sinister figure, wielding unprecedented political power over both the government and the monarchy. To all appearances he was a severe, upright figure of deep religious conviction, a pale lawyer dressed in black, close to power but wary of taking office for himself, suggesting the names of others for important government posts when one ministry fell and another had to be formed. Yet, here he was, Chancellor of the Exchequer and Prime Minster, Leader of the House of Commons and Chancellor of the Duchy of Lancaster. How had he done it?

A widely accepted view of his character, articulated by his private secretary J. C. Herries and echoed by his biographer, is as 'the model of a high-minded, high-principled, truthful, generous gentleman, *sans peur et sans reproche*'.[4] He was also an accomplished writer and something of a rival to Thomas Ashe as Caroline's 'ghost' until his untimely death. Robert Huish describes Perceval's 'Answer' in defence of Caroline as 'one of the finest examples of epistolary writing which the English language can produce.'[5] A more recent study finds his character more difficult to read because his conviction and high-mindedness were allied to a ruthlessness in achieving what he thought just: 'To achieve ends he decided were right, he would adopt whatever means were at hand, regardless of the consequences. That there were really no limits he had demonstrated in his defence of the Princess of Wales.'[6]

When the Prince of Wales refused to accept the implications of the Delicate Investigation's findings and placed further incriminating documents in the hands of his lawyers, Caroline threatened full publication in February 1807 to vindicate herself. As her lawyer, Perceval had first suggested publication in October 1806, though many in the opposition were against publication, including George Canning, who was implicated as one of Caroline's many possible lovers. Perceval had tried to use *The Book* as a lever 'by all the means in our power to secure some notice and attention ... which may satisfy the public'. How far short of blackmail is this? The Duke of Portland advised against publication on the grounds it might distress the king and affect his health. The king's letter of 10 February 1807 deferred receiving Caroline at court while he considered letters submitted by the prince's lawyers.[7]

Perceval's biographer Denis Gray describes matter-of-factly Perceval's extraordinary proceedings in relation to *The Book* in a way that allows us, just about, to keep our view of him as being highly moral: 'Only under pressure from the Princess did Perceval write again to Windsor Castle threatening publication within the week unless the Princess were received at court and restored to her old apartments.'[8]

Papers for the *The Book* were sent to printer Richard Edwards, then a further note reached Windsor on 5 March that publication would not be delayed beyond 9 March. On that day, a bill was introduced in Parliament on the Catholic Question, which caused the fall of the government, and Perceval became part of a new administration; the prince abandoned the Whigs and Perceval lost no time in burning the printed copies of *The Book* in his garden. Why did Perceval go to such lengths and with such speed to try to destroy all the copies of a book he had caused to be printed? Because, now that he was in power and had influence over the prince, he didn't need her anymore. There was no longer any need to risk inflaming public opinion against the family. This series of events is presented as the simple and obvious course of action for any high-minded man of principle. The new cabinet was invited by Caroline to dine with her at Montague House, but its members had no intention of continuing to champion her cause.

It is clear that Perceval's underhand tactics were well known and brought up by his political opponents, and that they hindered his attempts to form a ministry in 1809. The journal of Samuel Romilly recorded Perceval's overtures to Lord Grey and Lord Grenville. He knew they could not accept a place in a Perceval ministry, though his offer was 'not intended as an insult':

But surely no greater insult could be offered to any public men, than to suppose them so eager to be in office, that they would unite in an administration, with persons whom they had constantly represented as having supplanted them in office by a dark and disgraceful intrigue.[9]

The newspaper proprietor and author Francis Blagdon threatened publication of *The Book* in 1808 in his opposition paper *The Phoenix*, but he obeyed a government injunction not to and was rewarded with a Treasury subsidy for his loyal paper *Blagdon's Political Register*, established to counter the wild success of William Cobbett's *Political Register*. Doubts nevertheless remained in government circles about the loyalty of *The Phoenix*.

The Phoenix's editor, Thomas Ashe, thought he knew how Perceval had gained his control of the Commons and the royals. To him, Perceval was the arch-blackmailer who had gained his position and his grip on power through his blackmailing use of *The Book*. He called his own career of literary blackmail 'playing the Perceval game'. He justified his attacks on the government by citing the precedent set by the Prime Minister himself. Ashe's own version of *The Book* made him a household name.

Ashe's view of Perceval's actions was widely shared by contemporaries, including William Cobbett. It is difficult to reconcile with the public profile and official view of Perceval as an upright severe man of religious principle, but the Treasury Solicitor's papers point at Perceval very clearly as a man who had created a monster in *The Book* and then battled and bribed to control it, a man very much at home in the literary underworld rather than above it.

Perceval and Ashe not only shared tactics but also a subject: the love lives of the royals. It is entirely characteristic of the world the novel describes and the ironies at the heart of the life of its author that *The Claustral Palace* should have survived by virtue of being suppressed by the Treasury Solicitor. Perceval was then obliged as Chancellor and then as Prime Minister to buy up strayed copies and fragments of *The Book* to prevent their publication, as well as dealing with Thomas Ashe's threatened version of it. Papers of the Treasury Solicitor show the prodigious sums of money as well as time and effort spent in this endeavour. Sometimes the government seemed in control; at other times it was in a state of blind panic, usually after an interference in the process by the Prince Regent's solicitor or his own briber of writers, the Privy Purse.[10]

Ashe's autobiography, *The Memoirs and Confessions of Captain Ashe*, make pretty clear that the government's tactics were very much those of what is comfortably described as the underworld: hired hands, allegedly some of the Prince Regent's disreputable friends, were sent to relieve Ashe of his manuscript at his house near Bath. Ashe's story unfolds through secret sources who show how much the authorities at the time discuss his work and respond to it. Gradually it becomes clear that the moral outlook and tactics of the literary blackmailer and those of some of his targets were not so different, and that they recognised him not just as a nuisance but also as a particular talent they could put to their own uses. As Perceval's critics saw it, he had been corrupted by his domination of the Commons and his power in prosecuting the war against Napoleon. This in turn had financial consequences at home, which fed his unpopularity and ultimately led to his assassination.

After Spencer Perceval's death, his nephew John, Viscount Perceval and his wife Bridget, Lady Perceval, continued to fuel the campaign in favour of Caroline and Charlotte as the principal heads of a many-headed agency which Ashe called 'the Hydra', and for whom he was a prominent if problematic writer.

Thomas Ashe's literary approach combined the blackmailing techniques of Spencer Perceval with the epistolary form of the popular novel, both informed by the vulnerability of the royal family to revelations about their conduct and in particular the danger presented by their letters and confidences. After years of travel, honing his literary skills in Ireland and America, Ashe found his true purpose, and his financial opportunity, when the Prince and Princess of Wales challenged the loyalties of the family and the country by declaring war on one another.

2

Memoirs and Confessions

'The most delightful period of my life'
The Memoirs and Confessions of
Captain Ashe, ch. XXII

Looking back, it was unlikely they should ever meet. The third son of an Irish gentry family and a Brunswick princess destined to be Princess of Wales. The circumstances of their upbringing, their characters and their talents gave them something in common, but how did Thomas Ashe come to be attached to the court of Brunswick and, through that, Caroline's cousins and sisters-in-law, the princesses at Frogmore? If his memoirs are to be believed, it came about through a series of unfortunate love affairs and the good offices of Lord Edward Fitzgerald. Ashe's memoirs are disreputable, certainly, but likely to be broadly accurate for two reasons: he is not looking to protect his own reputation, and he publishes in 1815 when the stories are all fresh and the subjects of his anecdotes are still very much alive. Thanks to him, Caroline's true love, Captain Browne, comes out of the footnotes of her biography and the corners of contemporary satirical cartoons to take his rightful place at the centre of her story.

Even before her arrival in England, Caroline's life was shaped by the Royal Marriages Act. The court of Brunswick, anticipating a potential match in England, placed restrictions on her relationships not unlike those placed on her cousins at Frogmore. High-spirited like them, she bridled at the curbs placed on her ability to follow her own inclinations and tell her own side of the story in the face of the many rumours and allegations that circulated about her conduct.

James Harris, later Earl of Malmesbury, was sent to Brunswick by his friend the Prince of Wales to assess and prepare Caroline for her new life in England. Early in this endeavour, he recorded this famous view of her character:

> She has a ready conception but no judgement; caught by the first impression, led by the first impulse, turned away by appearances or *enjouement*; loving to talk and prone to confide and make missish friendships which last twenty-four hours. Some natural but no acquired morality and no strong innate notions of its value and necessity; warm feelings and nothing to counter-balance them; great good humour and much good nature – no appearance of caprice – rather quick and *vive* but not a grain of rancour. From the habits from the life she was allowed and even compelled to live, forced to dissemble, fond of gossiping.[1]

If this were an extract from a memoir, rather than a diary entry, one could accuse the earl of using hindsight to make his judgements seem prescient. There are so many positive qualities here, but they were to lead her into a lot of trouble because, though admirable in an ordinary human being, they were not suitable for a royal princess. Most of all, the description sets out clearly the kind of literary form of which she would be both the source and the subject. Like her cousins, she was raised in constraints that obliged her to deceive those who watched over her in order to indulge her warmth and love of friendship. Her quick wit and lack of scruples made her a natural mimic and satirist, but easily bestowed confidences made her vulnerable to those disposed to harm or blackmail her when friendship soured. Letters and memoirs were a natural outlet for passions, which could not find immediate physical expression, but these manuscripts too were vulnerable. They were also readily imitable by a writer like Thomas Ashe, who could produce books in epistolary form which read as if they came from Caroline and espoused her cause, but did not expose her to censure and were better spelt than her own letters were. The grain of rancour would come later. It was reported that Caroline had rebelled against her limited education in Brunswick and attended a College of Women secretly climbing out of her bedroom window at night.[2]

What we know of Caroline's early life is limited but largely confirms the account later given in Thomas Ashe's defence of her conduct in *The Spirit of the Book*. She was raised according to a regime similar to the English royals, a sheltered upbringing with an emphasis on morally upright behaviour rather than useful accomplishments. She was not bound by the Royal Marriages Act, but since the court at Brunswick had its eyes on matches for its daughters in England, they were brought up as if they were. Perhaps in both cases there was a tacit admission there is not much useful they could do with their lives even if they were not so constrained. Most importantly from Ashe's point of view was the figure of her lover in Brunswick before her marriage, a figure only hinted at in most sources, but a man well known to him, who his books would bring out of the shadows. According to her biographer, Joseph Nightingale, she was 'prevented from marrying the man of her choice, a man whose rank was not equal to hers 'a young officer who was a constant visitor, a native of Ireland'. This may be an indication that not just her seclusion and invigilation, but her love of this man, may have contributed to her failure to marry, despite frequent overtures and the keenness of her mother than she should do so. This is taken by Ashe as a source of initial fellow feeling between the Ill-starred couple George, Prince of Wales and Caroline of Brunswick. Both had been deprived of their chance of happiness by the Royal Marriages Act before their betrothal.

Her experiences made her naturally sympathetic to her cousins the princesses at Frogmore but the 'nunnery' was a step beyond that experience, an institutionalised group pining but passive. She wanted to share their confidences but she was constrained by their love for their brother, her husband, which made the relationship awkward as the marriage became bitterer. Joseph Nightingale gave his readers a little more detail about the handsome Irishman: 'Caroline herself explained her continued spinsterhood with the observation that her father preferred her to remain in Brunswick rather than marry on the Continent. But she also wrote of having been prevented from marrying the man of her choice, a man whose station was not equal to hers, so perhaps she was not eager to wed another.' It is not clear who this suitor was but a contemporary biographer referred to a 'a young officer who was a constant visitor at her father's court ..a native of Ireland... usually denominated "the handsome Irishman"'. In one martial engagement in hussar dress with a white plume floating from his cap, he was in the thick of the fray. 'Careless of life, and bent on victory, his arm scattered death and destruction around him, and he succeeded in killing the enemy commander and snatching the enemy standard. On his return to Brunswick, her Serene Highness exhibited a peculiar share and regard and solicitude.'

> That such an attachment had, at one time, an actual existence, I have no sort of doubt: that it extended to the degree of intenseness which some persons have amused the world by declaring, I am not in the least inclined to believe.

Nightingale might have believed that Ashe's account in *The Spirit of the Book* exaggerated the intensity of this early relationship and he was more prepared to concede the political necessity of the Royal Marriages Act, but he was just as clear as Ashe was, on its negative effect: 'But this much we may venture to assert, that, owing to this kind of state policy and practice, for one happy royal marriage, there are twenty of a contrary description.'[3]

Caroline's father, the Duke of Brunswick, concerned at the duchy's political and military weakness in the face of Napoleon's successes, was firmly in favour of a political marriage, instantly reinforced by the proposed match with England. Flora Fraser adds another note from another early biographer of Caroline, Robert Huish on the way the handsome Irishman came with her to England , becoming 'the stranger in the cottage' near her house at Blackheath, a mysterious figure who could not meet her openly but was never far from her. His presence, along with her marked preference for jovial rustics, led her away from the court and prying eyes. 'Calumny followed her to the cottage and in her visits nothing was discerned, but…a secret desire to escape from the prying eye of her family and the Court to enjoy the society of one to whom… her affections were already engaged.

Huish also says that Alleyne Fitzherbert, Lord St Helens was among the English visitors to Brunswick who spoke of 'stain' on Caroline's character, a fault spoken of in diplomatic circles but not written down.

> He thought the character of the Princess was such as to make it inexpedient to commit a sketch of it, and he feared that such an alliance was more calculated to ensure the Prince's misery than promote his happiness.[4]

While these early English visitors harboured doubts, Thomas Ashe emerged as part of a trusted group of Irishmen she had known in

Brunswick before her marriage, friends of her beloved Captain Browne, who supported her for her own sake rather than political advantage and appreciated her own passionate nature and skill at mimicry. They included Lord Edward Fitzgerald and after his death, the connection continued in the otherwise inexplicable relationship with his brother Henry, her remaining link to a happy and exciting time before her marriage, which according to Thomas Ashe included a planned elopement with Captain Browne.

Ashe could not emulate his friend's military prowess, though his memoirs are full of incidents of his conspicuous bravery in a doomed cause. Instead, his path to prominence came through his writing. His personal narrative and journalistic ambitions were to bring him to the notice, among others, of Thomas Jefferson and William Pitt, as a useful but potentially dangerous weapon. The king too, had a prominent if detached role in bringing about the circumstances in which Ashe could thrive. He is a benign but slightly ineffectual presence as an individual portrayed in Ashe's manuscripts, but this is not the whole story, he is the architect and the principal culprit. The Royal Marriages Act is his act, his scheme for the education and protection of his children, keeping Prince George from a military role and sequestering the Princesses. His own youthful indiscretions revealed in *The Claustral Palace*, his increasingly frequent bouts of madness, are the context for the gothic melodrama the horror of 'The Birthday' an excruciating celebration which obliges the court with all its deadening decorum, to overlook the monarch's extraordinary behaviour. He is a reluctant ally of Caroline by the time of The Delicate Investigation. He hovers over *The Claustral Palace*, sending his daughters into the power of their grotesque German husbands, unable to cope with the unintended consequences of his own actions. The effect of the Royal Marriages Act is to condemn his family to loveless unions with their cousins. Frogmore, the incubator of this curious and cruel state social experiment, is a source of sympathy for the inmates and horror at their plight on the part of both Princess Caroline and Thomas Ashe.

With the king's madness in 1788-9 came the first Regency crisis and with it, a focus on the political importance of the Prince of Wales and whom he might marry. His sisters the Frogmore princesses were never considered politically important enough to feed the caricaturists, but Caroline's confidences showed Thomas Ashe how they and she were the victims of political conspiracy.

Though less constrained than his sisters and properly educated in the business of government as the heir to the throne, George, Prince of Wales, had suffered his own deprivations. Protected from meaningful military service, he lacked a martial air, which might have appealed to his future wife. What was his job? To be good until he inherited the throne. His sisters bemoaned being separated from him at the age of seven while he was tutored in the serious business of kingship. But how serious was this role and how much influence could he have? His father had a legislative role, which allowed him to block things but not to initiate anything. His personal role seems to have been similar, to stop his eldest son from doing what he wanted to do without suggesting a useful alternative. From the first appearance of his madness, there was constant fear for the king's health. This had a profound effect on the mood and regime of the royal household, both when the bouts of madness came and afterwards. The stress and uncertainty darkened the Queen's humour. The king's lewd remarks and aversion to her during his illness stayed with her after his recovery.

Prevented by his father from doing anything useful, or anything he wanted to do, and fearful of the effect on his father's health of any conspicuous disobedience, the son was compelled to pursue his pleasures in clandestine fashion. His 'secret' marriage in 1785 to the Catholic widow Maria Fitzherbert was however no such thing and was satirised in caricatures. John Horne Tooke published 'A Letter to a Friend on the Reported Marriage' about the lack of precedent for The Royal Marriages Act. MPs, he pointed out, had no right to enforce monasticism on the king's children. This was a genuine gripe from a republican point of view. What have elected representatives to do with the love life of an unelected German? No action was taken (or possible) against the author. The lack of malice in Ashe's account of George's relationships is remarkable, given the level of popular opprobrium he attracted.

The Prince of Wales married Caroline, his first cousin, when presented with an ultimatum by his father, in one of his more lucid moments, to settle his life and his debts, his bride apparently being recommended to him by his mistress. The dreadful initial stages of their relationship and their clear ill-suitedness has been recounted many times. James Harris is our witness again for the Prince calling for brandy at their first meeting. At the marriage ceremony, the Archbishop of Canterbury asked twice if there was any just cause or impediment, looking meaningfully at the Prince.

In Ashe's sympathetic treatment, the pre-marital relationships on both sides are an initial cause of fellow feeling between George and Caroline; neither has been allowed to marry according to their own inclination and only malicious rumour undermines their mutual resolution to make the best of a marriage neither wanted.

Doing what they did best, the Prince's sisters involved themselves in the preparations for his marriage to Caroline – embroidering dresses for a proposed nuptial fete at Frogmore. Even Ashe's sympathy wanes in his narrative when George's mistress, Lady Jersey, is put in charge of Caroline's household. 'The Countess' as she is called in Ashe's *The Spirit of the Book*, he alleges, arranged the marriage to ensure George's constancy, in that the wife would be so abhorrent to him she would drive him to her. As well as his marriage to Mrs Fitzherbert, George had already had a catalogue of largely short-term relationships characterised by histrionics, threats of suicide and callous discarding. He was a Romantic in this sense at least.

Their daughter Charlotte 'an immense girl', was born precisely nine months after the marriage, though George reportedly spent the wedding night in the fireplace. She is presented in *The Spirit of the Book* as a cause of hope of a reunion between the warring parents and becomes in time the recipient of the confessional letters Ashe writes for Caroline in the book.

Famously, her father was taken with a sudden illness three days after Charlotte's birth and apparently fearful of his life, wrote a will, which left Caroline a shilling, giving everything to Mrs Fitzherbert, and removing Caroline from any role in the upbringing of her daughter. There was nothing for Charlotte either. This was followed by a mutual agreement never to have sex (with each other) again, part of 'the terms upon which we are to live' set out in a letter by her husband of 30 April 1796, which was in turn published as a prelude to the report of the Delicate Investigation that became known as *The Book*.

Lady Jersey resigned in the face of her lover's renewed attachment to Mrs Fitzherbert, her infidelities a joke to the king. The love lives of his sons could be a source of amusement as long as there were no dynastic implications. He made similar jokes about Mrs Jordan, the long-time mistress of William, Duke of Clarence; no wonder Caroline was confused in the letters of *The Spirit of the Book* by what she called 'British manners'.

Lord Glenbervie's diaries, gossipy and potentially vulnerable in themselves, are full of evidence of the power of aristocratic and royal letters and their routine use as the instruments of blackmail at the top of society. Letters given by Mrs Fitzherbert to the Queen precipitated the Prince of Wales's break with Lady Jersey; Lady Jersey herself was able to turn the Queen further against Caroline by intercepting letters to the Duchess of Brunswick containing derogatory comments. Caroline's frank and open manner meant she was quite good at eliciting and using the indiscreet remarks of others, but her own could be used against her. In his diary entry of 16 October 1796, Lord Glenbervie compared Charles II's Villiers mistress, Barbara, Duchess of Cleveland, with the Prince of Wales's Frances Villiers, Countess of Jersey, noting that Catherine of Braganza was content to become the subject of the mistress, but that Caroline was not. 'It remains however to be seen what will be the ultimate result in the present instance of a struggle perhaps as yet in its infancy.'[5] This was perhaps a salutary reminder that English monarchs had taken foreign princesses for reasons of diplomacy and rejected them in favour of domestic mistresses for many years, without the proscriptions of the Royal Marriages Act.

Weeks later, in November 1796, Glenbervie recorded that pro Queen Charlotte sentiments had been met with silence at Drury Lane theatre, when twenty years earlier they would have met with rapture. The Family were in need of a boost to their popularity. A royal wedding might have been expected to provide it, but the unhappy couple could not do so, instead their bickering and attacks on one another's reputations dragged the institution of monarchy further into disrepute. There was an element of enjoyment in the endless gossip about royal relationships and their often unlikely-sounding political significance, just as there was of the king's state of mind. Prime Minister William Pitt's maladies and his hopeless affair with Eleanor Eden at this time attracted very little coverage by comparison, though the fate of Europe hung in the balance. Perhaps his predicament was too important and not funny enough to gossip about. In 1801, Glenbervie reported that Pitt was more ill than the king.

Caroline moved to Blackheath, away from the prying eyes of the spies sent by her husband from Carlton House, but here, too, she became something of a spectacle. As Lord Glenbervie put it, 'Society took the road to Blackheath, partly out of curiosity and partly to annoy the Prince of Wales.' After her abandonment by her husband, Caroline endured a period of political isolation in which she was no longer deemed useful to any group with any hope of power. At first, Caroline's mother, the Duchess of Brunswick, insisted Caroline was included when she was invited to dine by the Family, later they also fell out and she no longer insisted. In 1799, a remorseful Prince of Wales, mad with desire for Mrs Fitzherbert, gave up Lady Jersey under pressure from the king, as the relationship was deeply unpopular. Lady Jersey turned so violently against him that she became one of Caroline's greatest supporters at her 'trial' in 1820. Therefore, she was not for very long the inveterate opponent and corrupter of her lover's wife that she appears to be in *The Spirit of the Book*.

The Delicate Investigation focussed on the prominent male visitors to Caroline at Blackheath, Sir Thomas Lawrence who came to paint her portrait, Admiral Sir Sidney Smith who fitted Caroline's favourite type of military hero and was at the centre of the allegations of impropriety made by Lady Douglas, another naval man, Captain Manby, and the politician George Canning. The blue room and the greenhouse at Blackheath gave plenty of space and her time alone with young men, plenty of scope for impropriety to occur. The revelations and the impetus for the Delicate Investigation came from Caroline's soured relationship with Lady Douglas. Caroline, as Lord Malmesbury's early assessment suggested, was in the habit of betraying confidences, sometimes to unwilling recipients, whom she subsequently annoyed. The danger was that they would then use those confidences against her.

The principal focus of the investigation was the allegation that thanks to the attentions of one of these men in one of the many more or less private rooms at Blackheath, Caroline had borne a child outside her marriage. Born in 1802, William Austin was the son of a Deptford dockworker and his wife who could not afford to raise him themselves. He was brought up by Caroline as her own and nicknamed 'Willikin'. This was charitable, but perhaps not wise, given the rumours that attached to it. Many of the rumours associated with him seem to have originated in Caroline's own hints and confidences. One was that he was the son of a Prussian prince, his later insanity if anything a proof of royal blood or perhaps the peculiarity of his upbringing. In Ashe's version of events in *The Spirit of the Book*, William Austin calls Captain Browne 'father', so 'the stranger in the cottage' was evidently a frequent and attentive visitor. In Ashe's version Willikin was presented as the son of 'Prince Louis of Prussia' and Melina, Countess of Weimar, given to Caroline for safe keeping, so the story of the Prussian princeling was in the public domain in fictional form ten years before Caroline's deathbed confession of it to Stephen Lushington in 1821. It was the job of Ashe's *The Spirit of the Book* in part to educate the English about Caroline's background and to explain her connections, attitudes and behaviour.

William Austin's birth record from Brownlow Street Lying in Hospital on 11 July 1802 was witnessed by Charles Watkin Williams Wynn, on 23 June 1803, and published in *The Book*. It was his copy of *The Book* or perhaps *The Spirit of the Book* that found its way to John Murray and from him to Lord Byron in the early months of 1813, which led naturally to the correspondence and patronage of Thomas Ashe by Byron.

There was an outbreak of royal marital rumours and mysterious births at about the time of Caroline's supposed pregnancy. On 31 March 1801, Lord Glenbervie reported that the Prince of Wales was going to declare openly his marriage to Mrs Fitzherbert. This he noted as a reversal of Henry VIII's actions, leaving his Protestant arranged marriage for his Catholic lover. Rumours that he intended to divorce Caroline when George III died circulated as early as 1802; in the event he had to wait until 1820 to attempt it.

In 1800, Caroline had reported that Ernest, Duke Cumberland, had fathered a child by his sister Princess Sophia and that the birth had taken place in secret at Weymouth. Or possibly the father was equerry Thomas Garth. Sophia had confided in Caroline, that great confider and elicitor of childbirth stories, that it was impossible to be sure which of them was father, even for her. In March 1801, Lord Glenbervie reported Sophia's 'interesting illness ... from the most authentic source' and then again in 1804, via Lady Sheffield that the child was Cumberland's, that the queen, Sophia and Princess Elizabeth had been to Blackheath, that the queen knew of the child but believed it to be Garth's. This might make Caroline the possible source for Ashe's 'Osphia, or The Victim of Unnatural Affections' in 1829, but there was no hint of this possibility in Ashe's exposure of the royal siblings' love lives in *The Claustral Palace*. Perhaps Ashe discounted it as a scurrilous rumour in 1811, but by 1829 it had become the centrepiece of 'Osphia' when Ashe had the financial and political motivation to believe it.

On 22 April 1801, Lord Glenbervie reported the king dining at Blackheath on 18 April and telling Caroline that she should consider herself a sister to Cumberland and a daughter to him. There was no disorder in his speech, no repeated, 'what, what' and he was reported to be in his senses. Princess Elizabeth was confirmed by Glenbervie to be Queen Charlotte's conduit to Caroline and the most appropriate of the sisters, therefore, to confide in her about the life and loves of *The Claustral Palace*. On 17 May 1801, Glenbervie learned from William Pitt of the reliance of the Prince of Wales on his Privy Purse, Colonel John McMahon, and his role in managing his affairs. As the king's madness came and went and the prince's marriage failed, information and disinformation flooded out about the state of the king's health and the blame for the marital discord. In today's political terms it would be called 'briefing'; cancelling the prince's engagements because of the gravity of the king's illness when the official bulletins report him improving, in a deliberate attempt to improve the chances of a Regency. McMahon was the spokesman who gave the reasons for the prince's absence and spoke for him on those occasions. The game of disclosure of letters continued when the Prince of Wales feuded with his brothers Ernest and Frederick and with the king over his father's failure to grant him a military command. He allowed their correspondence to appear in the papers through McMahon, leading the king to refer to his eldest son as 'the publisher of my letters'. On 29 June 1801, the king visited Caroline at Weymouth with princes Edward and Adolphus. The king in his madness had called for Caroline as soon as he was released by his doctors and he was reported to be 'lascivious in his addresses'. In this state, his visits and support become unwelcome and embarrassing, adding to her sense of a double standard in operation, that her behaviour was judged harshly by the Family, while that of the king and his children were not. Caroline turned down the offer of the ranger-ship of Greenwich Park, partly not to antagonise the queen, who had a traditional right to the title, but also because, as Glenbervie suggests, she was able to live 'with less restraint' at Blackheath. The king's visits to Caroline and Charlotte at Blackheath infuriated his son, her husband. She wrote graciously to him but rather dreaded the visits themselves. In his madness, he expressed his disgust with the queen and talked loudly of the mistresses he could take, noblewomen and servant girls. Little wonder he favoured his niece Caroline, who managed to combine the qualities of both.

But what of our hero himself? How did Thomas Ashe fit into the background of the disastrous marriage between the Prince and Princess of Wales, how did he come to know and write for Caroline? While Caroline evaded her uncle's advances, and the Duke of

Cumberland pursued his sister, Ashe evaded his fledgling military career and took refuge in literature. Luckily, those interested in the appearance and character of Thomas Ashe have his riotous autobiography, *The Memoirs and Confessions of Captain Ashe*, as well as the official sources charting his notorious career. Though by no means wholly truthful or accurate, his memoirs give us a clear-eyed view of his nature and his failings, since his mistakes propel the narrative. He is never still, quiet and prosperous for long. The memoir highlights the parallels between his own life and those of the great ones with whom he becomes entangled. Like them, he was not free to marry as he chose. He needed to achieve the rank of major in the army to be considered worthy to marry Angelica Brunswick Oels, one of Caroline's ladies in waiting and, according to Ashe, her confidante. His increasingly desperate attempts to gain suitable rank sent him on a series of unlikely and unmilitary adventures, since buying a suitable commission in the army seemed a much more likely route to promotion than earning it in the field of battle with the royal armies opposing Napoleon. His evolution as a writer in England, Ireland and America was built on a desperate need for cash, which might somehow revive, or supplant, his flagging military career. Eventually, the literary life took over, propelling him to a world of warring factions of journalists and cartoonists where Caroline's fate and reputation were again in his hands. The lack of real executive power of the Family and the rise of the press made journalists like Ashe suddenly, if perhaps fleetingly, more powerful and freer to act and influence events than the princesses at Frogmore and perhaps even their brothers.

In his 'Memoirs and Confessions' and *The Spirit of the Book*, Thomas Ashe sets out in some detail the progress of his literary career and its close association with the Royal Family, and particularly with Caroline as Princess of Wales and the princesses at Frogmore. The frustrations of the royal lovers faced with the barrier of difference in rank, a barrier made into a legal straitjacket by the Royal Marriages Act, were felt by Ashe himself and his books show a sympathetic drawing together of the satirist and his targets. Unlike William Cobbett attacking 'The Thing' – the corrupt establishment dispensing patronage on the basis of rank and connections – from the outside, Ashe was always on the inside extracting confidences and being the voice of his confidantes as well as making money from publication or suppression. He was at his most influential when writing pseudonymously, as the ghost of an illustrious patron, speaking in their voice. Then he was free of the faults of his personality, which make his petitions on his own account so tactless and all too often led him to fall out with those who supplied their confidences.

This period covered by his *Memoirs and Confessions* (1770-1814) *The Spirit of the Book* (1785-1810) and *The Claustral Palace* (1759-1811) gave Ashe plenty of material from which to create simple gothic horror or bodice-ripping melodrama, but this was not the course he chose. Somehow, through the farce and chaos of the events themselves and the bitter partisanship of the journalism and satire that commented on them, Ashe fashioned a coherent narrative. His books show how the lives of George, Caroline and even Ashe himself are shaped by the Royal Marriages Act and the damage this caused, both to them as individuals and to the nation.

After a brief homily on the superiority of truth over fiction, Ashe dares those great ones mentioned in the pages of his memoirs to deny their involvement with him or the truthfulness of his account, a bold thing to do as many of them were still alive at the time of publication in 1815. Ashe then tells us he was born on 15 July 1770, the third son of a gentry family, the Ashes of Glasnevin near Dublin with estates at Ashe Grove in Tipperary and Asheville near Limerick. He was proud of his ancestors and of his father but quarrelled with him, blaming his habits of temper and disposition, which he characterised as being typically Irish. His principal feuds in later years are with other Irishmen among the friends and dependents of the Prince of Wales, such as his Privy Purse, Colonel McMahon. More recently, his family could boast success in the military. Of his uncle, Major Lovett Ashe, he recorded 'there was not a man of more gallantry and spirit in the whole British army.' In the American War of Independence Lovett Ashe had been at Charleston and elsewhere, carrying letters of military importance. There was perhaps a family trait that invited confidence and led to the Ashes being entrusted with secret intelligence, whether by military commanders or aristocratic women.

Thomas joined the 83rd Regiment of foot at thirteen through the influence of his uncle, but the regiment having been raised by contract for three years for the American war, the men revolted on the cessation of the war and refused to go to India. So his regiment was disbanded before he had a chance to join it. He was sent instead to one Martin, a wine merchant of Bordeaux and from there to Marennes to a Monsieur Gaudette, whose daughter he seduces. When she dies, Ashe duels with and wounds her brother. He is imprisoned on accusations of seduction and attempted murder but is released by the father who had him committed, when the brother recovers and his offer of marriage to the sister becomes known. This episode is the first of many examples of ingratitude and treachery in the face of fortunate patronage, which becomes a pattern in his career. Her relatives he describes in rather harsh terms, they 'could not pity because they could not feel'. This is a characteristic shared by the royal princes when they are described by Ashe later in *The Claustral Palace*. His parallel life prepares him for the world of political forced marriage and the Royal Marriages Act, the foundation of his temperamental sympathy with Caroline. Shunned by his employer and his father, he is rescued by his brother Jonathan, the curate of St Andrews, Dublin, always portrayed by his younger brother Thomas as a deserving, pious man overlooked for promotion in favour of crafty place servers. Surviving letters show a rather different character and a career almost as colourful as Thomas's was.

Thanks to his brother's connections, Ashe gained a post with the Board of Education in Ireland under the Lord Lieutenant, the Marquis of Buckingham, tasked with investigating the state of Ireland's schools. Producing the Board's report as its under-secretary, Ashe first came to the attention of those in power through his writing:

> The report contained four hundred folio pages, all in my own hand-writing, and composed by me from the testimonies of the various persons who were summoned by the Board, and interrogated upon oath as to the value and utility of the schools in question. Nor was it the appearance of this report alone, which reflected credit upon me. The language was allowed to be elegant, nervous, glowing, and spirited; abounding in vigour and variety; now copious and splendid; now enlivened with apposite imagery; and again plain, concise, and acute, as the occasion demanded.[6]

When the regime changed, Ashe hoped for patronage under the new Lord Lieutenant the Earl of Westmorland, but followed his usual inclination when faced with the prospect of a reliable income, becoming a dandy. Through a mixture of misfortune and vanity he was the unknowing seducer of the mistress of his patron, at a masked ball. When they are discovered together at a house in Merrion Square, she is revealed to be Nora Stratford, the lover of the Lord Lieutenant, who promptly abandons her. She was the 'Dublin toast and the best horsewoman in Ireland' as described by Baron Glenbervie,[7] who knew the regime at first hand as Chief Secretary to the Lord Lieutenant. This episode again showed Ashe, albeit inadvertently, bite the hand that fed him. Before he leaves Ireland in disgrace, he cannot resist recording the eminent circles he moved in, including playing billiards with Lord Edward Fitzgerald, a relationship that would later become very important to him. This establishes another pattern in the memoirs, common in the lives of writers, that his facility with the written word and in conversation kept him in an elevated social circle, which would otherwise have had little time for a junior officer on half pay. It also gave him that network of connections that stepped in, or tried to, throughout his life, to preserve him from the full consequences of his own misguided actions.

This latest misadventure meant fleeing to Switzerland where he met Johann Kasper Lavater, who was then at the height of his fame for his nonsensical work on the way the faces of individuals reflected their character. Despite his politeness to Ashe, he satirised Lavater in a pamphlet as 'The Physio gnomonical Quixote'. This first satirical work established another pattern played out in later life, that anyone spending more than ten minutes with Ashe was likely to have a pamphlet produced about them if he thought there was money in it, whether they deserved it or not. After this success, he left Zurich for Lausanne and there met the historian Edward Gibbon:

> To the town of Lausanne I took an invincible dislike. It appeared to me to generate nothing but sloth and indolence; and was at the time infested by that order of Englishmen, who, having no resources within themselves, first get dissatisfied with their own home, and next go about complaining of ennui in the streets of foreign cities.[8]

Lord Byron, later Ashe's patron and hero, would be doing that very thing by the time Ashe was writing his memoir. In Switzerland Ashe has one of his brief periods of contentment and philosophical contemplation. Briefly, as Caroline did among the cheerful rustics of Brunswick or Princess Elizabeth on her farm at Windsor, Ashe espouses rural life as 'the purest form of human happiness'.

When he could bring himself to think about the world of political ambition, Ashe portrayed Edward Gibbon as the victim of place-hunters at home, men of lesser talents who were more prepared or better placed to exploit corrupt systems of political patronage. He cites as an example 'Mr Steele', Privy Councillor and paymaster-general of the army, who was the 'son of the Duke of Rutland's butler'. Furious though he seemed to be against the injustice of the neglect of Gibbon in favour of the less deserving, Ashe was not so much against the system as its beneficiaries. He was quite happy to hunt for preferment and dreamed of buying a seat in Parliament from the proceeds of suppression of his later blackmailing works. He was drawn into the corrupt network of patronage, which William Cobbett called The Thing, He then found Lord Edward Fitzgerald in Lausanne, when the energy of revolution was running through France. Lord Edward embraced that spirit entirely and gave up his title and his place in The Thing.

Ashe's connection to Lord Edward Fitzgerald may have brought him intelligence from the aristocratic families to which Lord Edward was most closely allied as he grew up, including the Dukes of Richmond. This may explain the wealth of detail about the relationship in the early 1790s of Charles Lennox and Princess Charlotte 'The Senior Recluse' of *The Claustral Palace* and the role of the compliant page, 'nephew to the Duke of Poormond' who is the agent of their love affair according to Ashe's manuscript.

In its early part, Lord Edward's career, though from a grander background, follows a similar path to Ashe's; a younger son propelled naturally into the armed forces seeing the world and forming ideas about liberty and oppression, sincere and unbending, unfitted for politics but to all appearance a raffish Irish half-pay captain with a love of women. It is possible, given his ideals, despite their difference in birth, that Fitzgerald would not shun the company of Ashe in whom he might see a younger, poorer, version of himself, whom he could guide, protect and help to form.

In Ashe's account, Lord Edward offered to take him to Brussels in his carriage on condition that Ashe first accompanied him on a walking tour in Switzerland. They see, preserved in the mountains, bodies of Burgundian soldiers killed at the Battle of Grandson in 1476, of which the Swiss seem very proud. Ashe is vaguely impressed and thinks Lord Edward will approve of this lasting testament to the victory of liberty against a powerful invader. In fact, he is shocked and horrified that the Swiss can be so callous as to take pride in such a spectacle. This leads Ashe to reflect on Lord Edward's own death and reputation. He notes, 'This noble subject is no more. He was carried off in the prime of his life and deemed a traitor to God and his country. Yet God never endowed man with a better heart than his. Blessed be his memory!'

In Ashe's version of events, Edward Fitzgerald was contracted to 'Pamela', the illegitimate daughter of the Duke of Orleans in France, who was sent by her father to a Swiss convent where Fitzgerald saves her from her vows with 'a handsome bribe' to the Abbess. When the married couple returned to Dublin it was in the company of Caroline's lover, Captain Browne and the Princess Royal, Charlotte, the 'Senior Recluse' of *The Claustral Palace*, at the beginning of 1793. Captain Browne was apparently as well known to the readers of the *Dublin Gazette* as his illustrious companions: 'Yesterday morning arrived the Princess Royal, Captain Browne from Parkgate, with the Rt. Hon. Lord Edward Fitzgerald, his Lady and sister and several other persons of quality.'[9]

Parkgate was the fashionable port on the Wirral for passage to Ireland. Without placing undue emphasis on the order in which the members of the illustrious party are named, it is quite striking that Captain Browne appears immediately after the Princess Royal and before Lord Edward himself. He seems as well-known to the readers of *The Dublin Gazette* as the lords and ladies he accompanies. There are hints in Nightingale's memoir of Caroline that her lover was a military hero who rescued the standard of Brunswick in battle, presumably motivated by his love for Caroline. Captain Ashe was not of the party because of his debts, which precluded his return: 'I had an insuperable objection to England because of my debts contracted in Ireland.'

As Lord Edward's biographer has it, the newly married couple, Lord Edward Fitzgerald and Pamela, went from the Parkgate packet boat, straight to gloomy Leinster House, the raffish half-pay officer now a committed revolutionary. Ashe was still hopeful of gaining a place in the oppressive society he ended up satirising, while Lord Edward had taken a principled stand and resigned his place in it. Captain Ashe was not one of the persons of quality arriving in Dublin. Instead, he stayed behind enjoying the comfortable patronage of Britain's allies among the German states. Through Fitzgerald's introduction, he became attached to the court of Prince Frederick of Hesse, then Governor of Maastricht, as 'a master of languages'. During his attachment to the House of

Hesse Ashe travelled to Brunswick, he says, for six weeks: 'By such means I acquired much of that information respecting the genius and character of the Princess of Wales which the reader may see embedded in *The Spirit of the Book*.'[10]

Through his own liaison (serious and enduring this time) with Caroline's 'principal companion' Angelica Brunswick Oels, Ashe is entrusted with a letter to the Duke of Brunswick and is then made a Captain and Aide-de-Camp in the Brunswickers and tutor in English language and general literature to the ladies of the Brunswick Court. This is the period Ashe refers to as 'the most delightful period of my life'. There is an implication in his memoirs that Ashe himself helped Caroline 'perfect' her English, though in *The Spirit of the Book* that role is given to her lover, Captain Browne. Ashe was part of the link between Lord Edward, Captain Browne and Caroline before she is brought to the attention of the British public as a prospective bride for the Prince of Wales.

Ashe recounted how he fought for Brunswick against France in a bad campaign, honourable but not well planned. Against his wishes, his forces withdrew at the siege of Maastricht. Then he was prevented by lack of an aristocratic title from preferment in the Prussian service, needing to become a Major in order to marry Angelica. His disgust at Brunswick 'neutrality' leads him to Lieutenant Colonel George William Ramsay, then raising the Duke of York's Rangers soon after the taking of Valenciennes and before they lay siege to Dunkirk. 'When a nation is much corrupted, bravery is a puppet show.' It was in this campaign that he received two severe wounds sustained in the chaos of retreat, These wounds, not only in his own account, but also in testimonials by well-wishers seeking mitigation for his many later offences, seem to have been long-lasting in their effects. He claimed in later Home Office records never to have quite recovered from these and to have been poor ever since, though it is clear they predated his period of greatest literary and journalistic success.[11] He was taken to hospital in Bruges and then Bremen. Eventually, back to England, in high hopes of further promotion in recognition of his services, he finds he has been reported dead and all the commissions full, so he has lost his company. His delusions of military advancement and his prospects of marrying Angelica evaporate at Horseguards.

Significantly, his recourse at this low point in his fortunes was to Caroline, already estranged from her husband with her own establishment at Blackheath. Here in pursuit of patronage at her alternative court, on the strength of his Brunswick service, he meets Lt Colonel Campbell and Colonel Courtenay of the Cheshire Fencibles. In that difficult mix of roles shared with his rival William Cobbett, military man and accountant, Ashe failed on a recruiting drive in Wales, paying bounty to men who then deserted. Inevitably, this led him into debt and yet another desertion, this time for the patronage of the Portuguese court and from there to Corsica where the British had just taken control under Lieutenant Governor Sir Gilbert Elliot.

Although he had begun to attract the attention of influential people through his writing, it could not yet be relied on as a source of income. Ashe's international odyssey in accountancy continued. He was befriended by John Fullarton Udny, British consul at Leghorn, best known as an art agent for his brother who sold Jan van den Hoecke's 'Triumphal Entrance of Cardinal Prince Ferdinand of Spain into Antwerp' to the Uffizi in Florence in 1791. Through him, he secured the office of Inspector General of Accounts in Corsica at £700 a year. Before he could try on his robes of office the British abandoned Corsica and Udny himself evacuated to Bastia in the face of the French invasion. Ashe made his way back to England via his hated Lausanne where he met a fleeing English Catholic en route from Douai with whom he split his remaining money to get them both home third class. This man, Ashe reveals, was called Maunde and later became a rich banker, who, when they meet again by chance in London, affects not to know him. This Maunde may have been Henry Maunde who formed the firm of Austen & Maunde with Jane Austen's brother, Henry. One of their moneymaking schemes was the lucrative trade in military commissions, of which Ashe was later a customer.[12]

Ashe presented a Corsican memorial setting out the circumstances of his latest lost career and seeking compensation and delivered it in person at Downing Street after it was twice refused. After it was rejected again, he libelled the Prime Minister William Pitt. As always, the power and style of his prose was too direct to work in the corridors of power. Sir Frederick North rescued him again and gave him good advice about his tendency to wage lone campaigns on matters of honour without friends or tact. Ashe acknowledged the wisdom of this advice but did not follow it.

Next, Ashe was recommended to 79th Regiment under Major Cochrane Johnstone with the promise of a company of Cameronians due to go with Lord Mulgrave to Walcheren. At that point

Johnstone left the 79th and Ashe's hopes of any promotion go with him as he is replaced by a Colonel Cameron, 'who has among his relatives twelve of the officers and two hundred of the men'.

It was a lucky escape; he would have had a strong chance of dying of disease as part of the disastrous expedition to Walcheren if he had succeeded in going. The most remarkable thing to Ashe was the vanity of his own ambitions: 'It is, indeed, truly astonishing, how great was my pursuit, how contracted my means, how various my calculations, how infinite my contrivances.'

Astonished he might be, but his contrivances continued and his mature self was just as just as reckless and unfortunate as the young man the narrator wondered at. Ashe left for Vienna and joined the forces of Archduke Charles at a time 'when every monarch in Europe was trembling on his fragile throne'. He reflected that early battles in this campaign were won by Napoleon's reputation before the fighting started. He was taken prisoner after desertion by his regiment's allies.

To escape prison he enlisted in the French service and deserted, coming back to England via the good offices of Mr Capsaw, consul in Bremen. After a long winter journey, enlivened by being shipwrecked, he arrived destitute as usual, but as usual was rescued by luck, this time by Mr Forbes of the Board of Education, his former employer in Ireland. He found sanctuary and income being employed to write for him, but 'being emancipated from the slavery of distress, I recovered my usual independence of mind.' His half pay from the 83rd Regiment, (lost after his recruiting embarrassments with the Cheshire Fencibles), was restored to him with five years back pay of one hundred and fifty pounds, enough to set himself up in inexpensive literary retirement on the Isle of Man. He spent it writing 'The Manx Monastery or Romance of Belville and Julia' dedicated to John Taubman and took up school teaching, setting up schools at Coventry, Henley and Hammersmith. He left to join HMS *Colossus* at Plymouth under Captain (later Admiral) Grindall, duelled with a fellow officer and fled to Ireland.

His Irish debts were now beyond the statute of limitations, so with his usual knack of finding a crisis, Ashe made his way back to Dublin in time for the great Irish rebellion of 1798. Here again he met his deserving curate brother Jonathan and through his connections as chaplain, became Assistant Commissary General under Colonel Handfield at the Military Hospital at Kilmainham for the army under General Needham. It is curious to think that

Ashe's core skills both in the army and in civilian life were as a teacher of languages and as an accountant, and that these skills should have got him into so much trouble. In this latest accountancy job, he became engaged in the guerrilla war in Ireland in 1798, earned the thanks of his superiors and was made aide-de-camp for engagements against the United Irishmen at Tara, Wicklow, Goree, Wexford, White Plains and Vinegar Hill. At Arklow on 9 June, fighting on the opposite side to his friend Lord Edward Fitzgerald, he made perhaps his most dramatic contribution to the campaign and one which with repercussions for his subsequent career: 'At Arklow it was my lot to save the life of Sir Watkin Williams Wynn, who was dismounted by the pike of a rebel.'[13]

Sir Watkin Williams Wynn, a powerful landowner politician and commander of the Ancient British Fencibles, earned the nickname 'The Prince of Wales'. He was conspicuously more valiant and active in military affairs than the heir to the throne. His brother Charles was the witness on Willikin's birth certificate in the Delicate Investigation and his copy of *The Book*, or perhaps Ashe's *The Spirit of the Book* passed from John Murray to Lord Byron. His gallantry may have earned him a certain amount of credit at the Home Department, where he was later to cause so much trouble.

Gazetted for his bravery, Ashe's accounts failed again, thanks, he says, to the dishonesty of his subordinates. Characteristically, he fled rather than face court martial, another coincidental link to William Cobbett, who left England in 1792 after exposing corruption in the accounts of his military superiors. Gillray's satirical sequence 'The Life of William Cobbett' shows this episode as an act of rebellion against military authority, with a portrait of Lord Edward Fitzgerald on a wall that wears a red Jacobin cap. In fact, though Ashe characterised Cobbett as a fierce, unprincipled rabble-rouser, both he and Cobbett took a British patriotic line in America and fell foul of Thomas Jefferson's pro-French sentiments.

Just as Cobbett had done after his accounting embarrassments six years earlier, Ashe took refuge in America. From Bristol, he travelled to Boston where he encountered freebooting customs officials. His account of his arrival in his memoirs is a word for word repetition of its description in his 'Travels in America'; being offered new ways of life and 'investment opportunities' as soon as he gets off the boat, hoping to find a liberal democracy he instead finds a nation of 'sordid speculators', pride and bigotry.

In his own account Ashe spent two years as a backwoodsman at the head of the Patuxent, married 'a woman of colour' called Faveen and was the father of two children, leaving them and his farm to her and her old lover when he returned and Ashe became bored. He claimed his hard work in establishing his farm was undone by the Indian wars, just as he began to thrive and settle 'in my third year': 'What I valued most, were the black and grey squirrels. These animals are large and numerous, are excellent when roasted, and make a soup exceedingly rich and nourishing.'

There is certainly an element of travellers' tall tales about Ashe's time in America, not only in his memoirs but also in his 'Travels in America' and 'Memoirs of Mammoth' his account of his fossil hunting expeditions. Elements of the broad chronology can be established from the muster books of his various regiments, but much of the rest is speculation.[14]

Perhaps wishing to fill a gap created by Cobbett's departure, Ashe was unable to resist the possibilities offered by a new capital city. Ashe was drawn to Washington, recently established as the centre of government after the movement from Philadelphia. Ashe was not impressed with Congress, but this was a significant moment in his development as a writer, as it saw his first attempt at political journalism:

> During my researches, however, my finances were considerably reduced, and I was now compelled to attend congress as a hired reporter of its debates; for I saw little probability of being otherwise engaged or officially employed. This was a dreadful task. The majority of the speakers were truly despicable and mere automata. Their puny oratory was pre-concerted and mechanical. They babbled from the obligations of necessity, but could not argue from the high and proud demands of virtue.[15]

Ashe says he was introduced to the President, Thomas Jefferson, by John Rutlidge, the Chief Justice South Carolina son of an Irish immigrant, elder brother of Edward Rutlidge, signer of the Declaration of Independence. Through his influence and connections, Ashe soon becomes editor of the *National Intelligencer*, only recently founded by Samuel Harrison Smith in 1800:

> In the way of immediate employment. I succeeded Mr. Stephen Pinckney, as editor of the NATIONAL INTELLIGENCER, and

soon became a splendid instance of literary power, by coercing Mr. Cobbett, the most insolent writer alive, and putting my foot upon a swoln aristocracy, which he was endeavouring to foster in the bosom of a republican land.

Countering William Cobbett's radical influence in America became Ashe's training for their later encounters in London. Both would claim to be the champion of Caroline's cause, when she grew to be a focus of opposition at home, but Ashe would claim a personal attachment to her cause rather than using her as a figurehead for radical attacks on the government.

While still editor, he says he was appointed précis writer to the Department of State. His usual independence of mind saw him refusing to follow Jefferson's pro-French, anti-British line, but he was 'too deeply versed in the secrets of Mr Jefferson to be discarded with safety' and was replaced on the *Intelligencer* by a French emigrant.

I hope Mr. Jefferson is an honest man and a true American, but I am not warranted by the tissue of his life, during my literary and official association with him, to afford him an unrestricted credit. His personal virtues have frequently absorbed his political errors.

As Cobbett did, Ashe took offence at Jefferson's negative view of Great Britain and saw his favouring of Napoleon as an affront. Ashe's own sense of nationality was fluid though, in keeping with his principles. Often he represented himself as an Englishman when abroad. At other times, he was taken to be one, for example, when he was in France. He was often rescued and protected by British diplomats, but he was very much opposed to the union between Britain and Ireland and in favour of Irish liberty, though he fought against Lord Edward Fitzgerald when faced with the 'anarchy' of the 1798 rebellion. There is more than history and religion to Ashe's loyalty to the Crown. He needed the British establishment and its structures to feed his social ambition and his satire.

Ashe then found the charges relating to the failure of his accounts were not to be pursued, so he was free to return home. He returned to a Britain ruled by the optimistically named 'Ministry of all the Talents' with an ailing Charles James Fox as Foreign Secretary. The cabinet was characterised by Ashe as 'the icy cave of Death'. He describes himself as 'clamorous and importunate for place'. To his credit, he never pretended to be above this scramble or against the system, though he rails against it when it fails him. Though he was obviously one of the many admirers of Charles James Fox, he believed government had come too late for him. He had fallen off from a great of opposition leader to a state of 'florid weakness', the same phrase Ashe used of the Prince Regent in *The Claustral Palace*. Ashe was still looking for a military position, presenting his Corsican memorial to the Duke of York. Ashe was good at gaining attention through his writing but tended to annoy his patrons in face-to-face contact, probably because of his 'independence of mind'. He had cause to reflect, as many place-hunters had before him, on the true nature of nobility: 'It is not in the higher classes of society that we are to look for models of worth and genuine intrinsic greatness.'

In keeping with Ashe's sympathetic portraits of the royal brothers, the Duke of York is contrasted favourably with the 'haughty and little' Lord Amherst, whose path he crosses at this point. The good humour of the Commander in Chief carries some weight against the 'barbarous inequality' of aristocracy. He is given money by the duke for travel to his regiment, but instead sets himself up 'to live in style' in Little Ryder Street, in fashionable St James's in London, having come into his inheritance, a sum of four hundred pounds and eighty pounds a year. His view of Lord Amherst's ability and character was widely shared. To some extent, Ashe anticipated the verdict of history. Amherst was not then in a position of power; his real failure came in India later, long after Ashe's memoir was published. Ashe's opinions of the great ones who cross his path are generally not written in hindsight. He often meets them early in their careers and publishes before their reputations are fully formed, and certainly while they are still alive and able to sue, or at least contradict. He was either very confident of his opinions, or careless of libel.

While he was still wealthy, Ashe felt there was an easier way to achieving his majority in the army than joining the Canadian Fencibles, the regiment the Duke of York had suggested he join. He felt he could gain a commission in a more fashionable regiment, by bribing Mary Anne Clarke with a diamond necklace. At this time, in 1805, she was seen to be at her most influential in securing military commissions through her lover, the Duke of York. Ashe had no objection to the corruption of The Thing when he thought he might benefit from it and only objected to it when it failed him.

Ashe's narrative consistently shows him blowing his money and life chances, just when fate appeared to have smiled on him at last. This suggests a willingness to be honest at his own expense and a genuine character trait he was aware of but could not change. To 'live in style' equated to a system of vice to which he would devote an entire novel in 1819, *The Charms of Dandyism, or Living in Style by Olivia Moreland*, a tale of the descent into poverty and disgrace of a woman of fashion devoted to material comfort at the expense of principle.

The necklace bribe he bought from a jeweller on the corner of Albemarle St and Piccadilly in London's fashionable Mayfair. Inevitably, when Ashe's suit for a commission through Mrs Clarke reached the Duke of York, he recognised Ashe as someone he has already supported in joining his chosen regiment. The Duke was not impressed and dismissed Ashe's claim out of hand. Interestingly, the duke is portrayed by Ashe as a man of integrity, ignorant of Mrs Clarke's trade. Later, in *The Claustral Palace*, Ashe ridiculed Colonel Wardle, who attacked the duke in the House of Commons for his part in the trade in commissions. Ashe's own blackmailing career would also bring him into contact with Davenport Sedley, a shadowy figure, who threatened to publish Mrs Clarke's memoirs. Ashe was not yet viewed in the same way as Sedley, a loner writing in dark impoverishment, possibly under a range of pseudonyms. Ashe at this stage was still hoping to use his wealth and connections to carve out a career legitimate by the standards of the day. He would soon join Sedley in the papers of the Treasury Solicitor and in the sinister and lucrative negotiations around the suppression of *The Book* and *The Claustral Palace*.

By now, the reader may be able to anticipate the trajectory of Ashe's career as an Ensign in the Canadian Fencibles. His resolution on arriving in Canada was to use his service as a front for some lucrative fur trapping. He left for Quebec from Portsmouth and found the Fencibles staffed with second-rate officers and offering no hopes of promotion. He took a recruiting party into the wilds with no intention of recruiting (after his Cheshire Fencibles disaster). He turned his drummer, soldier servant and corporal into junior partners in a fur trade venture. In spring 1806, he sold his furs in Montreal for, he says, over a thousand pounds, in hope again of buying a captain's commission. He finds he has lost his existing commission through desertion having lost contact with his regiment for fifteen months and mustered no recruits.

By chance, he met Sir John Johnstone, the naturalist, and he encouraged him to show his Indian curiosities from the St Lawrence River. Ashe was inspired to begin his own investigations in the river valleys of America and assembled six tons of fossils at the expense of all his fur trapping fortune. He claimed to have ended a raft of learned speculation about what the creatures known as 'mammoths', a term used for all massive fossil bones at the time, were like. Ashe realised he that he was dealing with not one creature but a variety that we know as dinosaurs. There is some dispute about whether he gathered the fossils himself or simply acquired the collection of another naturalist with the intention of profiting by them. His 'Memoirs of Mammoth', written on his passage home, certainly drew on recently published works on the subject, but the language in its characteristic passages was very much his own. The scope that the remains left for speculation gave Ashe a chance to leave science behind and revel in sensation. Presumably he did not spend time while editor of the *National Intelligencer* or as precis writer to the State Department discussing fossils with Thomas Jefferson, since that episode pre-dated Ashe's interest in 'mammoths'. This was perhaps a pity. Here he is describing Megalonyx, Jefferson's Ground Sloth, using the terms Jefferson had when he first described and named it as a giant clawed cat, though Jefferson had since revised his opinion in a paper to the American Philosophical Society:

> The great Megalonyx, the monstrous lion of the Greeks; the cruel carnivorous animal of this western world, who was 'huge as the frowning precipice; cruel as the bloody panther, swift as the descending eagle, and terrible as the angel of night!'[16]

The last part of this description was taken from Charles Wilson Peele, whose sons Rembrandt and Rubens are credited with bringing the 'mammoth' craze to Britain.

The collection Ashe had acquired was confiscated by Liverpool customs in the way of duty and fines. He sold them to Bullock's Museum, then based in Liverpool, for £200 when he had hoped to raise £20,000. They were curiosities for a paying exhibition, with no thought of scientific research, other than Ashe's own speculative work: 'It made the fortune of Mr. Bullock, an entire stranger to me and to the design, and it left me a wretch in a state of mental darkness.'

According to his guidebook, Bullock had formed his collection 'during seventeen years of arduous research at a cost of £30,000', though like Ashe himself, buying up other people's collections rather than arduous research seemed to be his preferred way of accumulating objects. Admission was one shilling or one guinea for an annual ticket.

When Ashe's Memoirs were published in 1815, Bullock's Museum now established in London was approaching its zenith, which came in 1816 selling Napoleonic items. The exhibition of Napoleonic relics in 1816 made Bullock £35,000. The crush at the exhibit was satirised by Cruikshank and Rowlandson, who drew the carriage and the crowds straining to view it. Napoleon's carriage was presented to the Prince Regent by the Prussian Field Marshal von Blücher following its capture after the Battle of Waterloo. The Prince sold it to Bullock. The bill of sale for the Napoleonic material shows that the carriage made one hundred and sixty eight pounds and his snuffbox one hundred and sixty six pounds nineteen shillings and sixpence.[17]

Nonetheless some of Ashe's finds way well have made their way to London's Natural History Museum after Bullock's collections were auctioned in 1819; some, still on prominent display there labelled as coming from Bullock may well have been brought to Britain by Ashe. Ashe, in London for the launch of *Charm of Dandyism* may have been in a position to attend the sale in 1819, though naturally he was not in a position to bid.

Having failed to make money from his finds Ashe turned again to literature. His 'Memoirs of Mammoth' had in fact been written as a guide to the fossils for Bullock as part of the deal, which Ashe felt was so unfair.

As always, his inspiration and ideal readers were women, their curiosity would bring them and their incurious menfolk to view the mammoth bones, their love of his prose would convince them of the validity of his account of them, despite its lack of scientific depth. The British Library's copy of 'Memoirs of Mammoth' comes with manuscript corrections by Ashe and a note apologising to a Mr Blair for mislaying the original and attaching the enclosed imperfect corrected copy.[18] 'Mr Ashe is extremely sorry to have mislaid a pamphlet of Mr Blair's. He will look for it with assiduity or obtain another in its place. In the meantime he begs the favour of Mr B to accept this incorrect production and excuse him.'

Ashe's 'Travels in America' was more about how to make a living and avoid the touts who greet you with wild promises of fortune as you get off the boat at Boston than a tale of adventure. Ashe had his own store of memorable phrases: 'Dr Johnson was never more solicitous to leave Scotland than I was to leave the Atlantic states.'

Though famously outlandish in his own claims, Ashe was wary of the travellers' tales and outright fraud that fuelled emigration. He told the story of a prosperous and successful Sussex farmer who emigrated to America because his admiration of the French republic made him believe himself a slave in England and thereby ruined himself. Forty thousand people, he claimed were drawn to settle in Kentucky by a pamphlet written in Philadelphia by a man 'who had never been there'.

Ashe's opinion of Thomas Jefferson was if anything more stridently expressed in the 'Travels' than it came to be in the 'Memoirs':

This gentleman was more theoretical talent than sterling political ability. And to show some respect to the cry of the world I call him a statesman, though he was certainly betrayed more dereliction and tergiversation than ought to be accorded to so eminent a name. During the whole of his two presidencies he has been fluctuating between the good of his country and his attachment to the French government.

His view of Congress too was more caustic when the experience as a reporter there was sharper: 'There is in America no real politics, the speeches you see in the papers are made by Irish and Scotch journalists.'

Defending Britain against Jefferson's pro-French foreign policy did not merit the grateful thanks of his country and he came back to a nation indifferent to him. On his return to England, Ashe met his brother Jonathan by accident in Bristol. He too was overlooked, still an unregarded curate, recently established in the parish of St John the Baptist there. Ashe repeatedly raised the subject of his deserving brother, conscientious, scholarly and upright, destined to poverty and obscurity because ecclesiastical preferment depended on social connections. Jonathan it transpired was not as otherworldly as all that and had his own colourful and adventurous history, military, educational and Masonic. Putting his moral outrage to one side, Thomas made fitful attempts to secure patronage for Jonathan from the Duke of Northumberland and Lord Byron that renowned supporter of clergymen. Jonathan would probably not have been wholly comfortable if these efforts proved successful.

Around this time saw the beginning of a fitful but sustained campaign by Ashe to extract money from the recently established Literary Fund. There is an element of irony about this since it was soon to become the Royal Literary Fund. Ashe's applications came at the same time as his anti-royal writing and blackmailing campaigns, many of them directed at The Prince of Wales, who became its patron in 1806, or in support of the wife whom he despised. The Fund had the noble ideal of supporting talented writers who did not have independent means. Since he had come into his inheritance but squandered it, Ashe no doubt felt he qualified.

On 12 July 1807, Ashe made his first application written directly to the founder of the fund, David Williams. The day before the application Williams received a letter from Sir Richard Phillips on the subject of Ashe and the application was rejected. Phillips was a bookseller, publisher and author himself, who had just become High Sheriff of London. By 1809, he was also in financial difficulties and soon afterwards was accused of insurance fraud when his stock was destroyed by fire. This established a pattern whereby Ashe's applications in themselves were well-worded, persuasive and often successful initially, but then rejected or offers of support withdrawn on the information of others casting doubt on his character.[19]

The Prince of Wales became a patron of the fund, eventually granting it royal status. Ashe stopped applying once he was king, not out of principle but because the fund had by then investigated him and found him too morally suspect to be deserving of its support. The Prince of Wales was the subject of unprecedented satire. He was at the head of a very uncomfortable system of bribery and suppression of literature but also a patron of the arts. It is difficult to tell sometimes which side Ashe is on and whether the difference is loyalty or quality.

Ashe wrote 'Travels in America' and 'Memoirs of Mammoth' based on what he considered to be the ground breaking if not methodical or scientific fossil hunting expeditions of 1806. They were eventually published in 1808 but with no great impact or enthusiasm on the part of the trade. Sir Richard Phillips, who wrote to the Literary Fund about Ashe, is recorded as buying the rights to 'Travels in America' for £50 when no other publisher would touch it. Perhaps even this modest success undermined Ashe's pleas of poverty to the fund. He found the booksellers only interested in royal scandal, blaming them in part for the course his literary life then followed. In his disillusionment with the publishing trade, he offered a useful summary of their various interests, including a view of Byron's publisher John Murray, for which he would soon have cause to be grateful.

> Messrs. Cadell and Davies preferred works on divinity and history; Longman, Hurst, and Co. published nothing but English classics, under the revision of Doctor Aikin; Law, Johnson and Rivington, confined their business to school-books; Murray was occupied by authors who engrossed all his trade; Hatchett would have purchased my manuscript had it been called the "Spiritual Light-horse-man;" Budd thought that a work called "Beauty put to its Shifts" would sell better; Tegg would give me much more for a pamphlet to be named "Adultery Anatomized;" Wilson dealt only in such titles as "Lucky Disaster Merry Medley, Sally Sable," &c. &c.; and Allen and Jones were of opinion, that "The Secret Cabal, the Royal Cuckold, the Petticoat Privy Council," &c. were the only compositions that merited their regard.[20]

Ashe might like to claim that he was forced by the tastes of publishers into the scandalous market Wordsworth despised, but he always seems to be in the right place at the right time to exploit it. *The Spirit of the Book* ended up being published by Mister Allen and was very much in the genre of the titles cited.

Despairing of the London booksellers for the moment, he sought alternative patronage again with another Prince Regent, this time the Prince Regent of Portugal in Brazil. His latest dream was to use the proceeds of Brazilian diamonds to purchase a seat in Parliament and then to 'send for Angelica' when he was established as a man of substance. He assumed the name of Morgan (a family name of his connections) and pretended to be a Chargé d'Affaires travelling in advance of Lord Strangford (Percy Clinton Sidney Smythe, Secretary to the Legation in Lisbon from 1803). Strangford had advised the Portuguese Prince Regent to leave for Brazil ahead of the French advance in November 1807 and coordinated the withdrawal of his court. Ashe traded on the gratitude of the Portuguese royal family for their rescue by the British to further his diamond scheme. The diamond mines in Brazil were a monopoly of the Portuguese court, an injustice that in his own mind justified Ashe in liberating them. He gained diplomatic papers, a passport and escort through the good offices of William, Viscount Beresford. He used his established interests as a naturalist to take him off the beaten track, skipping to San Salvador when Lord Strangford finally turns up with Sir Sidney Smith, Caroline's supposed lover when at Blackheath. Presumably, he was only too glad to be away from England and the sniggering following The Delicate Investigation. Ashe was betrayed by an accomplice and imprisoned. He escaped thanks to an Irish priest who took diamonds in return for the absolution of the miners who had stolen them.

Ashe claimed that most diamonds were taken but that some survived in a secret spring-loaded drawer of his desk. Shipwrecked again, he took the San Francisco River to Pernambuco. From Pernambuco, he discharged his remaining debts by selling his final three diamonds, then he travelled to the Azores to write his 'History' of those islands, arriving at Corunna in time to see the betrayal of Sir John Moore by his allies. This was a military disaster with surprising consequences for the love life of one of the princesses in 'The Nunnery' according to Ashe's *The Claustral Palace*. The Oxford Dictionary of National Biography entry for Timothy Joseph Haydn claims he wrote 'The History of the Azores' as a ghost to Ashe, which is entirely possible, though Ashe claims to have been there at the time. It is possible that the two men conspired to benefit from Ashe's greater reputation and output of this kind. We will see them together later, Haydn being Ashe's agent when dangling the synopsis of *The Claustral Palace* before the eyes of a horrified government.

When Ashe finally returned to Plymouth, rumours of scandal at Frogmore were mixed with frenzied speculation about what had been written of Caroline's conduct in the still unpublished report of the Delicate Investigation. Her gossip about the princesses in 'The Nunnery' became her way of getting back at the Family for their hypocrisy and her ill-treatment. Ashe was her chosen vehicle for articulating it. It had appeared since her marriage and move to England that Ashe had been at one remove from her sufferings while on his adventurous travels; but the Delicate Investigation and the report it produced, and its suppression, brought untold possibilities for political advantage, revenge and profit, bringing the Princess of Wales and her ghost back together.

3

The Book and *The Spirit* *of the Book*

"The Book."—Any Person having in their Possession a Certain Book, printed by Mr. Edwards in 1807, but never published, with W. Lindsell's Name as the Seller, of the same on the Title Page, and will bring it to W. Lindsell, Bookseller, Wimpole-Street, will receive a handsome Gratuity.

The Times, 27 March 1809

And that might have been that. With the failure of the marriage of the Prince of Wales to his German princess, the hopes of advancement at the English court that Captain Ashe might have entertained as the result of his connection with Caroline and her ladies in Brunswick appeared to have evaporated. In the eyes of the Prince of Wales and his agents in Carlton House, he was suspect, part of that entourage which had failed to turn Caroline into the princess he wanted. After their separation, Ashe had sought the patronage of Caroline's alternative court at Blackheath and military commissions under the Duke of York, scraps by comparison with real royal patronage. His commissions had sent him on a series of unmilitary adventures in the Americas, and with the predictable failure of his airy financial schemes, from dinosaur bones in the Ohio River to Canadian furs and Brazilian diamonds, he was now back in the hands of a tribe more ruthless than any he had met on his travels: the booksellers of London, who were fully engaged in the print war between the Prince of Wales and his estranged wife.

Ashe's adventures honed his literary skills against a background of convulsed Napoleonic Europe, reforming and replacing its political structures and a nascent United States evolving its own.

He fought against Napoleon but bitter experience had taught him to despise the military incompetence and complacency of the royal armies ranged against him. The disappointments and injustices of his military career and the parallel disappointment of Caroline at her life and marriage in England gave his writing a new edge and purpose. He wrote petitions for lost civil appointments and military commissions, and followed his political journalism in Washington with unreliable memoirs of American life. These brought him back to Caroline, not only as a companion of her beloved Captain Browne, but also as a writer.

He returned after the Delicate Investigation into Caroline's moral conduct to a life of journalism at the heart of murky negotiations, around the publication of the commissioners' report, known simply and notoriously as the *The Book*. Why did he come back? Partly the failure of his 'careers' in North and South America, but he was also drawn back to Caroline and to British politics. The fascination of *The Book*, and the use Spencer Perceval made of it, opened another avenue for his services.

Since Ashe, by his own account, was abroad for much of the years 1805 to 1808, his knowledge of the political machinations both leading to and following the Delicate Investigation must have come second-hand, perhaps from Caroline's own confidences. The Delicate Investigation, and the blackmailing literary milieu it created, were the perfect environment for Ashe. The deaths of William Pitt and Charles James Fox left a political vacuum and led to a struggle for power among lesser figures more prone to using and being manipulated by blackmailing literature. This coincided helpfully with the lapsing of Ashe's various debts incurred in Britain. A useful pen for hire, Ashe returned to Caroline's cause and her connections from Brunswick, lured by her or provoked by Spencer Perceval. Perceval emerges as a very different figure in the papers of the Treasury Solicitor from the one most often portrayed.

The Commissioners appointed to produce the report into Caroline's conduct were Lords Erskine, Spencer, Grenville and Ellenborough. Erskine was a loyal lawyer apparently ennobled for the purpose. The report was submitted to Sir Vicary Gibbs, one of the law officers consulted by Perceval later in relation to *The Claustral Palace* synopsis. Sir Nathaniel Conant, Lord Moira and others who loomed large in Ashe's later career were all key figures in relation to the Delicate Investigation.

The Treasury Solicitor, the government's principal officer tasked with dealing with troublesome authors like Captain Thomas Ashe, had an important role in assessing the evidence submitted to the Commissioners. He naturally had his own copies, some of which appear in fact to be the originals. One of his files[1] contains some evidence submitted to the Delicate Investigation of 1806, but is chiefly devoted to the expenses of the Italian witnesses to the Milan Commission in 1818. This was a later investigation, which compiled evidence of Caroline's infidelities after she left England in 1814, an indication that the investigation into Caroline's conduct was more or less a seamless, continuous operation until her 'trial' in 1820. It also includes a bound and gilt-edged booklet containing what appears to be Lady Douglas's original evidence of Caroline's relationship with Sir Sidney Smith between 1801 and 1803 along with a note insisting her evidence was given against her own inclination, under royal command.[2]

The Douglases were interviewed by the ever-willing and manipulative Privy Purse, Colonel John McMahon; there was only one likely outcome from questioning from that quarter.[3] Slightly unfortunately for her reputation, the file also includes Lady Douglas's claims for a pension in 1818 on the basis of her service to the Crown. Like so much of the evidence against Caroline, it gave the impression that it had been procured by the manipulation and bribery of her vindictive husband. The verdict of the Commissioners made no difference, and the campaign to convict Caroline of adultery and treason went on. The same file[4] also includes monitoring reports on Caroline's movements from August to September 1806 including her sojourn with Captain Manby at Southend, a further indication that investigation and surveillance by the agents of Carlton House went on after her acquittal. The report also noted Caroline's regular Sunday church attendance since the Delicate Investigation, infrequent before.

The Delicate Investigation was an extraordinary proceeding with tragic-comic consequences. Its findings, circulated to the Family in July 1806, were too weak for the Prince's liking, proving insufficient for a charge of treason; Caroline chose to believe that she had been exonerated. On balance, there was no conclusive evidence of adultery but definitely signs of conduct unbecoming in a princess and a potential royal consort.

In 1806, after William Pitt's death, Caroline adopted her husband's Pittite opponents, Spencer Perceval, Lord Eldon and

Lord Castlereagh, none of whom she liked very much. The government fell on Charles James Fox's death and Spencer Perceval and Caroline's other allies found themselves in government obliged to buy up and suppress copies of *The Book*, which he helped to compile. The Prince of Wales threatened to delay restoring Caroline's rights and access to their daughter Charlotte and the urge to publish *The Book* increased. The Prince, though obviously wronged, fell still further in popularity. Britain found itself with a future king and queen who had no grounds for divorce but were growing in mutual loathing. What was to become of Princess Charlotte, the promising result of this unlikely union?

Captain Ashe's immediate concern on his return to Britain was to replace his lost American fossils with domestic ones. In his own account, Ashe took a house at Broadway near Weymouth and established a museum built on his curiosities and fossils taken from Dorset and Devon, 'the finest collection of petrefacts in Europe'. These were contemporary with Mary Anning's discoveries at Lyme Regis. Ashe's museum appears to have been established in 1808 or 1809, two years before Mary Anning discovered her Ichthyosaur in 1811 and the Dorset fossil craze began. Like so many of his other ventures, this one was short-lived; his Brazilian creditors caught up with him and his funds evaporated.

He arrived in London in much-reduced circumstances and took up gardening under the good offices of 'Ellen H' in Manor Terrace, Chelsea. This brief semi-rural, or at least horticultural, sojourn filled him, as these things generally did, with improving maxims about the virtuous way to happiness. 'The shortest way to be rich is not by enlarging our estate, but by contracting our desires.' Ashe always quickly abandoned this wise maxim, his desires did not contract, and the search for fame and fortune began again.

Much though he praised his gardening interlude, quiet did not suit him. Ashe got bored, ran out of money, and took up his pen again as a 'public writer', declaring war on William Cobbett's famous newspaper the *Political Register* in Francis Blagdon's rival *Register* established as a loyal paper to Spencer Perceval's government in October 1809. His objective was to write against the radicals, who 'aimed at the destruction of society for the acquisition of personal interest, or the gratification of criminal ambition'. Blagdon had form in exploiting the financial possibilities of patriotic feeling, having written a graphic history of the life of Admiral Lord Nelson in 1806.

Ashe, an officer in the 83rd Regiment, disparaged William Cobbett as 'a sergeant in the Fifty-Fourth'. These were the same superior social terms the Tories used against Cobbett. Ashe also attacked Cobbett for his lack of principle, as someone 'who has been with unexampled versatility and licentiousness, all things to all men, who has flattered and abused praised and reprobated, enraged and defied all parties just as interest has happened to guide his venal pen'. Ashe was of course perfectly capable of doing this himself. Cobbett led a life parallel, in some ways, to that of Thomas Ashe. Cobbett was more comfortably on the outside of The Thing, more principled and consistent than was Ashe himself. It was certainly debatable whose pen is more venal. Ashe accused Cobbett of a malicious and scandalous libel on the military in repeating the allegations made against Mary Anne Clarke, even though he knew them to be true from personal experience, having recounted his own attempt to bribe her with a diamond necklace to gain a superior military commission. He claims, rather against the standard account of Cobbett's journalistic success, 'his Register fell as mine rose'. It is difficult to believe this happened for long, if at all.

> William Cobbett, enraged to think that his successful adversary was a mere newspaper contributor, fiercely attacked now Mr. Becket, now Mr. Canning, and Mr. Croker, to whom, as Treasury writers, he alternately attributed each of my compositions in Blagdon's Political Register.

At this stage Ashe was a loyal writer, writing under the pseudonym 'Albion', already known to the government as a political author in negotiations with Perceval in 1809 before he became the author of *The Spirit of the Book*. Despite his apparent success, Ashe then left Blagdon's *Register* to become 'Sidney' of *The Phoenix*. As usual, there had been an argument over money. Ashe believed he was enriching his proprietor while being paid just ten pounds per month. His chosen paper, *The Phoenix*, had been 'more corrupt and venal than the *Morning Post* or *Evening Courier*'. *The Phoenix* was another Blagdon venture, this one edited by Joseph Swan. Contractual obligations meant for a time he was both 'Sidney' of *The Phoenix* and 'Albion' of Blagdon's *Register*, writing against himself, partly carrying on as 'Albion' in order to convince Perceval it was worth supporting a loyal paper. He was on better terms at *The Phoenix* with a financial interest in sales.

Ashe recalled that Blagdon 'made me offer upon offer, and finally confessed to me that, on my menace to leave his paper, in consequence of the poverty of his supplies, he had informed Mr. Perceval who and what "Albion" was, at the same time stating that, as he (Blagdon) was unable to remunerate such a writer as "Albion," he begged ministerial assistance to that effect.'

Blagdon made renewed offers to Ashe after his replacement as 'Albion' failed, Ashe refused. Blagdon approached Perceval to provide funds for 'Albion', since if 'Albion' fell, Cobbett would triumph. Blagdon told Ashe he had been promised a pension of four hundred pounds a year from Spencer Perceval, through the Treasury Solicitor, to espouse 'liberty and the prosecution of the war':

> 'I have obtained for you the promise of an allowance of one hundred pounds per quarter, or four hundred pounds a year; and if you engage to write for my Register after your usual manner. I will go to the Treasury to-morrow by appointment, and get that promise confirmed by Mr. Litchfield and Mr. Arbuthnot, whom Mr. Perceval has instructed to treat with me.' On saying this, he laid before me several letters, particularly from Mr. B[rooksbank]., private secretary to Mr. Perceval, and placed such other evidence before me as left no doubt on my mind that his representation was correct in every point.[5]

Naturally enough, Perceval found out 'Albion' was also 'Sidney' and rejected any proposal out of hand. Despite being found out for writing for both sides at once, Ashe had no difficulty in blaming Spencer Perceval for his predicament. He determined to continue to attack Perceval as 'Sidney'. Perceval's position was perfectly reasonable, but it is important to note his role in bribing and threatening journalists. Ashe was a known force to him as he rose to office and in relation to *The Book*, which Ashe believed was his means of obtaining his political eminence. Perceval's biographer, Denis Gray, finds the claims of blackmail made against him absurd without saying why or how it came to be so widely believed at the time.

In Ashe's account, the funds available from the government to promote loyal literature and suppress sedition were much larger than the sums offered to writers by newspaper proprietors. To our eyes, it seems incredible that the government should expend so much time energy and money to attempt to control the press and popular sentiment in such a haphazard and uncertain way. It is even odder that the principal agent of this attempt is said to be Spencer Perceval, the pale evangelical lawyer described by King George III as 'the most straightforward man I ever knew'. Except of course that George III was a terrible judge of character and the Treasury Solicitor's papers are full of evidence of payments being authorised by Perceval precisely for this purpose. Ashe explained the style and purpose of his loyal writing:

> While the state was struggling with difficulties, that tended greatly to impede and affect its exertions, I, while a loyal writer, gave a new colour to the national complexion; banished gloom and despair, and exhibited the kingdom in a wealthy and prosperous condition almost beyond example. "Every wind that blows," said I, in one of my "Albion" numbers, "wafts an influx of riches into our ports. The seas are covered with our ships, laden with the produce of every clime, of which our extensive colonies, and the confidence that is exclusively due to our commercial character, secure us the consignment; and with the productions of our arts and industry, which their superior and unrivalled excellence induce the world to covet." In this manner, and by constantly urging the people to adhere to the crown and constitution, did I distinguish myself; and when Mr. Perceval, saw it proper to settle on me four hundred pounds a year. it is to be presumed that his existence as a minister, and his triumph over treason, were, perhaps, in some degree, owing to the advantages which he received from what was universally called "Albion's popular and powerful support.". But no sooner had Î an altercation with Mr. Perceval, than I felt myself at liberty to contemplate the condition of the country in another point of view.[6]

Ashe defended his change of heart with the explanation that it was perfectly normal among journalists. 'There is not a newspaper editor who would not change his principles to increase his means, nor any author who could not be employed in scourging and curbing the administration, or in exposing the opposition as the vilest characters that ever took rank in the society of man.'

Mr. Swan, the proprietor of the Phoenix, was first intimidated, and next bribed by Mr. Perceval. He called upon me, and told me I MUST qualify my language, to sooth the minister whose vengeance I had incurred, or I could no longer be employed by him. The only reply I made to this insolent observation was, by turning him out of my study, and charging him never more to come within the length of my cane.[7]

Thus, Ashe had a double animus against Perceval for his interventions with both Blagdon and Swan, which had lost him his columns and influence. His means of revenge was *The Book*. As a journalist, Ashe had begun as a defender of the government and its unreformed institutions against the radicals, but then his personal animosity towards Spencer Perceval combined with a growing sense that Perceval had become too powerful. Ashe's fresh fury at Perceval's exploitation of Caroline, rather than an enduring sense of loyalty to her, brought her back into Ashe's story,

As 'Albion' he had had access to Mr Lindsell of Wimpole Street, the publisher of *The Book* and through him to the printer Richard Edwards. Two thousand copies were printed but Lindsell was instructed not to sell or publish without further word from Perceval. Ashe went to Edwards the printer and got sight of the proof sheets; instead of publishing it, 'The Spirit' would give Caroline's view of it.

Without arrogating to myself the title of exalted character, or the possession of great parts, I may still be allowed to say, that I never felt more power of soul and vigour of mind than I experienced on finding myself equally remote from the drudgery of the opposition, and the venality of the ministerial press. In the choice of my subject, I had no difficulty. Mr. Perceval was the cause of my having lost the editorship of 'The Phoenix', and I from that moment resolved that the author of my misfortune should be the origin of my prosperity. Mr. Perceval was much in my power.[8]

Swan found William Cobbett a more enduring friend and ally than he did Thomas Ashe, since he is evidently the same Joseph Swan imprisoned in Newgate for selling seditious pamphlets, to whom Cobbett writes as an ally in triumph on the death of Lord Castlereagh in 1822.[9]

All but six copies of *The Book* were removed by Perceval for circulation to 'the family' and at least six more were removed by the staff, the rest burnt by Perceval himself. Lots of other imperfect copies, parts and even single sheets found their way back to Mr Lindsell looking for the 'handsome gratuity' from the Treasury Solicitor promised in *The Times*.

It was as 'Sidney' in *The Phoenix* that Ashe claimed his greatest success as a journalist. Perry, editor of *The Morning Chronicle*, praised 'Sidney' as 'the truest limner of character in our present age'. Success as an opposition journalist was not enough, however. He wanted to pursue his own personal campaign against Perceval. In his 'Memoirs', Ashe quoted in full his threat to publish *The Book* in *The Phoenix*. It is salutary to note that the entertaining claims Ashe makes in his memoirs about the negotiations around stray copies of *The Book*, his threats to publish it and the composition and circulation of the *The Spirit of the Book* are largely substantiated by the papers of the Treasury Solicitor. As well as buying off opposition writers and subsidising loyal ones, he was the government officer tasked with retrieving and paying for stray copies of the Delicate Investigation's report. He retained, luckily for us, a file[10] on the Attorney General's injunction against Francis Blagdon to restrain publication of *The Book* in *The Phoenix*.

In these papers, the substance of Ashe's allegations is borne out but the sequence of events is rather different. As early as February 1808, two and a half years before Ashe threatened to publish *The Book* in *The Phoenix*, Francis Blagdon had been stopped from doing so with an injunction, as the government's first act in attempting to retrieve the work it had printed. Only then was Blagdon bribed to start his *Register* as a loyal paper to rival and counter Cobbett's.

The original signed parchment injunction dated 11 March 1808 is on the file; it was served by the Prince of Wales's solicitor Charles Bicknell but in the king's name. With it are four extracts from weekly numbers of *The Phoenix*, 14, 21, (exhibit A) 28 February (exhibit B) and 6 March (exhibit C), with mounting, excitable claims to be on the point of publishing *The Book*. There are also official copies and legal opinion, including the Attorney General, Sir Vicary Gibbs' annotations for Lord Eldon on the Treasury Solicitor's copies of chancery proceedings. So Blagdon was restrained by an injunction not to publish extracts from *The Book* before Ashe arrived, and renewed the threat of publication in *The Phoenix*. It is possible that Blagdon's fortunes genuinely suffered as a result of his dealings with Thomas Ashe because he, too, received support from the Literary Fund in 1812 and further application was made by his widow after his death in 1820.[11]

The evidence for the suppression of other stray copies of *The Book* at this time also comes from the files of the Treasury Solicitor, a beautifully documented and preserved example of highly disreputable government. The care with which the various receipts and undertakings are preserved suggests it was public money being used to bribe those with copies, or bits of them, to give them up. There are occasional anguished notes from the Home Secretary. Lord Liverpool asking Perceval and his agents not to spend too much and to account for the money.

The Dramatis Personae of the Treasury Solicitor's files are worth introducing. William Lindsell of 87 Wimpole Street, bookseller, the man who produced *The Book* and the man to whom applicants for Perceval's reward money were directed to bring their copies. Richard Edwards, printer of Paternoster Row, the printer of *The Book* and a rather overworked and underpaid agent of Perceval in tracking down the stray copies. He was soon to be the author of 'The Diamond Testament', a blackmailing work on the relationship between Princess Amelia and General Fitzroy, which suggests that he had concluded that following Perceval's methods was more lucrative than working for him. H. C. Litchfield, the Treasury solicitor and George Maule Litchfield's assistant solicitor to the Treasury who succeeded him in that role, had the near impossible task of securing stray copies without spending too much money. William Playfair, statistician and pamphleteer, the inventor of the bar chart, who, the reader must decide, was either an innocent bystander or active blackmailer in the affair of *The Book*.

J. C. Herries was private secretary to Perceval from 1807. During the period of the suppression and retrieval of *The Book*, he also produced two short-lived government newspapers with John Wilson Croker. Judith Noel, Lady Milbanke Lord Byron's mother-in-law from 2 January 1815 makes an unexpected appearance in pursuit of *The Book*. (Timothy) Joseph Haydn, author and publisher, appears as an important ally and agent to Ashe, pretending to be, or perhaps just being, a concerned citizen buying up Ashe's works in the public interest.

Sir Nathaniel Conant seemed, on the face of it, on odd ally and adviser for Thomas Ashe, being a law enforcement officer and publicly declared enemy of vice; but has two important areas of sympathy with him, his belief that rank should bring virtue and not licence vice, and his connection to the book trade. He is described in *Dictionary of National Biography* as 'bookseller and magistrate', which may account for that odd mixture of admonition and sympathy, that characterises his relationship with Ashe. He was an apprentice printer dedicated as a magistrate to the moral reformation of society, part of an inner group of elite advisers to the Home Office, which prosecuted aristocratic gamblers, in the belief that rank should not protect vice. Was Ashe a campaigning journalist uncovering vice in high places or a blackmailer contributing vice of his own? It was not always easy to tell. Conant evidently believed Ashe's protestations that he could be saved from the booksellers and returned to a life of virtue. Conant, as a government law officer, used his connections with the print trade to track down copies of the book, and was later the recipient of Captain Henry Bell's 'contract' with Ashe re *The Claustral Palace*. Ashe later told Conant's son John, who succeeded him at Bow Street, that he possessed hundreds of letters from him. Whether these were a sign of respect or another veiled threat of blackmail was not clear.

Six months after the injunction on *The Phoenix*, evidence of the government's attempts to track down other stray copies of *The Book* began to emerge. In August 1808, a Fleet Street editor and a statistician pamphleteer threatened to sell their copy to Sir Francis Burdett, the prominent radical politician, for £3,500. This, the Treasury Solicitor supposed, was probably just a ruse to get the government to improve its own offer of £2,500.

William Playfair was reported to have a copy.[12] Playfair's defence, typically for a prolific pamphleteer, was to write a pamphlet, the 'Vindication of William Playfair', intended to clear his name and explaining his dealings with J. C. Herries.[13] Playfair, the inventor of statistical graphs, spent the years 1793 to 1814 in London involved in miscellaneous pamphleteering and financial schemes for the public good, but died in poverty. The characteristic complaint of his 'Vindication' that he was trying to do good in securing the copy for the government, only to be arrested for attempting to extort money from it. The government had reason to be suspicious of pamphleteers since that literary form was such a potent political weapon. The Treasury Solicitor's file dealing with the Playfair case mixes papers relating to the suppression of copies of *The Book* with those of 'a pamphlet', Ashe's circulated preface to 'The Spirit of the Book' and 'another manuscript', which, it emerges, is *The Spirit of the Book* itself. Part two of the file relates to the expenses of witnesses providing testimony for Caroline's 'trial' in 1820. This provides further evidence that the investigations of 1806 and 1820 ran together and were really part of a continuous government campaign against Caroline.

Claiming your 'handsome gratuity' was not a simple matter of accepting whatever Spencer Perceval or the Treasury Solicitor felt your copy was worth. It became an invitation to make demands, which in turn left you open to accusations of blackmail and criminal conspiracy. Further evidence against Playfair came from another Treasury Solicitor file[14] purportedly relating to the printing and publication of *The Book* in 1806, but which in fact gives considerable additional detail about the recovery of stray copies in 1810 and 1811. The editor of the *Morning Post*, Peter Stuart, gave details about his own copy and his consultation with Playfair about selling it to Sir Francis Burdett. Stuart met with with Herries, who demanded £1,500. Stuart admitted that the copy was stolen but no action was taken against him and Stuart concluded that Perceval's fear of a copy staying in the hands of a Fleet Street editor was greater than his own fear of punishment. Stuart protested that *The Book* was 'in his possession for eighteen months and [he] hath refused the sum of £3,000 for it rather than disturb the tranquillity of the country or the peace and happiness of The Royal Family' by what he strongly apprehended might be the 'improper use of it on the Continent of Europe or elsewhere'.

Stuart's undertaking not to publish forms part of another slim file[15] that contains only fourteen bonds of booksellers to return their copies and not publish any that come into their hands; gentleman's agreements in return for the 'handsome gratuity' promised by Spencer Perceval, which can have had little practical effect in restraining the signatories. Some come with annotations of the seller's whereabouts, who to ask for and where. The copies are priced at anything from £300 to £1,000 each. Blagdon and Lindsell the publishers were also noted as recipients of handsome bribes. The undertaking of Peter Stuart of 33 Fleet Street, here noted as the editor of the *True Briton*, in the file, dated 7 November 1808. This was the first of many, issued, one senses, with decreasing confidence. Further inducements were necessary; Stuart was reportedly offered a job in Perceval's ministry in return for his continued loyalty.

The possible circulation of *The Spirit of the Book* or a synopsis of it greatly complicated the Treasury Solicitor's programme of suppression. There were increasingly frequent and worried references to a 'separate work' by Ashe about to appear. There was understandably some official confusion between the various works to which Ashe had access, but his 'Spirit' was clearly not 'a version' of *The Book* but a ghosted celebrity memoir justifying and giving context to Caroline's conduct.

Denis Gray's biography of Perceval does not discuss the evidence of Perceval's involvement in the suppression of *The Book* as revealed in the Treasury Solicitor's papers, but he does suggest that Caroline wanted *The Book* published and that she had become impatient with Perceval's delays and political manoeuvring. She could have supplied the information for Ashe's 'Spirit of the Book' in that gap.

The under-rewarded printer Richard Edwards, perhaps with his own blackmailing schemes in mind, or aware of the massive potential workload of tracking all copies down, wrote to Perceval on 27 January 1809 arguing that the suppression of *The Book* did not mean suppression of the information contained in it in other forms; extracts, pamphlets, or Ashe's own work, based on the 'sight of the proofs'.[16] On 6 March Judith Noel, Lady Milbanke, wrote to William Adam looking to secure a copy: 'the owner might come to Portland Place and part with it for £600.' Adam wrote to the Treasury Solicitor in turn, with news of a 'person in Wimpole Street' asking £3,500 for a copy. Adam was in financial difficulties through his son's debts in India and dependent on loans from his aristocratic friends. Negotiations over *The Book* were a lucrative side-line. It sounds as if Byron's future mother-in-law was looking to secure a copy for herself rather than looking to secure it in the public interest. She was, it seems, prepared to outbid the government to do so. So Adam could pass on a copy secured by the government to make a profit for himself.[17]

On 9 March the judge and specialist in the suppression of Luddism and libel, Sir Simon Le Blanc, gave the Treasury Solicitor the first intimations of Thomas Ashe's negotiations around *The Book* and the possibility of *The Spirit of the Book*: 'I understand that the person who is in treaty with the booksellers and with Mr Lindsell has made a great many extracts from his copy upon which he inks a separate piece.'[18]

Perhaps Ashe was able to secure a 'handsome gratuity' himself, since a note of the following day suggested that Lord Moira had acquired this copy for the government. Le Blanc then confirmed to the Treasury Solicitor that 'a book stitcher at Edwards the printer is the source of the leaked information.'[19]

On 27 March 1809 the *Times* advertisement for return of copies of 'a certain book' appeared, though it is clear from the Treasury Solicitor's files that retrieval had been underway for six months before they resorted to this expedient. The advertisement was an extraordinary thing for any government to make. It later appeared on the title page of *The Spirit of the Book*, just as it appears at the head of this chapter.[20] As might be imagined, it prompted a flurry of offers. J. C. Herries, on behalf of Spencer Perceval, gave the Treasury Solicitor the kind of reasoned advice that everyone knew to be wise but no one followed: 'To give 700 guineas for the copy in question without any security for it not having been copied and reprinted would be virtually no better than throwing so much money into the fire.'[21]

This perfectly reasonable argument is repeatedly advanced in related papers but nonetheless considerable sums continued to be paid. Rather impossibly, Herries still wanted the Treasury Solicitor to look out for and obtain copies, but apparently without spending too much, not a welcome communication for H. C. Litchfield, a government law officer with nothing left in his armoury but threats and chicanery. J. C. Herries wrote again from Downing Street on 9 April outlining to the Treasury Solicitor the terms under which copies of *The Book* might be purchased, trying to rationalise and control the process the government had started, but the flaws were all too apparent..

William Playfair had obviously not cleared his name in the eyes of the government and resorted to writing to Spencer Perceval directly. He complained he was 'arrested 3 weeks ago, in that business I am totally ignorant'. Overhearing talk of a copy of *The Book*, he says he took steps to recover it. Spencer Perceval was unlikely to believe, still less recognise, that Playfair was acting from altruism. Playfair wrote again on the eve of his trial 26 April, then again from Newgate on 31 April and 4 May with the added veiled threat of taking his case to the Prince of Wales, 'to whom I am well known'. [22]

In 1816 Playfair stooped to extortion when he attempted to broker the sale, to Lord Archibald Douglas, of papers alleged to relate to the Douglas Cause of the 1760s, a spectacular legal scramble for the vast wealth of Archibald Douglas, 3rd Marquess and 1st Duke of Douglas. Perhaps these papers show he had descended to blackmail rather earlier. Playfair and his family were serial applicants to the Literary Fund[23] and had successfully received ten guineas in April 1807, just before Thomas Ashe was rejected in his first application in July.

William Lindsell, the publisher of *The Book*, then gave information on further copies bound up at the same time. He also warned of a publication about the scandal of the Duke of York and the selling of army commissions, possibly the Mary Ann Clarke revelations later threatened by Davenport Sedley.[24]

On 27 June, Lord Liverpool at the Home Department wanted to account for the disbursements in recovering copies of *The Book* and demanded details from Litchfield. Two days later Litchfield was authorised by Perceval via J. C. Herries to purchase another copy for £500.[25] The Treasury Solicitor became something of a piggy in the middle between Perceval's office and potential vendors, receiving notes urging him to acquire copies without spending too much.

Intriguingly, soon after Perceval became Prime Minister in October 1809, he received a petition from a 'Mr Ashe'. Perceval's reply appears in the collected correspondence of the Prince of Wales. Spencer Perceval sent a note to a 'Mr Ashe' returning his papers and saying he 'cannot now enter his petition in Parliament' but acknowledging receipt of his letter of 19 October.[26] Why should this letter end up with the Prince of Wales (the editor of the correspondence Arthur Aspinall rightly finds it strange) unless it comes from Thomas Ashe who was known to him? Was Ashe petitioning for his lost military commissions at the height of the negotiations around the stray copies of *The Book*? Perhaps Ashe was combining a petition related to his military service with a threat to publish a copy or his own version of *The Book* if his petition was not granted. Presumably, this rebuff at Perceval's hands strengthened Ashe's resolve to have his revenge.

In October, Richard Edwards, the printer of Crane Court, was still pursuing promised compensation for his losses in relation to *The Book*; both his own copies and those he was able to track down. He found himself passed from Sir Simon Le Blanc to Litchfield, then to Herries, with no one taking responsibility or paying him. In January 1810, Edwards was still complaining to the Treasury Solicitor about his expenses in recovering copies of *The Book* and the time and effort expended. He 'walked and rode 600 to 700 miles' and had consumed four months of his time.

Compensation for the loss of his own copy given to Simon Le Blanc had also not been paid.[27]

Ashe was not too busy with his apparently successful journalistic career to make a renewed application for support from the (Royal) Literary Fund in February 1810. Wary of his previous rejection he applied in the name of 'Charles Armitage' on 20 February and was awarded ten pounds on the following day but returned a receipt in his own name on 25 February.[28]

Then came the re-emergence of another shadowy blackmailer, Davenport Sedley, a figure so elusive many have doubted his very existence, though for a while he kept up a sustained correspondence with the Treasury Solicitor from a seemingly credible address in Grays Walk, Lambeth. He wrote to Perceval in April 1810, apparently when in possession of another copy of *The Book* obtained directly from the printer Richard Edwards. He wrote on behalf of Walter Honyford Yate. Yate was an ostensibly respectable rich man disaffected by bad debts owed to him by The Prince of Wales and Duke of York. Yate was a man with whom Thomas Ashe would have his own blackmailing relationship later on. Sedley wrote directly to Perceval fearing Herries and Litchfield as 'designing men', but naturally his note went straight from Perceval to Herries and then to Litchfield.[29] Attacking the problem from both ends he also wrote to Charles Bicknell, solicitor to the Prince of Wales, about his copy of *The Book*; that too ended up with the Treasury Solicitor.[30]

Ashe still threatened to publish *The Book* in *The Phoenix* in August 1810, despite the injunction against Blagdon not to print extracts. Ashe takes up the story in his 'Memoirs':

The Phoenix, which I conducted, was the instrument I employed. In a number of that paper, published August the fifth, 1810, I inserted the following notice:

"The Book."

"At a moment of dark mystery and bold imposition, a plan was formed for the absolute ruin and destruction of her Royal Highness the Princess of Wales. A council presumed to be called together for the glory of the crown and the good of the nation, summoned this amiable personage, interrogated her and all her domestics, and delivered their proceedings and decisions into the hands of the King. The Book, however, was compiled and printed by Mr. Perceval, her Royal Highness's attorney. He printed two thousand copies, but published no more than six. These six he delivered into the hands of the leading members of the Royal family: the remainder he held conditionally sealed up. The proceedings were no sooner seen IN PRINT by this illustrious family than they were filled with horror, remorse, and dismay. The Princess was innocent, the accuser criminal! Nothing could now be thought of but how to convert rage into friendship, or how to destroy every trace of a transaction, which Mr. Perceval, in his printed proceedings, made appear to be the most bloody and treacherous that history has upon record. To bury the proceedings of Council was the first suggestion; but it was adopted too late. "The Book" was printed. In this dilemma, Mr. Perceval was consulted. He admitted that "The Book" was printed, but denied that it was published. It was yet in his power to secure the reputation of the accusers. He could propose a scheme capable of producing this important consequence. Were he to be suddenly raised to the station of prime minister, to the chancellorship of the Exchequer, and to be secured of two of the richest sinecures in the kingdom, he would suppress his printed edition of the proceedings in council against his Royal client, and bury the whole transaction in so deep an oblivion, that it could never more rise to appearance and to light. This scheme was adopted: Mr Perceval was forming a cabinet, while Mr. Lindsell was setting fire to the two thousand copies of the Delicate Investigation, now vulgarly called "The Book." To this universal conflagration, there were some few exceptions: six rough copies had been purloined, and gone abroad. To correct this lamentable error, Mr. Perceval applied to the [Lord] Chancellor to send injunctions to the holders not to dare to publish them, and to discover the holders, rewards were offered for the extant copies, to a very large amount. Such being the case, and the importance of "The Book," the Editor of the Phoenix, who has access to one of the extant copies, is determined to give extracts from it in this paper, and to investigate the spirit and principles of the proceeding in such a manner as must eventually bring the whole question before the public eye.[31]

Handbills promising publication of *The Book* appeared on 2 August 1810. A note about it was forwarded to Perceval and sent to the

Treasury Solicitor with a covering note from Perceval dated 15 September 1810 'I suppose it is only an overture to a negotiation for a purchase.' The handbill itself was attached to a note from Charles Bicknell saying it was put in the Prince's hand and then forwarded to Perceval. Perhaps Ashe's threat to publish *The Book* in *The Phoenix* was put in the Prince's hand by Ashe himself. A government agent called immediately at the address of the proposed printing on the handbill (357 Strand) on 28 September 1810 and got no information nor from the printer of the bills themselves.[32]

The Treasury Solicitor found himself corresponding with Perceval from Cromer on 20 September 1810, finding there was no escape from *The Book* while on holiday with some useful Norfolk bankers. He suspected Davenport Sedley or Colonel Sinclair was behind the handbill threatening publication and was inclined to leave it, but he was recalled to town under pressure from Prince of Wales. Litchfield found on his return that Charles Bicknell the Prince's solicitor had left town as he had arrived. Now he was convinced that Davenport Sedley was the prime mover.

Sedley had written to Spencer Perceval on 23 August, not only about his copy of *The Book*, but also the conspiracy of an appropriately named Mr Trickey, an attorney of Rowland Street, and Colonel Sinclair of Paddington to have it reprinted. Presumably, this is the same J. G. Sinclair who had sent a blackmailing note to Perceval on 4 December 1809. Thus blackmailers began hoping to gain credit with the government by warning it about the designs of other blackmailers. Sedley wrote: 'Send this to Mr Litchfield with my compliments for him to keep, that if occasion should require, he may remember it.' But Thomas Ashe was the source of the handbill rather than Sinclair, Trickey or Sedley himself. [33]

Once again, the Prince of Wales became more directly involved through the returning Charles Bicknell, instructing the Treasury Solicitor to find grounds for prosecuting Davenport Sedley rather than simply ignoring him. Then on 13 November 1810 John Davies of No 1 Cannon Row, Parliament Street, gave an account of an interview with Davenport Sedley, in which Sedley boasted of his copy and made allegations similar to those made by Ashe, of the power Perceval had over the Royal Family and government because of *The Book*.

On 15 November 1810 came a more detailed letter from Davenport Sedley on the role of *The Book* in the change of ministry in March 1807 and in a new twist, the threat of a manuscript work (the title and preface of which he attached) by Mary Anne Clarke, 'an enemy to coercion', but in Sedley's own hand. This was entitled 'The First Chap of Revelations or A Political Mystery or An Inquiry into The Nature and Causes of the Unexampled Power and Influence of the Present Ministry'. There was more than one writer who believed Perceval had blackmailed his way to power and saw the financial possibilities as well as the moral justification for playing him at his own game. Mrs Clarke had little need of the income from a ghosted work by Davenport Sedley. She had appeared before Parliament in February 1809 and had her annuity reinstated at £7000, later raised to £10,000 for the suppression of her memoirs after 18,000 copies of the initial print run were burned. Her popularity fell when it was learned that she allowed herself to be bought off. Later she brought out *The Rival Princes* in 1810, which went over the same ground and added an attack on Colonel Wardle who led the campaign against the Duke of York in Parliament. John Joseph Stockdale later claimed to have sold the Duke of York her papers.

On 27 November the Treasury Solicitor received the unwelcome news that another copy of *The Book* was in the possession of 'Mr Rook' of 17 Cheyne Walk, who was brought to the Treasury Solicitor's chambers by Mr Swan of *The Phoenix*. We seem at this point to be very close to the Chelsea-based Thomas Ashe and his newspaper proprietor. It may even be that Rook is a rendering of Rourke, a suitably Irish pseudonym for the star writer of *The Phoenix*, Thomas Ashe. Like Ashe, 'Rook' was planning a publication based on extracts from *The Book*. The identification with Ashe seems to be borne out by what followed.[34]

With the latest letter from Davenport Sedley to Colonel McMahon, forwarded by Charles Bicknell to the Treasury Solicitor, the threat had extended from the publication of *The Book* itself to the revelation of the use Perceval had made of it to gain and maintain his power over the government and the Family. In response, Herries scribbled a querulous denial of any broken promises or wrongdoing in pencil on the reverse. He called it 'the opposition resorting to fiction for want of fact'.[35]

At this point, Ashe renewed his application to the Literary Fund, while at the same time circulating his blackmailing preface for *The Spirit of the Book*. The file relating to Thomas Ashe's applications shows that the fund had some difficulty in keeping track of them, since Ashe was in the habit of applying under pseudonyms once he was rejected. He wrote initially to the committee in his own name and to then to Richard Yates as 'Charles Armitage'. This led to Charles Monro writing to Yates following an enquiry into Ashe's character, after which the ten guineas authorised after his original application were withdrawn. In his application, he described his circumstances in the King's Bench Prison, asking not for money directly but for the Literary Fund to pay for a room on his behalf: 'In this prison I am doomed to pass the night in a confined room with twenty of the lowest order of debtors. If I be not removed then I must become a character like all the others in it, faded, fallen and lost! Save me! I beseech you save me!'[36]

His negotiations with the government over *The Spirit of the Book* are captured in the same file of the Treasury Solicitor's papers (TS 11/ 106) that contains the receipts and correspondence relating to *The Book* itself. There is substantial correspondence about the Preface and manuscript of *The Spirit of the Book* by Ashe and his agents with the Treasury Solicitor, senior ministers, and Caroline's solicitor. Joseph Haydn wrote directly to Perceval about *The Spirit of the Book* just as the government may have felt it had recovered most of the stray copies of *The Book* itself and compelled the acquiescence of the booksellers through bribery and threat. A fresh menace now emerged. The file contains a printed preface by Ashe and four letters of 18 and 20 March and 13, 16 April 1811, sent from Stafford Place, Buckingham Gate.

So the first attempt to extract money from the government for *The Spirit of the Book* came via Timothy Joseph Haydn, posing as Ashe's creditor. Haydn claimed to have acquired the book for the government in the expectation of being rewarded by them. On 18 March 1811, Haydn told Perceval that he had encountered Ashe in King's Bench prison and as his creditor had acquired a joint share in a proposed publication in 'large octavo', which he described as a 'Political Romance'. Mr Longman of Paternoster Row looked, he said, but did not buy (Mr Allen looked harder, later, and did buy). 'Captain Ashe as an author has much celebrity as a political writer much more he is an author of popular works,' he concluded, artfully maintaining an air of menace behind this apparently dispassionate estimation of Ashe's literary abilities. The reply from Herries was, as the government's initial reactions generally were, rather dismissive: 'Mr Perceval must decline having anything to do with such a work.' The notes became gradually less disdainful as the menace increased and pressure from the Prince of Wales was applied through his solicitor.

The government's measure of control seemed to have increased with the conviction at the Old Bailey on 3 April 1811 of Davenport Sedley. He was indicted for feloniously stealing, on the 18th of January, five bills of exchange for the payment of five hundred pounds each, a bill of exchange, value three hundred pound and two bills of exchange, value two hundred. each, the property of Thomas Taylor, Marquis of Headfort, yet another Irish aristocrat in our story, his notoriety resting on his elopement with the wife of a clergyman in 1803 and the subsequent law suit. Being committed to Newgate prison did not stop the flow of threatening correspondence from Davenport Sedley; increasingly varied and desperate attempts at blackmail.

Joseph Haydn was not deterred by Perceval's initial dismissal. He was no longer the concerned citizen presenting Ashe's book as a seditious work to be suppressed, but rather a literary agent offering it as a great work of literature, worthy to be published. On 13 April 1811, Haydn added a measure of urgency in the next letter to Perceval: 'a loyal and patriotic feeling pervades the work; it will merit well the patronage of The Royal Family and the approbation of mankind.' If suppression was not an option Haydn claimed, they must look to publication instead. The tone of the notes becomes harder. He would have sent the government the book on approval before but not now. This again carried a reply from Thomas Brooksbank, as from Downing Street: 'You must use your own judgement, Mr Perceval does not feel that seeing you upon the subject could be of any service.'

On 16 April 1811, Haydn increased the pressure again by enclosing Ashe's preface: 'Censure and reprobation have been heaped upon the innocent while sentiments of pity and commiseration have to this day been entertained for those who alone merit public indignation and disgrace.' Ashe's sources, Haydn confided, were *The Book* and, he hinted Caroline's confidences 'from sources equally authentic and incontrovertible'.

Then, on 7 May 1811, came the news that Ashe had indeed found a publisher, albeit, if Ashe's account is to be believed, at a much reduced fee. Haydn sent the Treasury Solicitor Allen's advertisement for the forthcoming *The Spirit of the Book*. Again, Perceval's calm indifference to the threat posed by Thomas Ashe was undermined by the blind panic he induced in the mind of the Prince Regent. The advertisement prompted a flurry of activity from the Prince of Wales through his solicitor and the indifferent tone of the government changed. Suddenly, it was not just the Treasury Solicitor and Brooksbank (because Herries was too busy) but also Charles Bicknell and Colonel McMahon, the Prince of Wales's Privy Purse.

The government's agents in dealing with seditious and dangerous writers could be as disreputable as the writers themselves. With the Treasury Solicitor, law officers and Bow Street magistrates, Ashe's negotiations are generally conducted in a tone of mutual respect and regretful necessity. It was a different matter with the personal officers of the Prince of Wales. The Privy Purse Colonel John McMahon, described as 'a sort of manager for the Prince of Wales', was an Irishman, talented, resourceful, rather like Ashe in fact. His range of tasks included encouraging loyal papers, discouraging hostile ones, and supplying documents damaging to the Princess's reputation.

The job of the Treasury Solicitor was 'to guide the subsidised newspapers', but the Privy Purse was needed to bribe and threaten the independent ones. Writers of all political shades could earn a government living in one way or another, rewarded with pensions or occasional payments for suppression. George Cruikshank in *The Scourge* had great fun with the large, ageing lovers of the lecherous Prince. 'The Court of Love' shows McMahon pouring sovereigns into a bawd's apron: 'Let her be forty at least, plump and sprightly.' Two related duties for the Privy Purse sort of meet: procuring mistresses and suppressing caricature.

Are they bribing Ashe or intimidating him? There were offers of patronage from both sides. McMahon was removed from office not for embezzlement, though he was rumoured to have left with drawers full of cash, but because his drunkenness and overconfidence might lead to indiscretion. He was eventually replaced by Benjamin Bloomfield. The new Privy Purse was no more exalted than was his predecessor. Lord Glenbervie, in his diary of 21 December 1810, reported with approval Sir Henry Englefield's description of Bloomfield as 'a canting methodistical hypocrite, always talking religion, but living, though a married man, in bare-faced adultery with the Marchioness of Downshire.' The Treasury Solicitor's papers and his collection of suppressed cartoons and seditious literature indicate how routinely satirists were bribed by these men. The practice stopped with them as Sir William Knighton, Bloomfield's successor, did not continue it.

Given his conviction that rank should not protect vice, Sir Nathaniel Conant must have been uncomfortable with his role in tracing stray copies of *The Book* to protect the reputation of the Prince Regent and Spencer. Nonetheless, he used his agent in Fleet Street, 'Robinson the bookseller', to track down yet another copy and enclosed with it a note from Prince's solicitor Charles Bicknell of 3 May 1811, which left no room for doubt as to who was the real force behind the attempt to track down all these copies. 'The Prince wished that you should be acquainted with all the circumstances.' Perceval's struggles to contain the monster he had created were made more difficult by the Prince, who was more prone to panic.

Information soon arrived to the effect that extracts from a copy of *The Book* were in the possession of a Mr Dobson. This came with an ominous note that Ashe expected to make three thousand guineas if publication went ahead. A chastened but still voluble Davenport Sedley was writing no longer from Lambeth but from the State Side of Newgate Prison on 15 May 1811, after his conviction on what he calls a vague charge of conspiracy. Perceval, he said, deserved 'every censure that can be thrown on him' for getting it printed.

> If the narrative of what passed between 5 February and 31 March 1807 between that gentleman (Perceval) and his Majesty were ever to be published it would reduce him, Lord Eldon and [Lord] Liverpool to the lowest ebb.[37]

On the seventh of that month, Sedley claimed, Perceval sent printed copies of *The Book* to the King, the Prince of Wales, Lord Moira and Mr Adam and blackmailed the Family to turn out Grenville's government under the cloak of the Catholic Question.

June 1811 saw celebrations of the Regency finally authorised under cover of a reception for the visiting French royal family. Neither Caroline, Charlotte nor the sisters in the Nunnery were invited. Mrs Fitzherbert was another notable absentee, refusing to sit at table with Lady Hertford. *Morning Post* editor Peter Stuart was offered a post in government when the Regent ascended.

The Prince of Wales might feel more secure as Regent, but the bribery to suppress *The Book* continued. The final items in the file of booksellers' undertakings included a covering note and a printed handbill for Ashe's *The Spirit of the Book*, which had reminded John Turnbull of the newspaper advertisements of 1809 for the return of *The Book* and that his copy might still be of value. On 12 July, Turnbull's undertaking and acknowledgement of £400 for his copy were duly recorded; still the happy recipients of the 'handsome gratuity' came and went.[38]

On 29 October 1811, there was a sample oath and bond that William Bays had given up his copy of the book and had kept no extracts. Bays had to wait some time for his money because on 2 May 1812 is there a receipt for £50 paid by the Treasury Solicitor to him for four specified pages.[39] This is the last transaction in the file and a clear indication that Spencer Perceval was the force behind the pursuit of the stray copies five years after they were printed. With Perceval's assassination on 11 May 1812, the pursuit of the stray copies of *The Book* ceased. By then *The Spirit of the Book* was going through its fourth edition and the government had a new Thomas Ashe manuscript to contend with, his Frogmore nunnery revelation, *The Claustral Palace or Memoirs of the Family*.

The *Memoirs of Caroline* published by Joseph Nightingale immediately after her death give a very similar account to Ashe's of the allegations in Parliament by Samuel Whitbread and others in 1811 against Perceval for his role in the suppression of *The Book*. Nightingale gives a verbatim reproduction of *The Book* and the debates in Parliament that followed Caroline's qualified acquittal. Perceval was then challenged about the expense of buying up copies of the book by the radical MP Samuel Whitbread:

There was a time when the right honourable gentleman, Mr. Perceval, not only thought it not inconsistent with his duty to give information on the subject of the 'Delicate Investigation', but when he took every pains to spread this information as generally as possible. At that time a book was prepared, which was intended to be circulated most extensively, both here and upon the continent. The Book, however, had been suppressed, and the outstanding copies had been bought up at a great expense, out of some fund or other, whether public or private he could not say. He could not conceive why the right honourable gentleman now remained mute, when before he had a thousand tongues.

If any man can satisfy the public upon this topic, it is the right honourable gentleman, Mr. Perceval. They believe him to have conscientiously undertaken her defence—to have written her vindication—to have perused that vindication—to have published it. That vindication is said to have involved in it an attack upon her royal consort. It was known to have been an attack upon his Royal Highness, and the Regent's first minister is known to have been the author of it: and after he had published it; after it had been read by one and one hundred, it was bought up at an enormous expense; bought up by the private secretary of the honourable gentleman. I ask him now; does he retain his former opinion of the unexceptionable conduct of the Princess of Wales? I ask him, if he did not lately in the House solemnly record his confirmation of that opinion?

When Swan was pressured out of publishing *The Book* in *The Phoenix* Ashe retired to Brighton to write *The Spirit of the Book* in six weeks, a book designed to give Caroline's account and defence of her conduct and to show 'nobility in adversity'. He wrote better than Caroline spoke. The manuscript was given to a printer called Carpenter; the son of a General Carpenter said to have drowned himself in hopeless love for Princess Elizabeth, debarred to him by the strictures of the Royal Marriages Act.

Ashe predicted the assassination of Spencer Perceval in office (albeit in his 'Memoirs' three years after the event, but claiming to have done so at the time) as a consequence of his shameful use of the *The Book* and his abandonment of Caroline after he had gained political power. 'It would bring the attorney who abandoned his client, to end the career of his vices and ambition in a death at once shameful, terrible and premature.'

Ashe was then called in by his Brazilian creditors and put in the Poultry Compter gaol and then in the King's Bench prison after being sentenced at the Mayoral Court in the Mansion House by Alderman Scholey. Davenport Sedley had been tried before the same court with Scholey on the bench in April of the same year, suggesting his trial, like Sedley's, was to some extent 'political' and the charges against him an opportunity for the government to constrain a potential blackmailer.

While in the King's Bench prison in January 1811, Ashe was not entirely dependent on the Literary Fund to improve his lot. He wrote a poem 'The Legal Vulture' about the machinations of his accusers, who then bought the poem from him in order to suppress it. His first circular to the booksellers about *The Spirit of the Book* came from the State House of King's Bench, perhaps an indication that the proceeds of 'The Legal Vulture' had enabled him to improve his accommodation and circumstances in the prison.

Ashe then recounted his meeting with Mr Allen the publisher who affected indignation at *The Spirit of the Book* to get the price down, though he admitted 'the language is musical.' Allen, Ashe claimed, paid £250 for the book and made £7,000 in three months.

Ashe's reputation as a journalist who sells was now at its height. Back at *The Phoenix*, he commanded, he says, fees 'unparalleled in literary annals', essentially for writing scurrilous attacks. He sold his 'Argument for Parliamentary Reform' to Walter Honeyford Yate for £300, his 'History of the Azores' for £250 and 'Ireland's Catholic Question' for £110. Sprung from King's Bench by unnamed (unknown?) friends in high places, later it was suggested that this was done by the Home Department and was the beginning of pressure on Ashe to abandon Caroline and to write for the Regent. It would be alleged that the government had freed him in order to write *The Spirit of the Book* as an anti-Caroline work, but he had clearly written it before his imprisonment and in its published form it was unashamedly pro Caroline. Papers in the Treasury Solicitor's files show that Ashe's agents offered it to the government for suppression before publication, as a work that would influence public opinion in Caroline's favour and threaten the Prince Regent and his government.

The title page of *The Spirit of the Book: Memoirs of Caroline Princess of Hasburgh* carried *The Times* advert for the recovery of *The Book* of 27 March 1809. The introductory note to 'The Spirit' found its way in draft form into the Treasury Solicitor's papers. Here *The Book*, properly 'The Delicate Investigation', was described as 'an unnatural guilty and malignant volume'. *The Spirit* articulated Caroline's voice in a rather more eloquent way than the letters defending her conduct in *The Book* itself.

Other titles advertised at the back *The Spirit of the Book*, also published by Allen & Co. (so squeamish about the scandalous content of Ashe's title) suggest it was in fact just their kind of thing. There was *The Monk's Daughter, or Hypocrisy*. It is not difficult to deduce what might be going on there or indeed in *A Peep into the Tuileries, or Parisian Manners*. The Ancient Regime was still fruitful ground for racy fiction after the Revolution had swept it away. Would *The Spirit of the Book*, a political and amatory romance, herald a revolution in England?

The Spirit of the Book fitted with Allen's other titles in the sense that it dwelt on personal and private life in high places. There is exaggeration and melodrama but *The Spirit of the Book* is not a bodice-ripper, it was designed to be credible and help restore Caroline's reputation. After all that legal negotiation and official panic, what was Ashe's 'separate piece' like? *The Spirit of the Book* takes the form of letters from Caroline to her daughter Charlotte, then only fifteen years old, explaining her conduct and countering the rumours about her still being circulated by her enemies, while the outcome of the investigation was still secret: 'But "THE Book" is suppressed, and you are told, that I, your unfortunate mother, am not to be estimated at any value since "the Enquiry" was thought necessary to be pursued.'

In the Preface Caroline gives a reasoned analysis to her daughter Charlotte of the Delicate Investigation and its effect: 'once agitated [it was] not presented in an honest way to the nation. It has robbed me of the society of my husband and my daughter.' Arguably, she had been robbed of her husband's society ten years earlier, but the rumour and secrecy had undoubtedly damaged her reputation. However, her allies and advisers counselled her against pressing for publication as the evidence against her might be damaging in the eyes of the public. Charlotte was reputedly shocked by the contents of the report when it was finally published in 1813. In the Preface Ashe also set out the motivation for the work, building on the hints in Joseph Haydn's notes to the Treasury Solicitor: 'Censure and reprobation have been heaped upon the innocent, while sentiments of pity and commiseration have, to this day, been entertained for those, who alone merit public indignation and disgrace.'

He also suggests that a stray copy of *The Book* was deliberately given to him and that this was augmented by direct personal information, presumably from Caroline herself:

> He fully pledges himself that his work is formed upon the basis of the suppressed Book, which was placed for that express purpose in his hands; and he also declares that the original facts and interesting anecdotes, with which his pages are illuminated, are derived from a source equally authentic and incontrovertible.

Early on in *The Spirit* Ashe dealt with the principal accusations in *The Book*, beginning with Caroline's supposed naval lovers Captain Penrice, Captain Manby, and Admiral Sir Sidney Smith, all examples of what *The Book* called her 'indiscreet confidences and acquaintances'. Ashe's whole career was spent in dealing in gossip of this kind so it was a new role for him to refute it. Evidently, he felt there was value in quoting from phrases from the *The Book* to lend an air of authenticity to his work as if his readers would recognise them, though his great selling point was that he has seen the proofs of it and they had not. Perhaps enough copies had passed from hand to hand for some of its phrases to become current, despite all the government's attempts at suppression.

Ashe could draw on his personal experience in Brunswick to give his readers the background to Caroline's liking for military men, which was in in part explained by Brunswick's military weakness, its failure in war with France and thralldom to Prussia. This cheapens the Brunswick sensibility, its sense of its worth of life and manners. Caroline resolved to insist on exceptional character and fame. Against this expectation Ashe introduced the hero of his narrative, Captain Browne, as an accomplished Irish soldier, called in Ashe's version 'Algernon'. As well as his military bearing, he is blessed with literary attainments allied to Caroline's, she tells us: 'I was celebrated for elegance, literature, and wit'. As well as engaging in elegant conversation, Caroline is tutored by him, 'perfecting my knowledge of the English language'. Satirists were apt to suggest that Caroline's English was never perfected and remained eccentric until the end of her life. Ashe is perhaps merging details of Captain Browne's relationship as Caroline's lover with his own experience described in his 'Memoirs' as tutor in languages to the ladies of the court of Brunswick. In *The Spirit of the Book*, Captain Browne becomes both, and Ashe as the author can step back as faithful chronicler, uniquely able to furnish his characters with first-hand accounts of conversation and situation, because some of it was his own: 'Instruction, thus carried on, became every day more delightful and interesting to me.'

The lovers then have a very slight falling out on the question of whether or not virtue can be taught. This sounds a bit unlikely but but is lent verisimilitude by it dullness. The first fly in the ointment and the precursor of Lady Jersey as a seeming friend determined to meddle in Caroline's relationships, is Melina Countess of Weimar. In the best Gothic tradition she is a model of 'seeming virtue' but has been tutored in vice and dissimulation by a corrupt priest. She and Algernon have a long dispute on the role of passion in religion, which again sounds slightly too dry to have been made up, but is clearly part of that literary tradition in which men and women spar in erudite conversation and the reader is given insight into their character and compatibility.

Caroline learns Alexander Pope's poem 'Windsor Forest' and complains 'I have seen Windsor and felt no pleasure. I have wandered in her forests, and was alive to every thing but delight. But I must not anticipate.'

The damage is already done, the claustral influence of royal Windsor estate and the celibate slough of Frogmore permeates the book before Caroline even embarks for Britain. We then have the full melodrama of Melina's declaration of love, Caroline's own declaration to her mother and the forswearing of 'political' marriage and Melina's confession of her own attempt to lure Algernon from her. Algernon leaves for Paris after a misunderstanding with Caroline over Melina. They are reconciled through Prince Louis of Prussia.

Warming to his theme, Ashe focussed on The Royal Marriages Act and narrow circle of possible candidates for George's hand. There is a very modern ring to Ashe's assessment of the publicity the royal children are subjected to and the means by which they cope with it.

By an absurd law, a law made in violation of the great charter, which expressly secures to each subject the uncontrolled right of disposing of his person and property, the sons and daughters of the House of Edinburgh are condemned to celibacy, or else to marry any foreign Protestant prince or princess, that may be deemed, after proposals, an eligible match.

In consequence of this law, the sons waste the vigour of their mind in the lap of enervating enjoyments; and, at a time when they ought to be married men, philosophers, statesmen, and warriors, they are found with the reins loosened at the call of passion; and, instead of rising in the scale of excellence, they are compelled to sink in vicious depravity below their fellow-citizens; who are secured from the subjugation of criminal pursuits, by the domestic society of British wives, who are a pattern of virtue, of honour, and of truth.

Strangers to the tenderness of conjugal love, the sons waste their affections in the embraces of harlots; or, if they enter into a political marriage, their condition is more miserable than what can well be conceived. Without knowing the temper, manners, and character of those with whom they engage, they enjoy no satisfaction; soothe or share no cares, and must aggravate and augment mutual defects and infirmities.

They cast their eyes upon their situation, and contrast the freedom they enjoyed in the company of prostitutes, with the tyranny imposed upon them by political wives, in whom their hearts have no manner of interest or concern.

If such be the case of the sons of the House of Edinburgh, the fate of its daughters is infinitely less capable to be endured.

Perpetually secluded from marriage with their countrymen, however nobly and highly descended, and condemned to consume their life in hopes of some beggarly protestant Prince applying for their hand, they are placed on a tottering eminence, exposed to a multitude of watchful and scrutinising eyes.

There is nothing they perform that is not known, and the notorious subject of conversation. Their amusements are examined with an attention which themselves do not think they deserve. Their foibles are magnified through a thousand censorious glasses, and their smallest levities considered as the utmost stretch of human crime.

An insuperable line of separation is drawn between them and the nobility and gentry of their native land. They are immured in castles. No man, but the invalids and servants of the state, can enter those castles; no one must behold their faces, but at church or at court. An inevitable death or perpetual imprisonment, awaits the man who shall attempt to intrude himself into their apartments, or address a few words to them on meeting them out of doors. And the smallest instances of their affability, partiality, or kindness, such as a smile, a nod, the return of a bow, or the extension of the hand for an embrace, are interpreted into the signs of a passion, which, if not checked, would infuse the dreadful contagion of love over the regions of the imagination and the heart.

Once her marriage to the Prince of Wales was arranged, Caroline and the court at Brunswick were visited by English politicians including Lord Grey and Lord St Helens. Among the English entourage, a lovelorn traveller made his way to Court of Brunswick, and with him, we have the first intimations in Ashe's work of the love life of Princess Elizabeth, his contemporary and favourite among the sisters. She was to be the narrator of his *Claustral Palace* and more of its chapters were devoted to her love for the young Dormer Montague than to the lovers of her more impetuous sisters. Dorothy Margaret Stuart in *The Daughters of George III* (2017) calls *The Spirit of the Book* 'preposterous' twice without further comment, and Ashe himself 'a vile insect', which perhaps seems a bit harsh at two hundred years distance with no other evidence before her than a wildly successful and entertaining book. Oddly, given this starting point, her reasons for citing him at all are generally to quote passages from the book that seem particularly apt or to be based on some inside knowledge, including the scene of Montague being told to travel for six years after his discovery at Frogmore and the associated gentle and intimate portrait of the Princess:

> As to the form of Lady E, without being thin and taper, it is limber and elegant; elastic and well contoured: and those attractive properties, added to the softness and fairness of her skin; to the freshness of her complexion, and the carnation of her frame, render her one of the most interesting women of the age.

The is much more about the relationship between Elizabeth and the 'Young Dormer' in Ashe's *The Claustral Palace* For now we must leave him, despairing of her love, thanks to the Royal Marriages Act, on his way to kill himself crossing the great Rhine waterfall in Switzerland.

Characteristically, Ashe mixes his references to her beloved brother George's well-known financial embarrassments with an appreciation of his finer qualities: 'The heir to the House of Edinburgh is a man of feeling and honour – he owes to his tradesmen about half a million and his father refuses to discharge that enormous debt unless the son will consent to marry.' For the Prince 'convenience was the groundwork of his consent' and drove him to forsake his real love, Mrs Fitzherbert, 'to violate the sacred engagements he has sometime made and performed with a gentlewoman of considerable beauty, merit and worth'. Something always denied but widely known and with no prospect of prosecution.

Captain Browne diplomatically leaves Caroline's court, realising that the pressure of Brunswick's weakness makes alliance with England a political necessity. Her father sets out the situation, her marriage the only way to restore the fortunes and prestige of the dukedom of Brunswick after its defeat by France. Caroline's reaction is 'I will never consent to a marriage cold, forced and political.' Her mother, in tears, counsels that marrying the 'Marquis of Albion', son of the Duke of Edinburgh, is the only way to keep Algernon from prison.

Ashe quotes an inscription from the Panthéon in Paris: 'Mankind are created equal. Under the government of law, innocence is secure.' This is a form of rebuke since the theme of the book is that innocence is not secure when the law is The Royal Marriages Act. The Act becomes an infringement of fundamental principles of freedom and dignity, which lends a sense of purpose and moral justification to the couple's last-minute attempt to evade it. Through the noble agency of Lord Edward Fitzgerald there came the idea of elopement to Ireland with Caroline dressed as a boy. Algernon is given leave by the Duke of Brunswick to visit his father, 'the man of nature and of truth' in Ireland. Part of Ashe's purpose is to have a narrative in which the Duke of Brunswick is forced by weakness to accept 'cold political marriage' for his daughter while Captain Browne's father is free to act on principle and in the interests of his child. Lord Edward was the perfect man to act as agent to the scheme, instinctively noble and impetuous with a disregard for the constraints and conventions of rank.

The moral atmosphere of the Prince of Wales's court is brought to Caroline in Brunswick by his chaplain, 'Dr R', who mixes antipathy and moralising. Once again, she is caught reading Alexander Pope, this time for pleasure and the chaplain wants her to give up Pope's 'Essay on Man' and to read the Bible instead. She beats him in reasoned theological argument, which he resents, a view of Caroline as a theologian and philosopher that would have come as a surprise even to sympathetic readers.

Caroline briefly believes Algernon to be shipwrecked, and then Lord Edward Fitzgerald brings to her her lover's plan of elopement to Ireland, as it is too dangerous for Captain Browne to come himself and for his intentions to be discovered. Lord Edward reveals that Caroline is to 'assume the garb of an English youth' and join him in Ireland. Setting off on her journey in the company of Lord Edward (and presumably Captain Ashe), she passes her grandfather's grave and is filled with remorse, remembering the likely effect on her family of her elopement. A search party sent by her father overtakes them. She is brought the slightly unlikely news of the brief skirmish that follows: 'Your Algernon and his banditti, while striking at your father's, brother's, and friends' lives, were destroyed or subdued.' Algernon nobly gives himself up and urges Lord Edward to flee rather than strike at Caroline's father. Imprisoned, Algernon will only be released when Caroline marries 'The Marquis', so Caroline does so to save him from incarceration.

There is a rapid proxy marriage and no farewell for the lovers, Caroline, unsurpisinglyly, predicts an end to the Royal Marriages Act. She then visits Algernon in prison in secret. The visit is discovered by her father and she hears her mother's strictures on marital behaviour, which directly contradict those of Lady Jersey.

Her voyage to England brings Caroline's encounter with Captain Penrice and the beginning of the slander; his pointing out the stars to Caroline and wrapping her in his boat cloak becomes a major incident in *The Book*. In *The Spirit* their conversation is mainly about politics and Bonaparte, the Captain comparing him unfavourably with Alexander the Great, in contrast to the English prejudice in Napoleon's favour at this time. Caroline's first view of England is not favourable: 'the annual process of vegetation [by which she meant spring] was not yet finished;' a rather dull event.

Caroline prattles in her fateful coach journey to London with Lady Jersey about her deep love for Captain Browne whom she could not marry because of the difference in their rank, hoping to win over a female friend and ally against the constraints of the Act; she gives ammunition to a deadly enemy.

> Perhaps it will scarcely be believed that at the commencement of the nineteenth century I should have been driven from my palace and separated from my husband and his family by the intrigues of a noble prostitute.
>
> This profligate adulteress is yet in existence. She is the author of all my degradation and despair! At the day of reckoning, and her account is large, she will find her persecuting spirit towards me, and towards you, my daughter, recorded against her in characters of living fire.
>
> I should have told you, that 'he Countess' commenced proceedings, by cultivating a particular intimacy with me, in order to draw from my breast those secrets which she thought necessary for the establishment of my future infamy and misery.

The countess advises that those in English aristocratic circles marry for form's sake and carry on affairs as if nothing has happened, enjoying 'unbounded freedom' after marriage.

> In this manner did the countess endeavour to exaggerate the incontinence of the English nobility, no doubt with the view of debauching my mind and veiling over the enormities of her own heart.

The Spirit of the Book is rather at odds with the standard account of the first meeting of the ill-starred married couple. Ashe has the Prince of Wales displaying considerable charm. At first he is nicer than she had been led to believe and more understanding of her predicament than most accounts of his behaviour credit him with. Their infamous wedding night is also quite sensitively done; George recognises her earlier attachment and his own. Their agreement not to live as man and wife is immediate, mutual and amicable, a more sympathetic view of George's reaction than is usually given, another indication that Ashe's sources are closer to the parties themselves than the standard caricature.

Nonetheless, Caroline quickly becomes a clear-eyed critic of English manners and the character of the King and Queen, 'The Duke and Duchess of Edinburgh' as they are styled in *The Spirit of the Book*. Her letters home to her mother were in this vein, with comic portraits of the King and Queen, including the Queen's 'absence of taste', but the letters found their way to the Queen via the Prince's Chaplain and Lady Jersey. Caroline complained of her treatment as 'an exile in my own family' and caricatures of the family spark The Delicate Investigation. Her literary skills evidence of her facility at observation, her characterisation and even satire helped make her a sympathetic figure to Thomas Ashe – but they were not suitable accomplishments for a royal princess.

Soured by the stories of Lady Jersey about Captain Penrice, the Prince of Wales begins to think that Caroline is just averse to him rather than committed to another and their relationship deteriorates. No doubt for Charlotte's benefit Caroline tells her that her birth temporarily restored the Prince's favour: 'He regarded you as the sweet tie of connubial bliss.' There is no hint in *The Spirit of the Book* of his sudden illness and his will in favour of Mrs Fitzherbert. Gradually Caroline is driven out to establish her own patronage and connections with military men. 'I was tried without a trial, arraigned without an accuser and acquitted without a jury.' All of the family apart from 'Lord William Henry' were still distant after Caroline's 'exoneration' and the king's circular urging the family to re-admit her. Hence Ashe's address to his ghost in *The Claustral Palace*.

The charges in the report are pronounced 'unfounded and vexatious' by the Privy Council but the 'Marquis of Albion' (the Prince of Wales) is not convinced. The suppression of the report of the investigation perpetuates suspicions. The King orders the printing of the report for the family and a meeting at Windsor. The Duke of Kent brings up 'Charge 18', Caroline's meetings with 'The Stranger in the Cottage':

> To this Lord Edward [Duke of Kent] speaking for the rest, replied—"It is the eighteenth charge, which states that a stranger resided in a cottage at Blackheath, for a length of time; that he frequently went disguised and armed to the residence of the Princess, and that during the investigation he abruptly disappeared. He has however since returned to the same cottage, and to the same course of life, from which we imply intentions of intrigue."

At this point Caroline finds she cannot deny Captain Browne's presence: 'They discovered MY MINIATURE upon his writing table, and sonnets and odes inscribed to "Caroline," lay upon the surface of his desk.'

Then, with an exquisite sense of timing, Willikin runs in calling Algernon 'father'. Algernon tells the royal brothers that the boy is the son of Louis of Prussia and Melina of Weimar and the Prince is convinced by his explanation. With this happy ending the narrative concludes.

Beyond Ashe's boasting, we can only guess at the true readership and reception of *The Spirit of the Book*. We know that copies, including individually bound personal ones, found their way into the libraries of royalty from the Duke of York to Caroline Murat, Queen of Naples and sister of Napoleon, as well as those of Mary, Marchioness of Downshire, and William Beckford. Flora Fraser notes that *The Spirit* increased Italian interest in Caroline even before she left Britain and came to live in Italy: 'Roman nobility were more influenced by "Spirit" than by the Delicate Investigation itself, a mediocre and fantastic work which they read with avidity, turned the heads of the Italian ladies.'[40]

Ashe also claimed a success with the circulating libraries, with single institutions taking sixty copies and through them a huge popular readership for the book in its twenty-two editions. Ashe's work gave a more colourful and personal defence by Caroline of her conduct than the carefully worded letters from her, which eventually appeared in *The Book* when it was finally published in 1813. For a modern reader looking back, it is difficult to believe there was ever enough in either work to bring down the government, but *The Spirit* gave clear evidence of what had been done by whom and why. It found its way into the libraries of a number of influential people and for a while became synonymous with *The Book* itself. By degrees, the government would be driven to defend its machinations in Parliament, but for now sales of *The Spirit of the Book* soared and Caroline's reputation was bolstered by it. The duration and detail of Perceval's attempts to use and suppress *The Book* gave Ashe the ammunition and motivation to write *The Spirit*. With Perceval's assassination in May 1812, the question of his use of *The Book* for his own political advancement receded in importance.

The prominence of Ashe's fiction and its revelations is attested by a couple of images recorded in the British Museum Cartoon catalogue. Published on 1 September 1812, 'The Coronation of the Empress of the Nairs' by George Cruikshank shows a military figure with Caroline's daughter Charlotte as the Royal Princes make off with their various lovers. He is tentatively identified as Charles of Hesse, but his speech bubble gives him a comic Irish voice 'Shure, and I'll to Wales', a tall army figure well known to her, taking her back to her mother. Surely, this is Ashe's Captain Browne. Is there a scurrilous hint in her look and their closeness that he and not the Regent was her father? Generally, he appears in this and in subsequent cartoons as the perpetually youthful hussar hero of the 1790s, the military hero and rescuer of the banner of Brunswick in battle. Here he is slightly closer to his actual age, a more credible father figure next to Charlotte. Captain Browne was back on the scene after Caroline's separation, a recognisable figure to a contemporary London readership.[41]

On New Year's Day 1813 came a more direct tribute to Ashe's influence, 'The Spirit of the Book or Anticipation of the year 1813'. The Prince Regent and Lady Hertford look on in horror as the Delicate Investigation comes back to haunt them, in the form of *The Spirit of the Book,* a volume with a pale face, arms and legs. Caroline appears to be appealing to the Spirit to proclaim her innocence. In a sense Ashe's book has become a character in Caroline's story, whose influence was still obviously current.[42]

Emboldened by his own power and success as a writer, Ashe could now help ensure that Caroline secured her position after the Delicate Investigation. In *The Spirit of the Book* he had bolstered Caroline's defence of her own conduct, but she was now an outsider in her Uncle George III's family and her husband remained determined to ensure she had no role in the upbringing of their child or the life of the nation. Her position sharpened her naturally satirical view of the moral hypocrisy of The Family and their many oddities in life and love. This would be her insurance policy against further attempts to undermine her. She had her own blackmailing project, another aspect of the royal love ménage that had not been the subject of investigation. Darker and more hidden than Caroline's love life at Blackheath were the longings, suppressions and punishments of the princesses in 'The Nunnery' at Frogmore.

BOOK II

Voices from 'the Nunnery'

4

The Claustral Palace

Captain Thomas Ashe had built his reputation on telling his illustrious patron's story in a way she could not. After being her ghost and champion in the phenomenally successful *The Spirit of the Book*, he could now turn the gossip Caroline had received from Princess Elizabeth about the life she and her sisters led at Frogmore into a new book, which would naturally take the form of confessional letters written to her by Elizabeth. Despite *The Spirit of the Book* redeeming Caroline's reputation in the eyes of the public, at least in the author's opinion, Caroline was not vindicated in the eyes of The Family. Even her sympathetic uncle, the king, had reservations about re-admitting her to court life because of the report's reservations, This, she felt, was hypocritical, not only in light of her husband's infidelities, but because of the king's own embarrassing 'attempts' on Caroline at Blackheath while he was recovering from his illness. There was also the wider hypocrisy of The Family in view of the scandalous love lives of 'the Nunnery' at Frogmore. She had the confidences of her cousins the royal princesses up her sleeve.

At the time that the Delicate Investigation reported to the King, in July 1806, the Prince of Wales took the opportunity to tell his sister Amelia of Caroline's blackmailing intention to reveal all about 'the Nunnery' if the Delicate Investigation did not find in her favour.

I tell you what, my dear Amelia, the Princess says, if things don't quite end to her satisfaction, she will bring forward many things she has seen and heard of your sisters and will say the K[ing] allows things here, which he finds fault with in her. Don't be uneasy, it cannot injure your plans, and perhaps it might prove a blessing and make you all much happier.[1]

Was this a concoction designed to turn the sisters against Caroline? Or a warning of a genuine threat? Either way, the concluding sentence seems extraordinary. Why raise the prospect of blackmail and the public revelation of their private lives, only to say it could not do harm? Perhaps it was to emphasise Caroline's bad character and his own power to protect them from it. There is also the possibility, which chimes in with Ashe's depiction of the Prince as a victim of the Royal Marriages Act as well as his sisters, that Caroline's revelations could demonstrate the absurdity and hypocrisy of the Royal Marriages Act and so hasten its end. He was in no doubt, it seemed, that Caroline's revelations were not rumour, but rather what she knew to be true at first hand.

Recent studies of the princesses have rightly tried to get behind the collective veneer of princessdom and show the sisters as individual women with full characters and sensibilities of their own at the head of their society. Admirable though this is, still the most remarkable thing about them is the peculiarity of their position, which made that kind of personal development, self-expression and public influence so difficult to sustain. Royalty, particularly unmarried princesses, had always been constrained as to whom they could meet and where they could go, but 'The Nunnery' at Frogmore struck contemporaries as well as our modern sensibility as being peculiarly restrictive.

In the final volume of his *Memoirs and Confessions* Ashe recounted the sequence of events four years before his autobiography was published, which had seen the composition of *The Claustral Palace*. In the summer of 1811, he left London for Bristol and the company of his sage and deserving curate brother Jonathan. He again asked the Duke of Northumberland and Lord Byron to elevate his brother from his obscure curacy. Byron certainly seems an unlikely source of ecclesiastical patronage. Perhaps Jonathan was not just the poor cleric Thomas made him out to be, since he was soon in league with his brother, pretending to alert the government to Thomas's bad character and his serious intention to publish *The Claustral Palace*. Jonathan's role is always slightly murky. Was he the outraged upright citizen, the learned clergymen seeking to warn the government about his brother's activities, or was he simply acting to solicit suppression money on his brother's behalf? Later evidence suggests the latter more likely.

Thomas Ashe complained that his serious books like *Travels in America* or *Henry Percy, or the Liberal Critic* did not command anything like the same fees or attention as his works of royal scandal. He felt swindled by the booksellers and returned, with apparent reluctance, but high financial expectations, to blackmailing novels written for suppression.

Here in Ashe's own words are the circumstances of the composition and initial reception of *The Claustral Palace*:

> Thus provided, I sat down, and, in the course of three months, composed a large work in four volumes, entitled, "The Claustral Palace; or, Memoirs of the Family." As I came to the close of the fourth volume, I issued a circular letter, descriptive of the springs and principles on which this work moved; and such was the interest this circular excited, that, before I had revised my manuscript, I received several proposals respecting it, and was visited by several violent characters from London, amongst whom were the noted [Davenport] Sedl[e]y, and Admiral and Colonel Graves. At length, weary of treaty and competition, I closed with the offer of a Mr. [Carpenter], and sold half of my copyright for the sum of seven hundred pounds. Mr. C—— was to print and publish at his cost, and give me half the profits, clear of all demands. In this manner was my avarice fully gratified, and my ambition on the road to unbounded success; for my plan was (and I insisted on Mr. C—— acting upon it), to play the Perceval game; that is, to print privately, and to issue but six copies to "The Family," until it should appear whether "The Family" would purchase the whole edition on our terms, and bury their memoirs in the oblivion of the grave.[2]

Ashe claimed four volumes for his revelatory work but the complete book as it has come down to us consisted of only three volumes. It is no surprise that Davenport Sedley (back again after being copiously documented in the papers of the Treasury Solicitor around *The Book*) was trying to muscle in on another blackmailing opportunity. But what of the respectable-sounding Admiral and Colonel Graves? They were pages to the Prince Regent, Lords of the bedchamber. It is striking how often Ashe comes up against his fellow Irishmen who have been more successful than he in ingratiating themselves into positions of influence. They were evidently more pliant and clubbable, less likely to abandon a patron on discovering their 'independence of mind'. Thomas North Graves, Second Baron Graves was a characteristic companion of the Prince Regent. Sir William Knighton, who succeeded Benjamin Bloomfield as the Regent's Privy Purse, wrote that Graves 'had a mind stuffed full of the vice of conversation and few men had dipped deeper into the scenes (in early life) of immorality. One of his accomplishments was to recall them at the King's table.' He was driven to commit suicide, on 7 February 1830, by luridly publicised allegations of his wife's adultery with the infamous Duke of Cumberland.[3]

Graves changed sides on the Catholic question in pursuit of preferment in the royal household. If the Admiral figure watching the woman embracing the Duke of Cumberland in the Empress of the Nairs is Admiral Graves, then that cartoon depicts not just Captain Browne but also one of the men who was deputed by the Prince Regent to steal or negotiate away *The Claustral Palace* manuscript for the government.

On 2 April 1812 came the shocked letter from Queen Charlotte to her daughters in response to their petition, via their dresser, complaining of the extent of the restraint of their lives. She warned them that to appear in public would risk appearing indecent, given the fragile state of the king's health (perpetually fragile at this point, so a reason for them never to emerge). Thus, the emergence and circulation of *The Claustral Palace* to The Family and the government came at a point of considerable tension, when the proscriptions of 'The Nunnery' were being challenged by the inmates. It also coincided with the collapse of the government following the murder of the Prime Minister.

So four days before the assassination of Spencer Perceval by John Bellingham, his principal law officers were discussing the much greater danger posed by Captain Thomas Ashe. Sir Nathaniel Conant, the bookseller and magistrate, had dismissed Bellingham's warning letter as an idle threat, but Ashe would occupy him for years. Following, as promised in his memoirs, the example of Perceval with the *The Book*, Ashe had circulated a synopsis to members of the royal family and the government through an agent and with it an opportunity for them to buy the full manuscript. The blackmail the government faced posed a familiar problem. Would paying the money and gaining the manuscript be the end of it?

John Wardroper in his book on the life of the Duke of Cumberland, *Wicked Ernest,* cites both the synopsis of *The Claustral Palace* and the Claustral Palace poems offered for sale at Sotheby's in 1999, believing them to have been sent to Ernest as part of or precursor to the campaign against him. This may partly be because the Treasury Solicitor put papers about Ashe's 'Osphia or the Victim of Unnatural Affections' together with those relating to *The Claustral Palace,* but it is unlikely that *The Claustral Palace* was part of a campaign against Ernest as he barely features in it. Sotheby's lot description confuses Ashe's account of the fate of the novel, as recorded in his memoirs, with these poems of the same name, which came afterwards.[4]

Flora Fraser's Princesses also notes that the synopsis of *The Claustral Palace,* titled the 'programma' was sent to the royal family and the surviving copy is filed among the papers of Princess Elizabeth. Was it sent as a threat or for approval? Why did she retain it when the others were destroyed? Its chapter headings hint at Princess Augusta's attachment to Charles Lennox, linking it to Lennox's duel with the Duke of York on Wimbledon Common. These relationships are given much greater detail in the full work.

The synopsis gives a clear indication of the fine line Ashe is treading if this kind of tactic is to be successful. His revelations have to be credible enough to be worth suppressing, and Ashe we know had excellent sources, also horrible enough to be damaging to the reputations of those involved and the institution of The Family, but not widely enough known to be superfluous. This is a very delicate balance and we often find that Ashe paints a more sympathetic and human picture of his subject's character than the caricaturists do, only to shock us more when he details the behaviour they are driven to by the peculiarity of their situation. The occasional German nobleman aside, there are few monsters in Ashe's gothic melodramas.

The unprecedented power of the present ministry as Ashe and Davenport Sedley saw it was not just based on Perceval's blackmailing power over the royal family, but also Perceval's power over the men in his own administration. The lawyers concerned with deciding what to do about Ashe's synopsis were personal adherents of Perceval who had no great attachment to office when he died. Thomas Plumer, whom the Dictionary of National Biography tells us 'showed himself opposed to reform proposals of almost every kind' wanted to leave office after Perceval's assassination, though he had only succeeded Sir Vicary Gibbs as Attorney General on 26 April 1812. Gibbs and Plumer delivered their joint legal opinion to Richard Ryder, Secretary of State for the Home Department, who 'combined personal feebleness with reaction'. He also served the administration out of loyalty to Perceval, and succeeded in resigning after Perceval's assassination on 11 May. Ashe's synopsis was therefore one of their last pieces of combined official business:

> We do not see any steps which can be advisable for government to take in order to stop this publication, whether it be considered in regard to the prudence of their interfering at all or with a view to the probable attainment of the only end which they can look to, the suppression of the threatened pamphlet.
>
> What security can there be that the author, being such a man as he is represented by his brother, and indeed as he represents himself, will not threaten similar publication next year and what is to prevent him from carrying his threat into execution? The gaining of the manuscript is nothing, he may retain a copy of it or recompile the supposed history.[5]

From the description of the threatened 'pamphlet' it looks to be only a synopsis, the chapter headings with summary contents probably circulated before the main text was actually written, a means of gaining suppression money without the trouble of writing the full work. This was a perfectly clear-headed analysis of the problem, but not particularly helpful from a practical point of view.

The government was still not sure what to do about Ashe's synopsis for *The Claustral Palace* a year after it was written, so it was not in possession of the full manuscript and printed version of the novel at this point, or was perhaps fearful that Ashe would simply produce another. Evidence elsewhere suggests it was still being prepared for the press or at least circulated in the hope of suppression in December 1813 but was out of Ashe's hands by May 1814.

Another of the lawyers involved in the deliberations, Sir Vicary Gibbs, had been involved in the attempt by the government to prevent Francis Blagdon and Thomas Ashe from publishing extracts of *The Book* in *The Phoenix*. He played a zealous role in the government's battle against writers it did not like. He was notorious for his use of ex officio information in cases of seditious libel, which allowed a defendant to be tried without a grand jury indictment, without oaths being taken or the normal protection of jury and witnesses. They were tried before a selected special jury and the Attorney General could defer the trial indefinitely if the special jurors failed to turn up. The Attorney General had a financial interest in the system as he received fees from it. Lord Folkstone in Parliament on 28 March 1811 had noted the particular effect this system had on writers: 'In all other cases where an individual has to contend with the Crown, he is fortified by the rules and forms of the law, which rules and forms serve as a bar against oppression.'He complained that a related judgement by Lord Ellenborough saw writers as the source of libel but not its object. 'Now, Sir, I cannot see why the feelings of an author should be held less sacred than those of any other person; or why those of a statesman should be particularly spared.' Editors, he complained, were sent to prison for libel for stories supplied to them by the Treasury, while papers backing the ministry could commit libel with impunity

The murder of Spencer Perceval on 11 May 1812 may have halted the pursuit of stray copies of *The Book* but it did nothing to resolve the problem of *The Claustral Palace*. Lord Liverpool tried and failed to form a government, resigning on 22 May. The Prince Regent now fell back on his old government without Perceval, an administration safely anti-Catholic emancipation and in favour of the prosecution of the war. Ashe was sure his hush money would be as great as Perceval's. He planned to buy a seat in Parliament, not the ambition of a reformer, and to use the example of his own behaviour from his new position of respectability to say 'beware of writers against the King.'

At some point, with the first edition at the press, Ashe received a note from Carpenter the printer: 'Dear Ashe the game is up. I am off to America. By this time, your Claustral Palace is burnt to the ground. Success! GC' –Carpenter's note implies something other than the manuscript being stolen by government agents, rather that he had bought off and his passage to America funded by the government.

In the end, whether stolen or negotiated away the manuscript and first printing of *The Claustral Palace* came into the hands of the Treasury Solicitor. Thanks to the care taken by him and by the National Archives, it is still possible after two hundred years to hold *The Claustral Palace* (suitably supported and protected) in your hands and to describe its physical appearance and condition.[6] It is strongly bound in three volumes (produced in two separate boxes, volumes one and two together and volume three on its own) with marbled endpapers, but the text block itself is on poor quality paper, which has a slightly fibrous and tacky texture. There are some tentative administrative annotations as to date and provenance. The text is a revised manuscript in Ashe's familiar hand, the majority of the revisions being retrospective attempts to turn the names of the central characters into transparent pseudonyms and to replace 'England' and 'English' with 'Denmark' and 'Danish' at all the points Ashe originally forgot to do so. It is written in a strong copperplate hand, educated and consistent, not unlike that characteristic of members of The Family themselves. It begins with a history of the Hanoverian succession and the youthful indiscretions and political marriage of George III through the passing of the Royal Marriages Act to the love lives of his children from Charlotte Augusta Matilda, 'the senior recluse', to the youngest, favourite – and very recently deceased – Princess Amelia. Perhaps the fourth volume was a separate valedictory essay; a plea from Elizabeth to Caroline to end the Act when she became Queen, or like *The Patriot Princess* which followed it, a plea directed at her daughter Charlotte. It is just possible Ashe exaggerated the extent of the book when he described it in the 'Memoirs & Confessions'. By the time he published this autobiographical work in 1815 he believed *The Claustral Palace* had been destroyed and he could impress us with his great productivity in three months at Bath without fear of being contradicted.

The Claustral Palace is melodramatic and at times sentimental, there is lots of sighing, swooning and poetic recitation. It is sympathetic to the princesses and gives inside information and detailed descriptions of their lovers, their situation and even their clothes in particular scenes. Underneath it all is the corrupting power of the Royal Marriages Act which makes a gothic horror of relationships of all kinds, preventing love matches with pitiless brutality and enforcing political matrimony with a range of unsavoury ghouls from the obscurer royal houses of Germany.

Setting the book in Denmark was not just a device to allow Ashe to write about the love lives of the Frogmore princesses with greater safety. Denmark was a suitable place of ill-omen after the failed marriage and suspicious early death of Caroline Matilda of Denmark, George III and Prince William Henry's sister, who had married Christian VII of Denmark, a cold political marriage arranged for him while he was still Crown Prince. A sequence of events followed, many parts of which would become familiar to the followers of Caroline of Brunswick's fortunes in England: political intrigue, affairs, and evidence against her taken from her servants. Other precedents set by the earlier Caroline for the later one were still to come or remained a possibility: instituting her own order of chivalry, a 'trial', conviction, removal from the liturgy, imprisonment, divorce and premature death. Caroline Matilda's trial had been in 1772, the year of the Royal Marriages Act. George III's concern about the unreliability of his brothers in their relationships seems to have made the fate of his sister more likely for his own children. A partial restoration of her rights and freedoms had followed intervention by the English navy, and then came a plot to restore her. She died of scarlet fever, its symptoms exacerbated by the family disease porphyria, in 1775. Her death was politically convenient and therefore regarded as suspicious. Her fate meant that moving the action of the novel to Denmark was not simply a random displacement by Ashe to protect himself from libel. Rather it was a specific frame for the action, reminding the reader that 'the Nunnery' had its roots in the previous generation and that the fate of Caroline Matilda might await the Frogmore princesses or Caroline of Brunswick, the recipient of Princess Elizabeth's letters.

One of the conceits of *The Claustral Palace* is that the royal children are being raised to be good but not to be useful for anything. This seems to have been a more general feeling about them. One of the strengths of Ashe's novel is the intimate and sympathetic way he narrates terribly discreditable events. The corrupting power of the Royal Marriages Act lends coherence to the narrative and gives a reason, other than personal inadequacy, for the predicament in which the royal children found themselves. Part of the appeal of *The Claustral Palace* is that the gothic melancholy and suppressed sexuality so common in the romantic novels Wordsworth despised here has a political cause and purpose. Similarly, the epistolary form was not just a structural device, but drew on the power and vulnerability of letters and their trade in blackmail. Even Ashe describes *The Claustral Palace* as a potboiler, but is it just gratuitous populist melodrama, or was there something more to it? The atmosphere of the book seems justified by the context. Lord Glenbervie, for example, described the weird, enhanced emotion of the *bon ton* mourning the King's illness on 14 April 1801. His madness and the restrictions of the Royal Marriages Act lead to a truly gothic atmosphere at the top of society, and *The Claustral*

Palace in this sense a truer reflection of that society than was the official version. Ashe the literary recluse in Cumbria living in real poverty was in that sense closer to real lived experience and further from melodrama, than Wordsworth's carefully crafted lyrics about the simple folk of that county.

The method and style adopted by Ashe were very much Caroline's own, since, as Baron Glenbervie confirmed, Caroline wrote lively pen portraits of leading English political and social figures (in French) and read them aloud to Lady Glenbervie. Her husband's diaries also preserve Lady Glenbervie's own skill in this regard, including her comic impersonation of her friends and acquaintances reacting to news of her death. This was obviously a desirable skill in Caroline's household.

The administrative history and catalogue description of *The Claustral Palace* is rather notional and elusive. It sits in a class of Treasury Solicitor case papers ostensibly concerned with ongoing Crown interest in unclaimed deceased estates (*Bona Vacantia*) but since the novel was never published the financial benefit to the estate was presumably nil. Perhaps no means of disposal was considered secure enough and the Treasury Solicitor's ongoing interest was to ensure that the novel never saw the light of day. Perhaps, instead, the Treasury Solicitor had a locked cupboard of potentially embarrassing cases that was added to but rarely weeded.

The title page is marked indistinctly in pencil in a brief explanation of the circumstances in which this extraordinary book came in to the possession of the Treasury Solicitor:

NB The Whole of this volume was printed and in boards
Sol[icitor] use and destroyed along with prospectus etc.

Was there only one printed copy or did the Treasury Solicitor destroy the entire initial print run? The note suggests that there were further copies of the 'prospectus' or 'programma', beyond those six sent to The Family, either printed or in preparation. Perhaps Carpenter got as far as printing the first volume before he got cold feet, or he was bribed or intimidated. The Treasury Solicitor then destroyed the printed versions and kept the manuscript, possibly by buying rather than stealing it.

Beneath this note is the undated stamp of the Treasury Solicitor's Library. This implies again that it was kept as a work of political sensitivity or perhaps of amusement, rather than with case papers for some financial administrative purpose. I believe I am the first person to have read the whole of *The Claustral Palace* since its author and perhaps the Treasury Solicitor did so over two hundred years ago. To convey its quality I have made liberal use of quotation since there is no other way to draw the reader into its unique and peculiar world, not to mention its particular style. Its power at the time would have depended in the accuracy with which Ashe identified and portrayed the princesses' lovers. There is no doubt that the government was concerned that 'blowing the roof off the Nunnery' would expose the hypocrisy and weakness at the heart of the state. To us it reads so gently compared to modern royal revelations that we would be forgiven for thinking it had no blackmailing purpose at all, but was rather an elaborately constructed plea against the Royal Marriages Act, designed to move the successors of the king who designed it, to repeal it. Luckily, the circumstances of its composition and its purpose were so lovingly and copiously preserved by Ashe and by the government that we know the fear that it engendered at the time was genuine.

The first page carries the pre-title 'The Claustral Palace; A Political Romance, in a series of letters from Elizabeth, Princess of Denmark to Caroline Princess of Hasburgh'. Then on the full title page:

The Claustral Palace or Memoirs of the Family, a Political Romance upon the basis of the Royal Marriage act of Denmark. By Thos. Ashe, Esq. Author of *The Spirit of the Book* &c &c &c

This title page carries an epigram taken from Shakespeare's Henry VI Part 1 Act 5 Scene 5, a fitting plea from that greatest literary authority against the Royal Marriages Act:

Marriage is a matter of more worth
Than to be dealt in by Attorneyship
For what is wedlock forced but a Hell
An age of discord and continual strife?

If in nothing else, Ashe is a little like Shakespeare in *Hamlet* using the Danish context as a structure within which to explore domestic issues.

His prefatory essay addressed to 'Prince William Henry of Denmark' is presumably to the ghost of the Duke of Gloucester who had died in 1805, having married outside the terms of the Royal Marriages Act, so he is invoked by Ashe as a presiding spirit of defiance. In it, Ashe set out his political, if not his financial, reason for writing, the repeal of the Royal Marriages Act, 'which is found, after a long and fatal experience to be totally ineffectual for its intended purposes'.

> And, Sir, although there are some of The Family but little disposed to consider my writings as the inspirations of a prophetic spirit, still I am persuaded, that the time will come when I shall awaken their feelings. Rouse their attention and convert their resentment into sorrow and their antipathy into respect.

At the beginning of volume one, the contents pages give a precis and judgement on each letter and they betray evidence of last-minute revisions including two changes of mind about whether to refer to Lord Bute as 'Scotch' or Scottish'. The precis of that letter (Letter 4) also crosses out an authorial interpolation 'Portraiture of a Political Marriage – Horrible Portraiture, as the author wrote he trembled.' This was the marriage not of the Prince and Princess of Wales but of George III to Queen Charlotte. The cycle of political marriage had begun in Ashe's narrative before the passing of the Royal Marriages Act in the nuptials of the King himself. Most of the other revisions are Ashe remembering to alter proper names and titles to maintain a spurious distance from the real figures depicted. This includes in the relationship of the Marquis of Tavistock with the Princess Royal, an alteration of Tavistock to 'Vistatock' (sometimes 'Vastitock') as well as the forgetting to write 'Denmark' for 'England' throughout. The contents page summaries were sometimes revised in the light of revisions to the letters themselves. The summaries are reproduced, in rather worse handwriting, at the start of each chapter.

Before we begin there is another Shakespeare quotation, on the half-title page facing letter one:

> [But] man, proud man,
> Drest in a little brief authority,
> Most ignorant of what he's most assured,
> His glassy essence, like an angry ape,
> Plays such fantastic tricks before high heaven
> As make the angels weep.

Measure for Measure Act ii. Sc. 2

Letters one to eight deal with the historical background to the succession of the House of Hanover and the weakness of its claim to the throne in the framing of the Royal Marriages Act. Then the focus shifts to early relationships of George III, his marriage, and the establishment of 'the Nunnery'.

The summary for letter one reads, 'Elizabeth "O'er the past too fondly wandering", expresses in this epistle to Caroline the regrets of a truly virtuous and indignant heart. She looks down with disdain on the Pride of Palaces. She envies those who are permitted to enjoy the pleasures of an innocent and rural life.'

The quotation from Robert Burns' song 'Raving winds around her blowing' immediately introduces a note of despair at the future and anguished female solitude, which is characteristic of *The Claustral Palace* as a whole. The next line of Burns' song is 'On the hopeless future pondering'. It is a stark and eerie note on which to begin a scandalous romp through the affairs of Elizabeth and her sisters and a clear indication of Ashe's sympathy for their plight and for Elizabeth in particular. By letter 37, the climax of the first volume, the revelations are coming thick and fast and the summary becomes breathless, 'Reader! Read! This letter is too pregnant of interest to be subject to expression in a preliminary head.' For all the excitement about the youthful affairs of the king and his eldest son, it is to his sisters that *The Claustral Palace* truly belongs, as they were much more confined by it.

Elizabeth begins her first letter to Caroline:

Tis only to you that I break that silence which I had resolved with myself inviolably to observe. Without giving an answer to all those infamous libels, which have been sent into circulation against me. I will impart to you the motives of my conduct and the sentiments of my heart. You are not my enemy [presumably countering the suggestion she might be] your heart is too tender.

She identifies pity as being Caroline's defining virtue and views her as the victim of a campaign of calumny which she has borne with patience and a little help from Thomas Ashe: 'the world has leagued against you, it has attacked you with more than common fury. Every one has shot his bolt at you … The first flash appeared in your ungrateful country, the thunder burst in England. What has been the consequence of all this combustion? As vapour which your patience has dissipated. *The Spirit of the Book* has also defended you from many blows which otherwise must have overwhelmed your peace.'

There was no harm in having Princess Elizabeth attest to the power of Ashe's books. As well as a love of literature. they have a shared love of rural simplicity, Elizabeth's at Frogmore, Caroline's at Blackheath, 'Lodged in a humble cottage on one of our Blackest Heaths', a rural retreat from court life and 'the extraordinary reports which circulate about the family'. Elizabeth sets out to 'correct' these 'extraordinary reports' with the true version, which is of course equally extraordinary.

George III *and the* Royal Marriages Act

Elizabeth begins her history of The Family with her father, who, like his son the Regent after him, leaves his real love for a political marriage. 'Jemima' the beautiful Quakeress as she appears in *The Claustral Palace,* is a version of a well-established early connection of the king. There is a hint of her in the 'Fair Quaker of St James's market' who is called Abigail in the *London Evening Post* story about the relationship in 1771, though this may just be a generic name for a young maid. The newspaper cited this relationship, alongside numerous misalliances by the king's brothers, as an example of the 'natural depravity' of the royal family and the lack of moral high ground of the king over his brothers, which makes the Royal Marriages Act seem even more indefensible. Ashe refers in *The Claustral Palace* to long continuance of this dalliance and 'many beautiful children' but not marriage. It is interesting that Ashe does not suggest a marriage ceremony, given his supposed marriage to Hannah Lightfoot 'another beautiful Quakeress' in a secret ceremony in 1759. The relationship with 'Jemima' is suppressed by the minister and mentor of his early reign, Lord Bute, for reasons of state. His well-attested love for Sarah Lennox before his accession, who marries Mr Bunbury in 1762, is not mentioned in *The Claustral Palace.*

The Royal Marriages Act was instituted by ministers concerned that royalty should not marry beneath themselves. Ashe gives us historical context for the inability of the English to govern themselves and arrange their own succession going back as far as the Wars of the Roses, the Houses of York and Lancaster ('Royk' and 'Casterlan' as they appear in the text). There seems little to be gained by disguising an ancient conflict in this way, unless to get the reader used to his transparent anagrams of proper names for the juicy scandal later on. Perhaps too, the Wars of the Roses were not that distant and irrelevant, since, as we have seen, the king himself traced the socially destabilising effect of royalty marrying commoners back to that conflict. Ashe quickly moves on to William III and the 'Glorious Revolution', when 'a foreigner was called in to govern a nation which could not govern itself.' A reference to her father as 'George Guelph' was evidently considered by Ashe to be on reflection too revolutionary and was hastily crossed out. George III was uncharacteristically virtuous compared to other English kings and many European monarchs, lacking a mistress after his marriage makes him something of an oddity. His relationship with 'Jemima' is principally there to establish the pattern of true love blighted by political necessity even before the Royal Marriages Act makes this a legal requirement. It makes the king, as its proposer, seem still more unnatural as he himself had suffered by its precepts. In Ashe's narrative, Elizabeth sets out a character for her father that has been echoed elsewhere since:

> A mind determined and obstinate, views not always correct, but always virtuous, a devotion pious, a morality pure and popular, in private life most of what is amiable, in public little of what is great. Flattered and reviled alternately and intemperately, he was been worshipped and branded as saviour and tyrant, that exaggeration, this falsehood. In peaceful times he would have been adored and useful to his country.

This was a somewhat damning assessment for a daughter to make, since the implication was that he had been less than useful in both the American War of Independence and the Napoleonic Wars. (Letter two.)

The summary of the third letter is heavily and, in places, illegibly crossed through, with detail written and withdrawn of the relationship of Elizabeth's father and the lovely Quaker girl, called by Ashe Jemima. The overwritten version marries with the summary on the contents page suggesting the contents page summaries were fair copies of the final version of the summaries at the start of each letter, written when the book was complete. Perhaps the original version gave too much away about 'Jemima's' identity.

As Elizabeth tells the story of Jemima and 'my father', the girl is described as possessing 'peculiar grace and captivating ease'. The young prince, little more than twenty years old when the relationship took place, is shown 'making too free with wine in the company of his gay companions'. He is admitted to her by a faithless servant in the middle of the night 'not that this intercourse was confined to this particular night; it extended itself through the space of three years, during which time she became the mother of many beautiful children.' Naturally, the principal function of the relationship in Ashe's narrative is to establish the governing theme of the misery of forced marriage for dynastic reasons and the true love foiled by it. 'The dynasty of my father was not sufficiently established to permit of plebeian alliances.' The father cannot risk a 'plebeian' marriage as his own blood is 'inferior' some other 'Danish lords'. 'The glory of the dynasty opposes plebeian alliances. Ah, poor Jemima!' Jemima is about seventeen years old with 'long flaxen tresses' and performs the 'office of nurse' when he is 'dangerously sick'. (Letter three.)

'A scotch adviser' the minister who dominated the king's early life and reign, Lord Bute (rendered by Ashe, more or less consistently as 'Tube') counsels marriage in the interests of policy. He conveys the news to Jemima, who then 'shrunk and died' in solitude, though presumably not instantaneously. Ashe is particularly hostile to 'Tube's' Scottish hard-heartedness, he 'could not pity because he could not feel', a phrase Ashe later uses in his memoir to describe the family of the girl he seduces in France. Thus, the cycle of cold political marriage and the death of love begins with the king's own marriage, even before the Royal Marriages Act is passed and, in Ashe's version, becomes an explanation of it. His own marriage has been forced on him and his true love killed by it. Why should his descendants be able to escape that fate? (Letter four.)

In Ashe's version, the king was disappointed in Queen Charlotte, but carried off the marriage with dignity: 'he was so amiable as to dissemble.' Jemima's memory was a ghost of perfection. As ever in Ashe's sympathetic view of the plight of those married for dynastic reasons, Queen Charlotte also knew her marriage was a 'political necessity', rather than a love match, and resolved to make the best of it. It is suggested that the groom's 'bulging eyes and stutter' stemmed from his attempts to articulate his marriage vows. George's characteristic infirmities thus become part of a divine judgement on his cold political marriage, rather than a product of disease. (Letter five.)

What was it like just be brought up to be good with no other obvious purpose? Elizabeth's complaint against her upbringing and that of her sisters is considered and beautifully worded. Whatever the status of Ashe in the minds of the later critics, and whatever their view of the novel they knew he might have written but none of them has read, it reads in places less like the satire of a money-grubbing blackmailer and more like the heartfelt reported words of the Princess herself:

> We were brought up as if God had created us merely for himself and that our only business was to prepare for immediate residence in Heaven. One would have thought that we had no blood, no bodies all the pains being taken with our souls or that Providence had enacted a Salique [Salic] Law and excluded us from every inheritance of the earth. (Letter five.)

Elizabeth's seventh letter charts the move to Frogmore, and with it, she records her own preference for the rural life against that of the town. Elizabeth is noted by Olwen Hedley and others to be the chief rustic among the sisters and the most comfortable with their semi-rural confinement. She is also noted as the best route to the queen, her chief confidante and a reliable source of information about the other sisters.

The severity of the queen in enforcing the regime of 'the Nunnery' and the stolid uniformity of the sisters' days is confirmed in other sources, their routines of art and music and the limits placed not only on their movements but on their self-expression. Their Monday essay results in the compilation of confessional volumes of 'Memorabilia': a work, Ashe tells us, which was 'stopped and sealed at the third volume'.

Charlotte, Princess Royal

Letters nine to twenty-five detail the loves of the eldest sister, the Princess Royal, Charlotte Augusta Matilda, a lonely figure in Ashe's narrative, held responsible by her mother for the behaviour of her sisters, which tended to distance her from them, and allowed them to consider her to be her mother's spy.

Flora Fraser describes her as 'discontented and solitary', with 'all of her sisters favoured over her'. To Ashe she was 'The Senior Recluse'. Charlotte's relationship with Francis Russell, Duke of Bedford, 'a close friend of Fox and a very handsome man', is treated as a sudden revelation and brief infatuation of a few months, or even as an exercise in wishful thinking on her part, quickly dismissed by her brothers as impossible for political as well as legal reasons. In *The Claustral Palace*, this relationship is portrayed as of much greater importance and duration. Ashe devotes more chapters to it than any other of the revelations in the book, partly at least because it sets the theme and pattern for the others. The Crown Prince of Prussia is brought in as a largely illusory alternative to put her off. The princess tries to win over the queen thinking somehow that she could evade the Royal Marriages Act.

There was no room for ambiguity though. Olwen Hedley in *Queen Charlotte* times the relationship to 1790-1 and suggests the full force of the Royal Marriages Act was against the union between Charlotte and Bedford. She cites the register of the Chapel Royal, which records the Duke of York's marriage on 23 November 1791. The gist of the Act is recited in the register and compliance with it is implied by the signatures of the parties and witnesses.

The Claustral Palace details the violence suffered by Charlotte at the hands of her husband in Württemberg, the subject of rumour at the time but only known about outside The Family much later. Charlotte, as described in Elizabeth's narrative, was 'The first to feel she was neither angel nor saint but a mere mortal woman' and not suited to the life prescribed by her parents and by the Act. She was strong-minded and strong-willed, 'She began to consider the Claustral Palace in the light of a state prison,' agitating, for her own sake and for her sisters, for the rights and freedoms of ordinary subjects. 'An Elegy on Liberty' in twelve stanzas composed by Charlotte for the 'Memorabilia', includes the line 'freedom [is] as noxious to tyrants as daylight to owls.' It ends with:

> Vain wish! These walls whose turrets pierce the skies
> With frowning aspect, tell the hope is vain
> Till, freed by death the purer spirit flies
> Here wretched Charlotte's destined to remain

Perhaps Ashe's fictional version gives us a clue as to why the 'Memorabilia' were stopped at the third volume and self-expression of this kind by the princesses was discouraged. The volumes were discovered by the queen, 'The Old Lady', as she is described throughout *The Claustral Palace,* whose 'feelers' and ability to scent scandal among her daughters are a theme of the book.

Charlotte's elegy is addressed to Albinia, Countess of Buckinghamshire (hastily crossed out but still legible), a society hostess of Hobart House, Ham Common, famous for lavish parties, gambling and, latterly, a gift to caricaturists because of her size. She was an embodiment of freedom in her lifestyle and in her relationships outside her marriage, which the unmarried Charlotte had no hope of enjoying. (Letter nine.)

In a further letter to the Countess, she compared their fates, she being 'doomed to eternal celibacy'. She became convinced that the Act could be bypassed if her father chose, but that Bedford's politics were the real barrier keeping her from her happiness. The Duke of York laughed at the Foxite leanings of the princesses and their lovers. They were abhorrent to the king. Charlotte pleaded that the king's own experience and chosen education for her made her feelings inevitable; she wrote 'extolling her lover's virtues, but the letters between them were intercepted.' (Letter 10.)

The Royal Marriages Act, 'disgraceful to the statute books of a free country' as Ashe describes it, was still very much in force and Bedford was written to by The Family via a confidential page and reminded of its provisions. (Letter 12.) Bedford's letter of protest to the king, circulated among The Family, asks them, and in Ashe's telling, it partially succeeds, to see themselves as part of English society and not something set apart from it. (Letter 13.)

The response of The Family is to place the Princess Royal under an even stricter regime and closer supervision: 'Charlotte is held in a state of bondage.' There is a good description of the fierce governess set to guard Charlotte:

> Poor Charlotte was confined for a time to the dominion of as fierce a Duenna as was ever bred for the Seraglios of Turkey or the Tyrant husbands of Spain or Portugal, a creature 'never having been known to have wiped a tear from the cheek of misery'.

This state of affairs is the cause of some wider philosophical reflection on the part of the narrator; a voice which sounds less like Princess Elizabeth and more like the later Thomas Ashe writing in defence of her niece Charlotte in his next book *The Patriot Princess*: 'Nothing is more offensive to a bigoted Cabinet than the blaze of philosophy and the illumination of Truth.'

The most trying period of her confinement prompts another poem by the Princess Royal about herself, entitled 'The Recluse':

Ye verdant Patriarchs of the Wood
That veil around these awful glooms
That many a century have stood
In verdant age, which ever blooms (Letter 14.)

These sentiments are compatible with Charlotte's letters to her brother George about the slavery of her unmarried state, to which any marriage would be preferable. She complained in those letters of her 'tiresome and confined life' and 'the violence of her mother's temper'. [7]

Despite these precautions, Charlotte was still meeting 'Vistatock' when introduced to the unsavoury Frederick, Duke of Württemberg, nicknamed 'the Great Belly-Gerent', six feet eleven inches tall and twenty stone, a test of her resolution that any marriage would be preferable to celibacy. Whatever his sources, Ashe seems confident about the timing and sequence of events:

Never before had she beheld such a vile production of nature! His height was gigantic and his person swoln with fat to an outrageous excess. His bloated visage was crowned with a wig of extravagant dimensions; his complexion was of an olive, inclinable to a brownish puce. His eyebrows were long and bushy seeming to have a strange wild position upon his front as if they had been rent by some violent and sudden shock. (Letter 15.)

'Vastitock' is shattered by the Marriage Act, Charlotte faints into his arms when Wurttemberg kisses her hand. This scene is precisely dated to the king's birthday in 1796. The description of the nuptials gives us a virgin sacrifice to a beast of prey. The transaction prompted James Gillray's cartoon 'The Bridal Night', which focussed on the £80,000 dowry. This was perhaps the prime example of the 'stupid German tragedy' in Ashe's work, but Ashe could argue this was not melodramatic fiction but the reality of the life of the royal family. (Letter 16.)

The real horror begins in Württemberg, when the 'stupid tragedy' moves to Germany it becomes frightening. The events at the Nunnery produced a 'matter of fact' if rather colourful narrative of events, but now imagination, fuelled by the drama of the events themselves, takes over. First, there is Charlotte's ghostly appearance on the night of the wedding, and then Elizabeth shows Caroline the parallels with her own marriage in the preceding year. The queen their mother, reproaches Charlotte's for her aversion to and

Top: 1. *The Claustral Palace or Memoirs of the Family* title page. An unusual public record. Thomas Ashe's three-volume blackmailing novel, retained, but definitely not created, by the Treasury Solicitor. Despite his claim in his memoirs to have written four volumes, the three which have come down to us were all he promised in his blackmailing notes to the royal family. (TNA TS 17/1388)

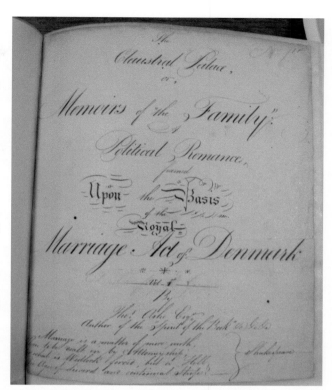

Middle: 2. 'The R--l Bruiser or Bloomy Floor'd!!!'. The queen's return to England is heralded by her handsome hussar, possibly the still-remembered forever-young Captain Browne whose courage contrasts with the panicked figures depicted. Wellington fears her return more than Napoleon. Benjamin Bloomfield is thrown to the floor. (TNA TS 11/115/326/42)

Bottom: 3. 'The Coronation of the Empress of the Nairs' by George Cruikshank. A satire on the scandals relating to the Regent, his brothers, and Lord and Lady Hertford, it is an assembly of the characters of the world of Thomas Ashe. The British Museum catalogue tentatively identifies the soldier with Charlotte as Captain Charles Hesse but cannot account for his Irish voice. Is there a suggestion that Captain Browne, and not the Prince Regent, is Charlotte's father? (Plate from the *Scourge*, iv, 173)

Above: 4. *The Spirit of the Book or Anticipation of the year 1813.* Ashe's ghosted memoir appears personified as the guardian of Caroline's reputation. Seven years later, being its author still made Ashe 'the only man who can save her'.

Left: 5. Spencer Perceval by George Francis Joseph. His legal team were too preoccupied with the threat of Thomas Ashe's *The Claustral Palace* to worry about the threatening notes of his assassin John Bellingham. Later Ashe threatened to emulate Bellingham's feat with the Duke of Cumberland. (Wellington Collection)

6. Caroline of Brunswick. The Lonsdale Portrait. Ashe's 'lovely, suffering Princess of Wales', the narrator of *The Spirit of the Book* and the recipient of Princess Elizabeth's confidences in *The Claustral Palace*. By the time of her 'Trial', despite Ashe's pleas to her solicitor, she had come to rely on other writers.

7. Princess Elizabeth by Thomas Gainsborough. Thomas Ashe's contemporary and his favourite among the royal sisters. The narrator of *The Claustral Palace*, she retained Ashe's synopsis among her papers. (Royal Collection)

Above left: 8. Charlotte, Princess Royal by William Beechey. 'The Senior Recluse', as the eldest daughter she was the archetypal victim of the Royal Marriages Act. Ashe devoted more letters of *The Claustral Palace* to her plight than to that of any of the other royal children. (Royal Collection)

Above right: 9. Ernest Augustus, Duke of Cumberland by George Dawe. A source of financial assistance to Ashe the wounded soldier, a suitor to his 'Persecuted Peeress' and the wicked object of Ashe's final blackmailing campaign. (National Portrait Gallery)

Left: 10. Princess Sophia by Sir Thomas Lawrence. *The Claustral Palace* gave copious detail to the scene and circumstances of her seduction by Thomas Garth. No doubt, Ashe's *Osphia* did the same for the circumstances surrounding the 'unnatural affections' of her brother.

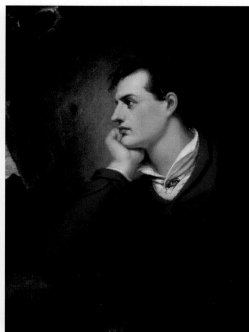

Above left: 11. George, Prince of Wales, later George IV by Thomas Gainsborough. Though Ashe's most sustained work was written in favour of his detested wife, Ashe never descended to the character assassination of the Prince Regent favoured by so many writers and cartoonists. He needed the system of literary patronage, which the government operated. (Royal Collection)

Top right: 12. Lord Byron by Richard Westall. Despite his own financial difficulties, Byron supported Thomas Ashe with £10 per month, believing he was the only man who would help him. He was wrong. In spite of his own scandalous conduct, he was the source of sage moral advice to his fellow writer, which Ashe, as always, ignored. (National Portrait Gallery)

Above right: 13. William Cobbett. Engraving by Francesco Bartolozzi. Ashe attacked Cobbett for the venality of his pen but wrote against his *Political Register* in Francis Blagdon's *Register* as a loyal writer then switched to *The Phoenix* to write against himself. Compared to Ashe he was a model of consistency.

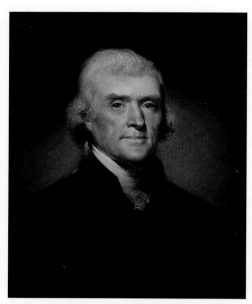

14. Thomas Jefferson painted by Rembrandt Peale at the time Ashe knew him. Both president and artist shared Ashe's interest in ancient megafauna but Ashe distrusted Jefferson's foreign policy.

Above left: 15. Lord Edward Fitzgerald by Hugh Douglas Hamilton. Ashe's early patron, who saw in him a younger, poorer version of himself. They fought on opposite sides in the great Irish Rebellion of 1798, but Ashe never lost his reverence for his memory.

Above right: 16. Princess Charlotte by George Dawe 'The Patriot Princess.' In 1814 Thomas Ashe urged her to take his patron Lord Byron into his ministry when she was queen. Within three years, Byron had left Britain never to return, and she was dead.

On the 1st Day of January next, 1813, will be published a Work, in Three Volumes, price 1l. 10s. entitled

THE CLAUSTRAL PALACE,

OR MEMOIRS OF "THE FAMILY,"

A POLITICAL ROMANCE FRAMED UPON THE BASIS OF

THE ROYAL MARRIAGE ACT OF DENMARK,

By THOMAS ASHE, Esq.

Author of the "SPIRIT OF THE BOOK," &c. &c.

"Marriage is a matter of more worth, than to be dealt in by Attorneyship, for what is Wedlock forced, but a Hell, an Age of Discord and continual Strife?"   SHAKESPEARE.

Programma to the Claustral Palace, &c.

THE DESIGN.

IN a Moment of dark Mystery and bold Imposition, an Act of Parliament was passed, which compels the Children of the Blood Royal of Denmark, either to marry foreign Protestant Princes, and Princesses, or else to consume their Lives at Home in the filthy Kennels of Prostitution, or in the stagnant Slough of Claustral Celibacy and ignominious Ease.—As the Author considers this to be a mere Act of Power, contrary to the inherent Rights of Nature, and pregnant with civil Discord and Confusion, he loudly and honestly proclaims, that the sole Design of this Work is, to cause the Repeal of that most illegal and unrighteous Law!

THE DRAMATIS PERSONÆ.

The many Fictions which have been lately imposed upon the World, under the specious Titles of Delicate Enquiries, Royal Memoirs, and Secret Histories, have given but too much Room to question the Veracity of every Work that has the least Tendency towards the House of Denmark: The Author, therefore, thinks it highly necessary to make known, that nothing will be found in "The Claustral Palace," but what has been collected from the original Letters, and personal Communications which he has been favored with from those illustrious Characters, who have sought him out, and honored him with their Friendship, ever since the Publication of "The Spirit of the Book," or "Memoirs of the Princess of Hasburgh."—It is also his Duty to state that his Dramatis Persona consists not only of the HEADS AND INMATES OF THE CLAUSTRAL PALACE, BUT OF EVERY CHARACTER AND OF EVERY PERSONAGE CONNECTED WITH "THE FAMILY," and who have been conspicuous in the Council or in the Field, in the Court or in the Cabinet, in the Boudoir, the Drawing-Room, or the Saloon, ever since the Origin of the existing Dynasty down to the present Time.

MANNER AND COMPOSITION.

The Author of "The Claustral Palace" has availed himself of the Passion for Novelty, which governs the Taste of the present Times, to convey the most delicate and exalted Sentiments, on most subjects, justly interesting to the human Heart, in a Manner, that promises fairest to fix an influencing Attention, by the Fame of "The Characters," to which they are ascribed.—He details with a loyal Delicacy all the Facts in his possession, and never attempts to supply the Deficiency of his Information either by bold Conjecture, or shameless Fiction.—He has indeed endeavoured to distinguish his Writings by energy of Thought, perspicuity of Style, felicity of Images, and brilliancy of Wit, but he never strove to render his Composition either scurrilous or malignant.—In the whole Course of so voluminous a Work, he never wounded the Feelings of a Father, the Dignity of a Mother, the Honor of a Gentleman, or the Modesty of Innocence, with a remorseless and guilty Intent: no,

17. Printed pre notice of *The Claustral Palace* sent to Princess Elizabeth on 23 May 1812 threatening publication in January 1813. Ashe prudently directed enquires to his curate brother in Bristol while affecting to write from the Ashe family estate in Limerick. He was in fact in Bath. (Royal Archives GEO/ADD/11/213)

Right: 18. Handwritten 'Programma' of *The Claustral Palace*, dated by Ashe to July 1812. Ashe repeated the substance of his printed notice, but increased the pressure with brief summaries of each relationship covered in the book. (Royal Archives GEO/ADD/11/214)

Below: 19. Title page of *The Claustral Palace*. This final foretaste of the book included reproductions of the full chapter headings of the finished work. The title page differs from that of the full manuscript at The National Archives (plate 1) in affecting to be a translation from German. (Royal Archives GEO/ADD/11/215)

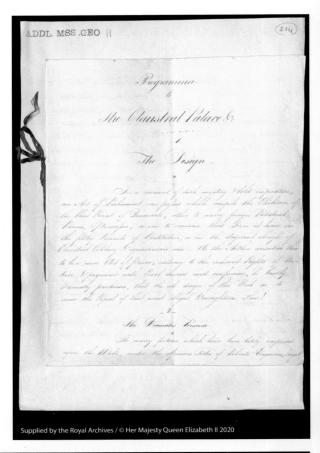

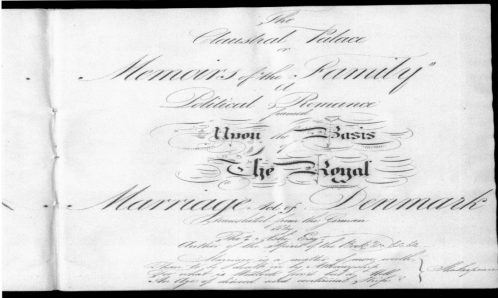

flight from the Duke. The couple then leave for Germany within three days, their exit concluded with indecent haste. (Letter 17.) Charlotte voices her impotent dread and valedictory longing.

> Yes I must tear myself from my friends, my Tavistock [hastily disguised again as 'Vistatock] my home and everything that till now has been dear to me. But a tyrant commands and a father implores me!

Characteristically, Ashe portrays her father the king as sympathetic, noble, and hopeful, but weak and impotent in the face of the tragic implications of his own legislation on the fate of his daughters:

> 'I am going,' said my father 'to confide one of my greatest treasures upon the earth into your hands. I repose with confidence upon your honour. I believe you are a noble generous and virtuous man, do not give me cause to think otherwise, but remember that I am your friend as well as her father. Do not embitter my remaining days and under the load of life, which I have hitherto borne with some degree of fortitude, too wearisome for me to endure.' (Letter 18.)

This is not an optimistic speech to a bridegroom and son-in-law and one full of foreboding.

Charlotte in Germany is generally accounted to have been be a picture of domestic tranquillity. Ashe's account suggests this was the result of Charlotte's spirit being cowed by her husband's brutality. Since Elizabeth can no longer witness Charlotte's sufferings at first hand, she does so by means of letters received from Charlotte herself. She is led by her enormous husband through a succession of large, gloomy, ill-lit palaces. At last, she is taken to her lavish apartments and asked by her husband if she 'still continued to object to him for a bedfellow, at the same time that he smiled most monstrously upon me and gave me a glance that awakened all the former emotions of horror in my bosom.'

To this point, she had evaded the consummation of the marriage and still hoped to be 'an amusing companion' rather than a wife. In her closet, she is greeted by a picture of her husband's first wife, her cousin, Augusta of Brunswick-Wolfenbüttel, concealed by a veil. Her death was unexplained but rumoured to be by poisoning. She is told that the fate of the first wife awaits the second, 'her death was slow and lingering.' Charlotte is threatened with a swifter fate if she is not obedient. Commanded by a dagger, she swears love and obedience she does not feel, while only half in her senses through terror. There are visions of her dead cousin and of her impending violation by the monster. (Letter 20.)

He accuses her of abhorring him, she counters with the horrors of 'political marriage' and barricades herself in her chamber, he breaks in, she sees him off with a sword, She asks him to kill her, he tells he would prefer to violate her, and then have her commit suicide. (Letter 21.)

There is then a last-ditch attempt to teach him what love consists of. 'I fell prostrate in a fainting fit, not recovered, till the innocence of my virgin state was polluted by this remorseless and sanguinary tyrant.' Ravished unconscious, she is henceforward dutiful. There is a slightly awkward shift in the narrative from the full dramatic horror of suicide or murder threats to apparently tranquil co-habitation. Ashe explains it in terms of the breaking of Charlotte's spirit:

> I found the violator hanging over me with an expression of savage ecstasy on his countenance and which he endeavoured to express by the incoherent and broken detonations of voice which a tiger employs while contemplating the prey that he holds between his fangs.

In these circumstances, the victim promised obedience: 'I did myself the violence to return his endearments in the best manner I could… A miserable German slave.' (Letter 22.)

In Ashe's narrative 'Vistatock' then arrives incognito in Württemberg. Charlotte's English entourage is banished out of jealousy when he is discovered. As seems inevitable in this gothic tradition, Charlotte becomes pregnant following her encounter with the 'tiger'. In his jealousy, he hits her with the flat of his sword. He leaves for Paris, and never touches her again. She gives birth to a stillborn child. (Letter 23.)

Flora Fraser cites evidence for some of this from no less a person than Napoleon: 'I had the pleasure of interfering to her advantage when her husband, who was a brute though a man of substance, had ill-treated her, for which she was afterwards very grateful.'[8]

In her husband's absence, Vistatock renews his advances, but she cannot return them, partly because of the fact of her marriage, but also because of the pitiful condition to which it has reduced her. She returns his ring with the words, 'Leave me, leave me, I am lost.' He returns to England vowing celibacy. (Letter 24.)

Charlotte's plight is really the exemplar of the destructive power of the Royal Marriages Act. She is compelled into a brutal and unhappy marriage and denied a happy one for political reasons. It comes first and at greatest length, partly because Charlotte is the eldest sister, and partly because her story sets the pattern. Ashe leaves her at this point, naturally with more pleas against the Act, but 'Vistatock' later Duke of Bedford (or 'Fordbed' when Ashe remembers to correct himself), reappears in the later narrative as a reminder of the consequences of the Act, and a reproach to the conscience of The Family. (Letter 25.) The Duke of Bedford's biography mentions a mistress, Mrs Palmer, with whom he had two children but no marriage. His sudden betrothal to Lady Jane Gordon, an intimate of William Pitt, in 1802 shocked his Whig connections, but the marriage was prevented by his sudden death. She married his brother and heir, Lord John Russell.

Before embarking on the story of the next sister, Augusta, Elizabeth pauses in her narrative and takes the opportunity to analyse the effect of their upbringing on the character of her brothers and in particular on George, Prince of Wales. Elizabeth tells Caroline 'You know the vices and follies of my brothers without knowing the causes that bewilder them.' Again, he does not see the disreputable events in isolation or as wilful but as the product of the Royal Marriages Act. *The Claustral Palace* affects at least not to add to the ignorant calumny of the Prince but rather to explain his predicament, a potentially more dangerous angle. 'The genius and character of her seven illustrious brothers' as she calls it, stem from enforced indolence, their vices rooted in impatience with their 'debauched and enervated' state. Forbidding legitimate domestic relationships before dynastic ones provokes illicit ones. 'In the lap of celibacy the vigour of the brothers' minds was enervated, while the indulgence of criminal pleasure completed the victory.'

The brothers petition their father to be allowed to serve in the army on the outbreak of war with France when 'cruel discord threatened the very foundations of the Claustral Palace'. As heir to the throne, George must be protected and is refused permission. Their lament takes the form of a terrible poem.

To find that France can make so bold a stand
And rapines, rapes and blood deform the land.

They invoke the spirit of Agincourt, but though they are given commissions and uniforms they are not allowed near any real fighting. This proscription on military service is presented as being a primary cause of their degeneracy. Occasionally, as Ernest was, they are given proper service, but are then recalled to sinecures. They were 'treated like overgrown children'.

Caricature tended to depict the brothers as revelling in their own indolence and smug in their own security. Ashe chooses a possibly better sourced and more sympathetic line, which may well have come from Elizabeth herself in her confidences to Caroline, of them chafing against the constraints placed upon them, but doomed given the statutory and moral background of their upbringing. 'It would be dangerous to give my brothers too much power, so it is proper to treat them as slaves.' Rendered useless by royally invented legislation. She describes her siblings as 'Great State puppets only to be employed for the amusement of the public'. (Letter 26.)

Elizabeth, in voicing this very modern-sounding and cynical view of royalty raises the central question of 'What are they all for?' This is what makes Ashe's work dangerous; this legitimate question was potential political dynamite in revolutionary times.

George, Prince of Wales

Characteristically, Elizabeth's letters to Caroline on the subject of her estranged husband are sympathetic, designed to help her understand his predicament. Her descriptions are still damning, perhaps more so because they arise from sympathy rather than satire. 'Even his separation from you, my dear Caroline cannot make him contemptible in your sight.' The description of George at the time of his marriage is echoed in Ashe's description in his 'Memoirs' of Charles James Fox in his final cabinet 'in his latter Spring and in a state of florid weakness'. She continues: 'The archives of the Claustral Palace do not record a single blot stain or imperfection against his private character.' (Letter 28.) This is perhaps a unique and unexpected remark to be found in a blackmailing novel, but perhaps not too surprising given the novel's overall purpose of demonstrating the corrupting power of the Royal Marriages Act.

As a demonstration, if not of his purity, then at least his capacity for remorse, Elizabeth gives us examples of George's poetic and oratorical powers. There is a monody on the death in 1802, of 'Vistatock' now 'Fordbed' in his later incarnation, and The Family's pangs of conscience after his plea against the Act during his affair with 'The Senior Recluse'. There are pages of it. It is not good poetry.

> Excellent Man! Whose bosom was the sail,
> Where every grace and every virtue throve
> But chiefly those, the gentlest, sweetest, best
> That humanize and dignify the Breast
> Thy filial, fraternal and country's love!

Does Ashe make all of this up, or is it like something George might actually have written and his literary sister might have copied and shared? (Letter 29.)

The Prince of Wales we all thought we knew and loved has to be explained and be seen to emerge somehow from this unfamiliar poetic paragon. Falling off because of the effect of the Act on his upbringing and relationships, he lapses into debauchery and the 'petty crimes' of the 'court fop' under the tutelage of 'profligate wretches'. (Letter 30.) More generally, 'The jealous policy of your venal ministers renders your sons odious to themselves and burthensome to the state.' (Letter 31.)

We then go back in time to George's early life and loves. Exile educates him in foreign vices. Fragments of his letters show pangs of conscience in reply to the Duke of Bedford's reproachful correspondence. There are two years of decline, then we are told of the mysterious relationship of George and 'Ethelinda' and their secret marriage. This is certainly not the secret marriage to the widowed Mrs Fitzherbert, since she is referred to by a thinly disguised name later in the narrative. 'Ethelinda' is the son's equivalent of 'Jemima' to his father, the perfect early love who might have made him happy had reasons of state and the Royal Marriages Act not intervened. The relationship may be part of a destructive cycle wrought by the Act, but it still has its own character and detail. Ashe gives the precise terms of Prince's letters to her 'If fortune should happen to prosper my designs... Of what use is greatness to those who are already happy?' (Letter 32.) They go to a masked ball, at Thatched House Lodge in Richmond Park, she as a Persian Princess, George as the fallen Angel. There are repeated 'Paradise Lost' quotations. The girl is then only 22.

'George was ever in pursuit of adventures, to bring Virgins into distress and violate women of condition.' He arranges an assignation under the assumed name of Augustus St George.

'Ethelinda' it transpires is also a feigned name, there is 'a ravished kiss' (Letter 33) followed by an exchange of notes, her offence at the kiss and his penitent note, 'the game of skill begun'. (Letter 35.)

She is detained by a cold from her intention of leaving for the country, which might have ended the affair. This has the flavour of 'Perdita', Mary Robinson's sudden stress-related illness, in one of his well-attested early relationships, but then so many of his romances followed a similar pattern. (Letter 36.)

We are given tantalising glimpses of 'Ethelinda's' true identity, often hastily crossed through in the manuscript but not entirely effaced. There is a meeting at Countess of Bessborough's house where 'Ethelinda' reveals herself to be 'a daughter of the house of Cavendish' (again hastily deleted) 'and Countess B her father's sister'. Which of Caroline, Countess of Bessborough's brothers is supposed to have sired this illegitimate beauty is not made clear. Caroline Cavendish married William Ponsonby in 1739 to become Lady Bessborough, none of her three younger brothers, all unmarried, are recorded as having issue, whether George-Augustus, Frederick, or John. John, a man of passion and feeling, was probably the most likely. Again, there are parallels with the king's relationship with 'Jemima'; he is ill, she nurses him, then he abandons her for his disastrous political marriage.

George, labouring under 'pecuniary embarrassments', finds Caroline of Brunswick can settle £50,000 on him just as his debts come to the king's notice. Then comes the ultimatum from the king to marry Caroline and clear those debts. Elizabeth describes to Caroline in clear terms her view of Caroline's marriage to her brother: 'A union to which beggary and death would have been preferred... I am told that you are driven from your home to take refuge among the ordinary citizens, that a vulgar and abandoned adulteress may be left to the undisturbed enjoyment of your matrimonial mansion, it is added that the sums which ought to be divided among his creditors are squandered on infamous objects of his lascivious attachments.' She also knows the marriage came when she was still bound to Captain Browne. George was 'united to you whose heart was irrevocably engaged'. George in turn, in deference to 'Ethelinda's' memory, disports with only wives, not virgins, hence his attachment to 'the old Herbertfitzes (Fitzherberts) Seyjers (Jerseys) and

Yarbouches (Yarmouths, later Lady Hertford) of these strange and infamous times'. (Letter 37.)

Augusta

Volume two begins (letters 37 to 49) with the second sister Augusta Sophia and her lover 'Lonex' Charles Lennox, later Duke of Richmond. Lennox's duel with the Duke of York is often glossed as being a disagreement about military appointments, here it has a different cause. There is little in *The Claustral Palace* of Augusta's hope of marrying Sir Brent Spencer, about which she was still writing to the Regent in 1812 at the age of 43.

Ashe's narrative sets the relationship with Lennox against a background of the gradual erosion of liberty of the sisters by their mother and of them growing older and more desperate. 'No company but our mother who was perpetually inveighing against the follies and indecencies of Love and no servants save old maids and foreign Eunuchs.'

Augusta 'had led this solitary life with singular piety and patience'. Then she is dropped a secret note in fairytale fashion from 'Lonex' on his return to England. Elizabeth admits some jealousy of his attention to her, and her letters imply 'intercourse of a considerable standing'. Lennox was an athlete and cricketer, a founder of the Marylebone Cricket Club, so the wall leaping recorded in the narrative below may be credible. (Letter 38.)

Ashe adds some colourful grotesque to the circumstances of Augusta's confinement at Frogmore. There she was guarded by a dog trained by General Frederick Maitland in Jamaica, a flesh ripper bred to hunt escaped slaves. 'A dog fleshed in blood and reeking in the carnage of the Maroon War'. Elizabeth lures the dog away with stolen food while Augusta goes to her assignation with Lennox; she urges him to flee and the dog gains the scent. 'Lonex' gallantly kills the dog. (Letter 39.)

'Augusta had scarcely given vent to the dictates of her joy for the Victory of her Lover when the garden was thronged with a Court rabble.' 'Lonex' leaps the wall in time to avoid them. The rapidly invented 'unknown dog-murderer' alibi, which Augusta supplies, induces (not very credibly) a reflection on the part of those present about 'the dreadful tendency of the Royal Marriage Act to encourage vice instead of virtue'. (Letter 40.)

There are many hasty revisions in the text as the amatory adventures reach their climax and the escaped Lennox ponders his predicament:

> He perceived a vast difference between desire and enjoyment, between the full and vigorous light of the sun and the pale glimmers of the moon; and yet it was ruin inevitable, it was destruction, barefaced to attempt a private interview with the illustrious object of his choice.

Nonetheless, 'Lonex' contrives a personal interview, by flattery and bribery of Augusta's page who had been raised in the household of his uncle the Duke of 'Poormond' [Richmond] while the family is out, at Toadmore (Frogmore) Gardens. There is time for 'one moment of blessed intercourse' and Augusta is alone. There is lots of nice incidental detail as to interiors of the palace and Augusta's clothing:

> His mistress was seen lain down on a sofa apparently asleep or merged in the profoundest thought. The presumptuous Lonex softly entered this little chamber of repose. The weather violently hot, the Venetian blinds were let down before the window, the sashes open and the jessamine that covered them waved about and scented the room with a delightful fragrancy. Tuberoses, set in gilt and china pots, were placed fancifully upon marble stands; the curtains of the sofa drawn back to the canopy, made of yellow velvet... the panels of the chamber looking glass, upon which rambled artificial vines, displaying curling tendrils, verdant leaves and purple clustering fruit. Upon the carpet were strewed with lavish profuseness, abundance of orange and lemon flowers; and to complete the Ovidian scene, the young Augusta on the verdant sofa, lay supine lost in thought or sunk in sleep.
>
> She was in an undress composed of Carnation-Taffety stained with Indian figures, her beautiful long flowing hair...veiled over much of the beauties of her lovely form, yet sufficient of her entire person stood confessed to the view of her enraptured beholder. Her fascinating eyes seemed to be closed, her face, turned rather on one side, was obscured by the lace depending from the pillows on which she rested. Amazed and delighted, the Colonel gave himself time to gaze over Beauties so inviting; and which increased his flame to such a degree of enthusiastic ardour, that with an amorous sigh, he gently threw himself on his knees, close to the slumbering Angel, and dared. O daring youth! To lay his lips

to that part of her face which was revealed and lit up with the diffused light of joy, innocence and rapture. The burning Augusta was disturbed but not awoke. Her own emotions seemed to favour the Colonel's thefts. A change of posture exposed her bosom upon which he fixed his audacious mouth. She half disclosed, and then shut her lucid eyes with a languishing sweetness. Intoxicated and breathless with joy he grasped her to his ravished heart. 'Glorious destiny!' cried he, with a transported tone,' by what means, Fortune, hast thou made me the happiest of Mortals? I am in possession of greater joys than mortal sense can bear!'

This seems a slightly unlikely ejaculation at this point and of course, what was said cannot have been witnessed directly by Elizabeth unless she were hiding in a corner. It is just possible the wealth of detail came to Ashe from the princesses themselves; there is certainly plenty of it. Naturally, the lovers are interrupted before things can go any further, even before Augusta can go through the ceremony of pretended outrage and 'Lonex' can defend his conduct with a profession of love. The family returns, the queen is inclined to blame Augusta, her father the audacious lover. This prompts Augusta to confess her love: 'It was the fire of nature, it was the blush of love for him whose life is dearer to Augusta than the pride of fame, the wealth of palaces or the condition of kings.' She is dragged by the hair from the arms of her lover 'by her ensavaged mother'. (Letter 41.)

The queen and the evil governess 'Schwellenbergh' (the spelling varies) discuss Augusta's fate in German. 'A language Augusta so little understood that she could comprehend little more than that the former guardian of the sacrificed Charlotte had instructions to deny her any communication with the Family or with Society until she had "dragooned her" into the most perfect obedience to her Mother's will.' At this point, the narrative becomes Augusta's first-person account, either Ashe forgot for a moment he was writing as Elizabeth or just possibly, he got this account of her fate from Augusta herself. 'The Old Lady' appears to have an aversion to her daughters having relationships with Englishmen on principle as well as them being contrary to the dictates of the 'sacred Royal Marriage Act'. This prompts an exchange between Augusta and the queen:

When I was but fourteen years of age I formed an idea of perfection in a lover who could make me happy! I judged the men who visited the Claustral Palace by that standard, until Lonex met it.

Elizabeth witnessed the queen's reaction. 'My mother's eyes glowed with unusual fire, the instant of eruption was arrived, it burst forth and swept the dear girl from the sofa to the ground, she was trampled under foot; she was beaten almost to Death.' (Letter 42.)

Augusta, Elizabeth tells us, does not expect to survive and does not want to live in slavery. Her resignation to her fate denies Mrs Schwellenbergh the combat she enjoys. While painting this picture of despair, Augusta still communicated through the same compliant royal page. There are further stratagems; a ladder of silken cords let down from her window allows him to visit her again. Though this ruse does not appear likely, the athleticism of it, again, is characteristic of him. Since she has no means of communicating with him before the appointed hour of his visit, she faces a terrible dilemma, to betray her lover to discovery by not letting down the ladder, or risking another meeting, the consequences of which might ruin her:

> The Colonel was grown so dear to her that she could not bear the thought of parting with him without an interview and yet the means of the assignation filled her with horror and affright. Should she not let down the ladder in time he would be exposed to be taken by the patrol of the guard that relieves 'The Terrace' sentinels of the night; should she let the ladder descend she feared she could not control the emotions of her own heart. (Letter 43.)

There are many tears and lots of anguish. The lovers conjure the illusive prospect of freedom, the ability to marry as they choose, somehow evading the Royal Marriages Act. A further meeting is appointed for one o'clock the following morning. (Letter 44.) This time, inevitably, he is discovered in the grounds of Frogmore and Augusta swoons (again) at the Colonel's arrest there, 'in private clothes and without parole'. 'Lonex' volunteers to go back to the army. Augusta attempts to kill herself with her page's sword, but is prevented by her father. The king comes out of it rather well, counselling tenderness and placating 'The Old Lady' but still, as Elizabeth says, fitting his daughters for the next world rather than this. The unfeeling queen delivers a homily on the damage wrought by her unlawful love. 'Witness the shameful effects it has already produced, your character stained, the Claustral Palace mocked at and reviled.' (Letter 45.)

After the queen's lecture on the dangers of love. Augusta again takes on quietude as a cover for despair and produces an elegy on it. There is quite a long disquisition on the beauties of Augusta's poetic style, which may well be a case of the author praising himself, since she uses his name for Frogmore and repeats the rhyme in the second and fourth line of the third stanza:

Elegy on Despair

Farewell the liquid lapse of tinkling streams
Farewell the sun with noontide glory clad
Farewell in Toadmore shades delicious dreams
Farewell the mead in cowslip mantle clad

Things improve a bit in the final stanza, though her final union with her lover has a whiff of – what? – corruption, as well as presenting a difficult project for a weaver:

Beneath you, willow, eldest of the bank
By L ---'s meandering wave I'll lay me down
There mix my sad sighs with his vapours dank
And weave, ill-fated wretch, a Cypress crown.

At the end of this letter, Elizabeth regrets reproducing the poem, ostensibly because of its poignant emotive power. 'I sincerely wish, my dear Caroline, that I had closed this letter before I can called to mind this plaintive elegy of the fond and unfortunate Augusta.' Even at the distance of two hundred years, it is a regret that readers can probably still share. (Letter 46.)

Although this might seem to be the end of the relationship, there are further conversations between Elizabeth and Augusta about contriving further trysts. There begins to be some lenity in the regime after the extremes and violence of Lennox's discovery. Their loving father the king is conscious of the restrictions on 'virtuous love' of the Royal Marriages Act and is prepared to allow some leeway short of public scandal and vice, in the hope of avoiding further convulsions. Naturally, this becomes an invitation to further scandal rather than a safety valve designed to prevent it. (Letter 47.)

Under this new regime, the sisters are allowed walks into town and the freedom of the gardens of 'Toadmore'. Augusta composes a pastoral elegy and then hears 'Lonex's' song 'sweet as Milton's muse' in praise of her beauty and wit at the Temple of Trianon, presumably a rustic imitation of Versailles at Frogmore:

> In soft Augusta's form united shine
> Such female ease and majesty divine
> That each beholder must with awe declare
> Apelles' Venus was not half so fair
> But who the stores of judgement, wit and sense
> Her lips with graceful diffidence dispense
> Each hearer owns with pleasure and surprise
> That Homer's Pallas was not half so wise
> These different charms such different passions move
> Who sees must reverence but who hears must love.

This superiority of sound over sight immediately manifests itself as not only can Lennox sing his song audibly to them without being seen or exciting any curiosity about where he might be, but also Elizabeth is sure he cannot see the effect of the song on Augusta. 'What would not the Colonel have given to behold the heavings of her tender bosom?' Augusta wishes for a peasant's freedom to be disposed of in marriage by her father, in a way less constrained than her own father, the king, is. She complains 'my waiting women are happier than I!' It is just possible they would not have minded swapping places, even given the restrictions that would then imposed on them. (Letter 48.)

There follows a lovers' meeting during which Elizabeth's disclaims the powers of narration to reveal. She offers to leave them together, but Augusta cannot let her go. She is too conscious of her role as model to their younger sisters. His vows of honourable intention are followed by mutual ones of future fidelity. Other meetings take place to which Elizabeth was not a witness.

Elizabeth is then shown the 'infant coffin' of Augusta's dead child by Lonex and she learns of her attempts to end her life. Then comes Lonex's final letter, news of his compelled marriage and his posting to Ireland ('Landire') He died of hydrophobia following a bite from his pet fox in British North America. Perhaps it was in revenge for killing General Maitland's dog. (Letter 49.)

Frederick, Duke of York and Albany

The tale of Frederick, Duke of York begins with Medina (sometimes Melina) Amelia, a Maid of Honour, the daughter of an English lady of rank and a Hanover general, brought into the Queen's service through the offices of the Duke of Cumberland. (Letter 51.) She is seduced and abandoned. Frederick, 'a soldier, changeable and arrogant and unaffected by any gentle ideas, having gained the victory despised the victim.' The Queen is angry with her rather than with him, but also summons Frederick. (Letter 52.)

Frederick would be exiled if the truth came out. He wants to avoid this as he has already shifted his affections to another maid of honour. 'Though Fred could not be called a man of Wit, he had a good share of invention and was a great Master in the Art of dissimulation.' Fred blames the Royal Marriages Act for forbidding their love while having previously promised to obtain permission from The Fmily. (Letter 53.) Melodramatically, Ashe describes Fred's betrayal of Medina as 'Villainy beyond the annals of Peron nor in Sully's Memoirs'. Medina discovers Fred with the new maid 'Constantia' in a summerhouse at Toadmore. 'The Old Lady continually persecutes me about that little Bastard Medina and indeed it is with the outmost difficulty that I have got rid of that fond girl. Let us not waste the precious time.' Medina confesses all to the Queen. (Letter 54.)

Frederick is drawn to sudden an outbreak of truthfulness by Medina's state and his father's upbraiding. Both lovers are now melodramatically seeking death. The king is all mildness to Medina, consistently well intentioned and regal, despite being the framer of the Royal Marriages Act. (Letter 55.)

There is a consistent element of tragedy; the royal children are represented as of reasonable natural parts, not congenital idiots. Ashe is actually quite subtle about the difficulty and duplicity of the king's position. Ashe sees the background of the king's own youthful loves and his stern reaction to unsuitable marriages in Shakespearian terms; precedent and guilt, dramatic irony and doom. (Letter 57.)

With a soldier's first-hand experience, Ashe retells the story of some of the duke's failed campaigns, with detail about Bremen where according to *Memoirs and Confessions* he spent time in hospital. Meanwhile, poor Medina dies of shock at her rejection. The destructive power of the Royal Marriages Act demands it, but it has to be said that there are rather too many people dying of love and grief for the narrative to be entirely credible. (Letter 59.) Frederick is brought to account by Medina's father. There is lots more crying. (Letter 60.) She is buried in Bremen amid more tears and poetry. (Letter 61.)

A 'reformed' Frederick becomes Commander-in-Chief but the military disasters continue: 'the Dutch calamity was similar to his Flemish misfortune.' His marriage is weakened by his wife's disgust at his military incompetence and they have no children. (Letter 62.)

The Claustral Palace comes out on the duke's side in the Mary Anne Clarke scandal. He is forced to give up office by the campaign of Whitbread ('Blackbread') Burdett ('Dettbur') and Colonel Wardle' ('Dellwar') the pursuer of Mrs Clarke, who, like Ashe, fought with Sir Watkins Wynne in the Irish campaign of 1798. Ashe is rather more pro-monarchy than you might expect given the subject of the novel and his own experience. Elizabeth's language is very much Ashe's own in respect of Wardle's popularity in the 'venal papers'. 'Having traced Colonel Dellwar from the fountain of his imbecility, into the rapid current of popularity, I am now to show that he was encouraged to the most desperate acts.' There is the suggestion that Mrs Clarke's evidence against the duke is given in return for Wardle paying for the refurbishment of her house. The people, Ashe has Elizabeth say, are taught disloyalty by non-conformist churches, Colonel Wardle and the beggarly politics of William Cobbett ('Bettcob'). (Letter 65.)

Sophia

It is easy to see why Sophia would eventually merit her own book at Ashe's hands. The rumours about her were so extraordinary and her character set her apart from the other sisters. She is accounted the only sister to take Caroline's side in the marital war with their brother and their relationship seemed to be particularly close. Caroline acted as the go-between for Sophia in her relationship with Colonel Garth. Miss Garth, his niece and Sophia's confidante was in Caroline's household at Blackheath. Sophia and Caroline were also brought together by the king's alarming attention to them in his madness, Sophia then being subject to advances by her father as well as her brother. Sophia in her letters refers to the queen as 'The Old Lady' as Ashe does in *The Claustral Palace*. Given that Ashe devotes a book to the relationship between Ernest and Sophia eighteen years later, it is interesting that there is no hint of this relationship in *The Claustral Palace* and very little about Ernest at all. It is possible that Caroline, who may have had the story of Ernest's paternity of Sophia's child from Ernest himself, had not yet confided in Thomas Ashe. It is also possible Ashe knew of the rumour but held it back until new evidence emerged and a new political imperative drove him. It is clear from his *Memoirs and Confessions* that Ashe at this point thought relatively highly of Ernest and was obliged to him in a military capacity.

Princess Elizabeth is said to have been the source of the news to Dr Thomas Willis of Sophia's pregnancy, the Prince of Wales being the ultimate source; a confidence betrayed in revenge for Sophia's support of his wife. It seems an unlikely set of transmissions and motivations, but this is the strangest family.

'Amiable' is the adjective applied by Ashe to both Caroline and Sophia, a positive quality but with a vulnerable aspect when you cannot trust your family or your servants. General Garth, equerry and lover, is rendered as 'Tharg' with a reasonable level of consistency in *The Claustral Palace*. Sophia is described as 'one of the most lovely women that was ever condemned to a life of stagnant celibacy and claustral sloth... Humane and benevolent.' She exhibited from an early age a fondness for things which might do her harm. Her violent passions, led inevitably to confrontations with the queen: 'she braved the Old lady to her very teeth.'

Sophia bridles at the narrow discipline of her education and does not make the progress her parents wish. 'Tharg', who appears as something of a power behind the throne, is entrusted by The Family with the finish of her education. He 'aimed at something more than riches! He was in treaty with a Princess dowager and in hopes of being her husband and heir to her succession.' Ashe has Elizabeth address Caroline as 'Charlotte, my love' in error, as things hot up. Garth, a small, hideous man with a disfiguring birthmark, was perhaps an indication of how little it took to snare a princess mired in claustral seclusion. Garth talks virtue but pursues vice. He keeps Sophia away from romances and other corrupting literature, keeping her desires pent up so he can corrupt her himself. (Letter 66.)

'Tharg' becomes the principal instructor of all the younger princesses in a freer atmosphere than the one that had brought misery to Charlotte and Augusta. There are plays. Sophia acts the goddess Diana and the middle-aged General, in somewhat unlikely fashion, 'the son of Acteon'. 'Tharg', wrestling with his feelings, runs off to town to distance himself from Sophia, but returns to the Claustral Palace and her kisses. (Letter 67.) 'He changes the system of study of Sophia; he poisons her principles, before he contaminates her person.' Tharg reads his Machiavelli: 'None but great souls can be completely wicked.' If he corrupted her, would she fall for another? He starts her reading, predictably enough, with Ovid. 'Her virtue was becalmed or rather totally unapprehensive of her Mentor as its Invader... There are pleasures her sex were born for that she might consequently languish to enjoy... He drank in her tears with his kisses.' (Letter 68.)

The history of Sophia now comes not from Elizabeth's direct experience but 'Original Documents' to which she has access, so again Ashe is being quite scrupulous about his narrator's claims to knowledge, presumably reflecting his own sources. Sophia, inflamed by feelings she does not understand, is now bored by the Claustral Palace and longs for her former innocence. There is an encounter on a 'dangerous sofa':

> She threw herself down upon a sofa in only one thin petticoat, and a loose night gown the bosom of which was carelessly tied with a rose coloured ribbon, that corresponded with the green and silver stuff of her gown. She lay in a melancholy careless posture, with her head tilted on one of her hands.

'Tharg' gives way to 'the criminality of his desires' and 'the strength of her constitution at length failed her.' 'Caroline my love I cannot tell you what followed.' There is just time for another interlude on the futility of attempting to legislate against love. (Letter 69.) Elizabeth believes she is first on the scene after the 'dangerous sofa'. Sophia's face is 'covered in blushes, her bosom heaving with sobs'.

Sophia is entirely ignorant of the countryside and delighted by the journey to Weymouth to cure her 'dropsical' malady' after her encounter with 'Tharg'. This seems to be code for pregnancy among the princesses of the Claustral Palace since its principal symptom is swelling. It was a contagion common at the Palace and attributable to the Royal Marriages Act. (Letter 70.) In her recovery she 'assumes her former shape'. The Old Lady wants to send the baby to the workhouse.:'A curse rather than a royal blessing.' (Letter 71.)

Baptised at Weymouth on 11 August 1800, 'Thomas Ward' was a son to Thomas Sharland adopted by Garth, who made him his heir. The birth ends Sophia's hopes of marriage. Tharg's temple of love, erected for the christening of the boy who became Tommy Garth is somewhat fantastically rendered by Ashe as 'Alfred Fortunatus Tharg'. (Letter 72.)

'The Old Lady smells a rat' since the ceremony has all the trappings of a royal baptism; the queen will not allow Sophia to raise the child and gives him to a shoemaker's wife. The 'noise' of scandal prompts the family to leave town and return to the Claustral Palace.

Having denounced his own work as a potboiler, Ashe begins to make greater claims for it within its pages. There are eerie echoes of Wordsworth's Preface to *The Lyrical Ballads*. He makes a plea for serious literature and denounces 'poor deluded votaries' of popular romances. There is even a quotation from Milton's *Paradise Lost*: 'Can make a heav'n of hell; a hell of heav'n', justifying his use of quotation 'as much for illustration as embellishment'. He ends volume 2 with his favourite poet Horace, in the Latin: *si quid novisti rectius istis, candidus imperti; si non, his utere mecum*. This is translated for Caroline, whose Latin, Elizabeth is probably right to think might be rusty: 'Farewell and be happy, if you know of any precepts better than mine, be so kind as to communicate them, if not partake of these.' (Letter 73.)

Elizabeth

In Volume 3, the narrator, Princess Elizabeth, turns to her own story. She was Ashe's contemporary (they were both born in 1770) and his favourite. She was bookish and thoughtful, the one in whose voice he felt most comfortable speaking. It is tempting to view the surviving synopsis of *The Claustral Palace* found among her papers not as a threat but as a summary, sent to the work's source for approval. She was to be married in 1818, but that possibility had seemed to have already passed her by at the time that *The Claustral Palace* was written in 1811. Then she remained in the 'vile mire of celibacy'. There is some evidence from Flora Fraser that Elizabeth misunderstood the terms of the Royal Marriages Act and serially held out tentative hopes of relationships impossible within its terms. There is no place in Ashe's narrative for Elizabeth's doomed love for the Duke of Orleans, Louis Philippe, though this dates to the period immediately before the composition of *The Claustral Palace*. He was in exile, penniless, in Twickenham. She was now old enough to make her own choice within the act with the consent of Parliament. However, it was not just the Royal Marriages Act, but also the Act of Settlement that stood in their way. The marriage would not be consented to by Parliament because he was Catholic, even if the royal family could be persuaded to sanction it.

There is evidence for Elizabeth's increasing eccentricity around the time of *The Claustral Palace*: her praise of rural life, love of her cows, her social ease with farmers. Her voice in *The Claustral Palace* might simply be a satirist's device as in Virgil and Edmund Spenser to contrast the simplicity and virtue of rural life with the corruption of courts; but in this case, it actually reflects the kind of statements Elizabeth is recorded as making.

As narrator, Elizabeth gives her own love life a lot of space (letters 74-91), the most of any of the sisters, despite her having no widely attested relationships before her marriage in her late forties. This suggests that Ashe is either making them up to make his heroine appear more interesting or perhaps that they are based on genuine confidences given to Caroline or to Ashe directly.

Elizabeth bewails her eighteen years 'in this gloomy mansion'. She outlines her staid life at Windsor and Frogmore, longing for the gallantries of the merry days of King Charles II. Elizabeth's letters give some amusing detail of the limitations of their male society, generally 'cold, exhausted courtiers'.

> They favour us indeed with their presence for a short time in the evening, but no sooner is the tea equipage removed, than they betake themselves to their political disquisitions over the bottle, while we are obliged to have recourse to a game of whist, or to pass a considerable part of the night looking at one another in savage silence across a table. Whilst we are pining away in secret desires, our courtiers are busily employed in settling the affairs of the public, while we are meditating the conquest of the heart, they are ruminating the downfall of some popular advocate of a deluded people. (Letter 74.)

Elizabeth reprises her thrall to the Royal Marriages Act and its role in Caroline's predicament. She designs a remonstrance against the act to be devised by princes who can 'feel as well as write'. (Letter 75.) She contrasts peasant freedom and royal slavery, composes the inevitable bucolic poems – 'Where proud Windsora blest with long repose' – and records 'Sophy's' rebellion against the tyranny of the Act, which at that point she believes she will never have the opportunity to emulate. (Letter 76.)

Then, playfully in their rustic setting, Elizabeth and Amelia disguise their identities and ramble beyond the pale of the Claustral Palace. They discover the cottage of the Young Dormer and his sister, Maria and describe it and him in loving detail, including his 'martial aspect' despite wearing a 'milking frock', 'vigorous' despite being wounded in his left leg. (Letter 77.) They learn young Dormer's name is Montague ('Muetagon') and that he was a Captain at the siege of Valenciennes in 1793, where he suffered a bayonet wound to his side and a musket ball to the left knee. Maria conducts Amelia and Elizabeth around the farm the brother and sister share. Elizabeth contrasts Dormer's virtue with the general behaviour of soldiers. (Letter 78.)

Naturally enough, he is also a poet. There follows Young Dormer's ode 'To a Nightingale' as 'the love-lorn poet of the glade'. It is not Keats, but it does at least pre-date Keats' ode rather than deriving from it:

Now fairy twilight slowly steals
With shadowy tints across the sky
Whilst radiant sol his visage screens
Beneath your clouds of purple dye.

Is Elizabeth breaking the Royal Marriages Act in taking his arm to support him? (Letter 79.)

Although the sisters' escapade is not discovered, their absence invites suspicion. 'The smellers of the old lady' again begin to wave. 'The dear old lady has no dominion whatever over the muscles of her nose.' The queen fires a warning shot, a pre-emptive tirade against love: 'there is no illicit enjoyment without disgrace.' (Letter 80.)

Elizabeth conducts her own 'Delicate inquiries into the character of the Young Dormer', a type from the novels of Samuel Richardson, though 'not as immaculate' as Sir Charles Grandison or Joseph from *Pamela*. He is a classical scholar with favourites similar to Ashe himself, Homer, Horace and Virgil. Elizabeth uses that great standby of the Georgian leisured lady, the literary commonplace book, to express her admiration for him, through the poetry of her own favourite Dryden rather than risk her own words: 'We echo but the voice of Fame/That dwells delighted on his name.' Then another, this time from Shakespeare's *Venus and Adonis*: 'Love is a spirit all compact of fire/Not gross to sink, but light and will aspire.' This is obviously as close to a confession of love as she can go and she ends 'Caroline, burn this letter!' (Letter 81.)

Elizabeth plans to bring Maria into the household as a maid of honour, and Dormer under the patronage of Prince Frederick, Duke of York. Up to this point, the princesses' identities are unknown to the brother and sister. The daughters give their surname as 'Filleroi', 'daughter of the king. You would think Dormer might work it out, given his command of Latin poetry, though perhaps he shunned translating simple French after his wounds fighting Napoleon. Then comes Dormer's declaration of love. They 'sealed the bond with a thousand innocent and endearing kisses'. (Letter 82.) It might get a bit less innocent, and possibly less enjoyable after the first five hundred or so. The feigned loss of her royal identity liberates her: 'To know that I was adored as a woman not adulated as a Princess'. They take high tea in his military tent lined with Persian silk. (Letter 83.)

Elizabeth is beset by what Ashe calls 'Claustral qualms'. Love assumes the urgency of the present tense in Elizabeth's letters to Caroline, with reflections relevant to her Delicate Investigation, that a woman's reputation cannot survive the charge of departure from virtue never mind the reality. Elizabeth learns she is the Nightingale of his ode. (Letter 84.)

Dormer suggests elopement to Gretna Green ('Gretnaverde'). There are mutual vows never to marry another. (Letter 85.) She refuses the runaway match, but cannot tell him her true identity or the restrictions placed on her. He falls to his knees a lot, musket ball injury notwithstanding. A miniature of her father 'blazoned round with diamonds which I always carried in my breast' falls to the ground in Dormer's embrace and she confesses her identity. He flees; she implores him not to leave the farm and cottage. (Letter 86.)

The Royal Marriages Act, as Elizabeth reflects, licenses 'political rape'. She contemplates possible mechanisms of evading its punitive measures:

> I had often heard it whispered behind the claustral scenes that there was no act of Parliament but what a dextrous driver could wheel his coach and six directly through and through. I took the hint and resolved to drive my chariot through this famous law, to the temple of Hymen, and there get married privately by a regular clergyman of the established church. Give a poor curate a small pension to exile himself beyond the law, or it were necessary to keep his name a profound secret from the officers of state.

Elizabeth writes to her brother Frederick to ask for a majority for Dormer. Perhaps not entirely coincidentally, this was Ashe's own long-term military ambition, following his own wounding in the same campaign. Perhaps it was the similarities in the biographies of the writer and the lover that led Elizabeth to confide in Ashe, or perhaps he simply embellished the lover in his own image. (Letter 87.)

Emboldened by this resolution Elizabeth tries to pretend that his farm is a retreat from her status where they can behave as they did before he learned of it. Dormer starts composing pastoral idylls addressed to her, apparently as a shepherdess, but her royalty gets in the way along with other bits of awkwardness, as if he would somehow like to trap her or tear her to pieces:

> Low her glossy tresses twine
> Like the tendrils of the vine
> Like the hind before the hounds
> Through the silent lawn she bounds
> And with lightsome foot she treads
> When the winding dance she leads
> Tell me shepherds have you seen
> My delight my little queen? (Letter 88.)

Their former roles in wooing are reversed by her royal status. Elizabeth is converted to the idea of private marriage: 'You have triumphed over the cold political maxims of the state.'

Dormer, now presumably fearful as well as respectful, becomes set on his duty to The Family. She renounces her status:

> I abhor the title and the trappings of my royalty, I behold the elevation of my rank with horror and you must either deliver me from those odious objects by means of private marriage, or you must kill me with your own hand.

Now she is in a position to command and her love converts him. Despite his infirmity, he is soon on his knees again with an impassioned vow never to leave her. Once again, the Act is portrayed as the sole barrier to the happiness of a royal princess and this resolution of the lovers will defy it but come to nothing soon. (Letter 89.)

Maria joins the household and Dormer joins his regiment, Elizabeth buys his farm to prepare it for them. She turns it into a Temple of Love fit for his return. It is admired by the Duchess of

Devonshire who had 'almost forgotten the charms of Versailles' in comparison and Lady Jersey 'began to have her doubts whether it was not to be preferred even to the third heaven and to her native constellation, the brightest luminary in the firmament of love'. The family becomes so attached to it her brother George temporarily stops talking about Brighton Pavilion.

The farm becomes a Temple off Hymen with a prayer book open at the marriage ceremony. It features the Triumph of the God of love painted by Benjamin West from Elizabeth's sketch, which she describes in detail. 'Underneath was scrawled that emphatic phrase of Dormer's, when I subdued all his remaining scruples: "Love levels all distinctions".' Sympathetic members of the family are witnesses to their love, including the family's conscience, the Duke of Bedford ,who conducts Elizabeth to the altar. 'The Birth and Triumph of Cupid' as it was devised in 1795 became 'The Birth and Triumph of Love' when it was published in 1796. The change showed the wrong type of love being brought within bounds and hints at her natural inclination and her obedience. The marriage ceremony includes a song in praise of wedlock, ending in a grand chorus:

> Every doubt and fear averted
> Love and pleasure's all our own
> Bliss, on solid basis founded
> Shall the happy lovers crown. (Letter 90.)

Elizabeth's purchase of the farm was sanctioned by the king so long as it was visited by day only and improved only within the means of Elizabeth's pocket money. It gave an outlet for her creative energies which did not interfere with the Queen's regime at Frogmore where she wished to make 'alterations' but where the Queen wanted to retain control. It brings a brief period of happiness during which Dormer comes to her at the Claustral Palace in disguise.

Their last meeting comes via the trusty ladder to her apartment from 'The Terrace' while the guard changes, as Augusta had contrived with Lennox, Since no one in the saga is permitted the enjoyment of their illicit union, it comes as no surprise, when 'The Old Lady' enters the chamber by means of a master key. 'To attempt to soften my mother by lamentations and tears would be as absurd as to attempt to quench the fires of Etna or the storms of the ocean by the same means.'

The 'Old Lady' traps and exiles Dormer. Sent to Switzerland, he is killed in a suicidal attempt to cross the falls of 'Chapfhausen'. Presumably, these are the Rhine falls at Schaffhausen, Europe's largest waterfall. He is journeying there in his melancholy exile when we meet him at the Court of Brunswick in *The Spirit of the Book*. The aftermath of Dormer's death sees Elizabeth take comfort in her designs for 'The Birth and Triumph of Cupid' and in Bath buns. Her marriage to the Landgrave of Hesse Homburg is still far in the future. (Letter 91.)

Edward, Duke of Kent

It is with some reluctance that the reader moves from the sympathy and pathos of Ashe's favourite among the royal sisters to his least favourite brother, Queen Victoria's father, Edward, Duke of Kent. 'There is little in his character to admire and less to imitate; he spends his youth among common Prostitutes.' Although of 'abject insignificance' and full of 'arrogance and stupidity', he hoped to supplant his brother Frederick as Commander in Chief of the army. Writing with the disgust of a former soldier, rather than in the sympathetic voice of a sister, Ashe, through Elizabeth's narrative, details Edward's relish in drilling his troops to death well out of the way of the enemy. His military prowess consists in being fiendish about tailoring and haircuts. His mistresses are procured for him by his German valets. His Parisian mistress, 'the daughter of his banker', Thérèse-Bernardine Mongenet, became his 'chanteuse' and long-term mistress, known as Madame de Saint-Laurent. Prevented by the Royal Marriages Act from marrying her, much later he is driven to a loveless marriage in the general scramble of the brothers to secure the succession. (Letter 92.)

William, Duke of Clarence

Ashe calls Clarence 'William-Henry' so it is possible that he, rather than the Act-defying but dead Duke of Gloucester, is the dedicatee of the *The Claustral Palace*, though the sketch of his character makes that unlikely. The relationship of William Duke of Clarence and Mrs Jordan brings ten Fitzclarence children in something like conventional domestic happiness, a rather unregal arrangement moulded around the duke's naval career and punctuated with his naval slang. (Letter 93.)

William loves theatrical entertainments and there finds his actress mistress whom Ashe describes in naval terms. 'He falls in with the 'anjor (Jordan) frigate, he boards her; she carries his flag for upwards of twenty years.' Reasons of state and the requirements of the Royal Marriages Act then interrupt the domestic bliss. With the king's final decline and disappearance from public life, and with his two older brothers showing no signs of producing legitimate heirs, William is prompted to end the relationship. What happened next must have been very recent news when *The Claustral Palace* was written in the summer of 1811. He began to hunt for an heiress. In *The Claustral Palace* this is Miss 'Tilney-Short', presumably Catherine Tylney-Long., sister and co-heir of Sir James Tylney-Long, baronet, of Draycot, Wiltshire.

Ashe takes considerable trouble to describe the dress Catherine was wearing when she was introduced to William and how costly it was:

> She was dressed in a robe of two-coloured satin embroidered with silver and her fine hair was interwoven with cordons of pearls and studded with diamonds and other precious stones. Yet she owed more to her natural beauty than all these artificial embellishments. (Letter 94.)

Only the Tylney-Long wealth will allow William to live like a prince so he thinks it worth applying to Parliament for consent to marry outside the Act. He abandons Mrs Jordan before he has their or her consent. A violent sailor's wooing alarms and repels her. Her eventual husband, the fourth Earl of Mornington, William Pole Wellesley, appears in Ashe's list of her admirers carrying items she had given them. He got the reticule. Perhaps the enforced change in his circumstances and relationships would be sufficient to make William an advocate for the end of the Royal Marriages Act, though he had tired of Mrs Jordan by many accounts

The section on William ends with a plea for justice for Mrs Jordan. He only marries in 1818 following the succession imperative of Charlotte's death. The remaining brothers are treated very briefly. Augustus Duke of Sussex 'fearful of claustral traps...proceeds to Rome' to marry Lady Augusta Murray outside the terms of the Act. Adolphus Duke of Cambridge barely features, though he is described to Caroline (Letter 96) in unflattering terms.

Ernest, Duke of Cumberland

Ernest Duke of Cumberland, whose dark personal history was to be the centrepiece of a complete work by Ashe in 1829, escapes lightly from *The Claustral Palace* in 1811. He too is disposed of in a single letter, in this case as a 'tea table general', a carpet knight, a busybody and a generally disagreeable man. His military interest is mostly in fashion – 'the largest military hat and the prettiest fancy sword knots' – brought from Germany, his spiritual home. 'One that has more learning in his heels than in his head, his tailor and his barber form his cabinet council.' One of this council of servants was Joseph Sellis.

> All the knowledge he has of Denmark (i.e. England) was acquired from a late valet, who made a bungling attempt to cut the throat of his master, while he lay immersed and unprotected in the deepest sleep. Italians are proverbial assassins. How this vagabond failed in the science of murder has never been satisfactorily explained.

This is a way of looking at the suspicious death of his valet, which is curiously sympathetic to Ernest. This notorious incident had happened only the year before *The Claustral Palace* was written. Officially, the death of Sellis in mysterious circumstances was represented as being suicide, to escape arrest and disgrace, but an odd document in The Royal Archives suggests Cumberland later, in 1815, confessed to the murder because Sellis threatened 'to propagate a document'. This certainly suggests blackmailing him was a dangerous business. We also learn that Ashe was reluctant to attack Cumberland, a fellow soldier, who had helped Ashe when poor and injured returning to Britain from hospital in Bremen.

There are hints of Ernest as a sexual menace to his sisters, without there being a direct accusation of physical abuse. He is described as an unwelcome visitor to the Claustral Palace, 'he interferes in his sisters' little practices and meditations... Never was there such a meddling court pup in this world.' His sisters had no privacy at Frogmore while he was there, he was 'in every room taking inventories and terrorising the servants'. At least for now, his boasts are represented as being worse than anything he has actually done. (Letter 101.)

Mary

At last, we come to the scant two letters devoted to Princess Mary. It would easy to overlook that she features at all, given the space and detail lavished on her sisters. Her story begins somewhat unexpectedly with a satire on the male view of women in the mouth of the Prophet taken from 'The Female Right to Literature, in a Letter to a young Lady' by Thomas Seward.

> Women, the toys of men, and slaves of lust,
> Are but mere moulds to form man's outward crust;
> The heavenly spark, that animates the clay,
> Of the prime essence that effulgent ray,
> Th' immortal soul is all to man confin'd,
> Not meanly squander'd on weak woman-kind.

It is an ironic testament to the Royal Marriages Act that it manages even to keep the beautiful Mary in claustral subjection, robbed of an opportunity to be an example to society. Even Mary, represented as less warm and less sexually frustrated by her seclusion than her sisters were, forms a connection with a boy at Eton. ('Oten'). The sisters attend an Academic Exhibition and dramatic performances at the school and a particular pupil comes to her attention. Ashe gives him the name of 'Refre', presumably a transparently disguised version of 'Frere', in this case John Hookham Frere, a friend of George Canning who went on to Cambridge and a life divided between literature and the diplomatic service. Like the Duke of Bedford with Mrs Palmer, Frere is generally credited with an established long-term mistress, Lady Errol, with no indication of a long-standing relationship with a royal princess. (Letter 102.)

Frere first impressed Mary in an Eton school play where he performed the part of a Roman patriot in French. Ashe quotes the lines, which won her heart 'falling from his roseate lips'. There follow verses addressed to Mary as one of the 'claustral graces'. A very condensed final page of the letter takes Frere from lisping Etonian poet to diplomatic disaster twenty years later. Elizabeth cannot dwell on Mary's happy youthful passion and moves quickly to the effects of the interdict of the Royal Marriages Act on their relationship and later lives. 'Mary's historical limner needs much less the touches of a Titian than the pencillings of a Rembrandt.'

Ashe's narrative attributes Frere's appointment in Berlin in 1807 to Mary's influence. Frere then moves to the Peninsula, his embassy is a contributory factor to the defeat of Sir John Moore at Corunna in 1809, as witnessed by Ashe in his 'Memoirs'. Mary recoils from him in horror: 'She renounced her lover from that hour.' (Letter 103.)

Princess Amelia

The final chapters (letters 104–110) concern the youngest sister Princess Amelia and her lover Charles Fitzroy 'Fitz-rex' in Ashe's barely disguised version. Her visit to Weymouth ('Weybouche') sees Amelia's first release from the Claustral Palace. She greets her new surroundings with lines from her favourite poet, Alexander Pope in 'On Windsor Forest'. Our view of this poem is probably supposed to be coloured by Caroline's reaction to it, as recorded in *The Spirit of the Book:* 'I have seen Windsor and felt no pleasure.' After all, Frogmore itself was on the royal estate at Windsor and there is a clear indication that Dorset represented something markedly more bucolic and attractive than that. Tellingly, the quotation has been altered. Where Pope has: 'Rich Industry sits smiling on the plains/ And Peace and Plenty tell a STUART reigns,' Amelia's version has 'And plenteous peace announces George's reign' which sounds slightly more hopeful than likely.

Amelia's sea bathing gives rise to anonymous verses of a slightly less elevated kind, beginning: 'When sweet Amelia takes a dip/I envy Neptune's peeping.'

The author of these 'gallantries' is later revealed to be her lover 'Fitz-rex' himself. The visit serves to make Amelia more conscious of their previous confinement at Frogmore and she confides in Elizabeth. 'Surely our lives have hitherto been spent rather in state prison, rather than in a kingdom abounding everywhere with such lovely prospects and inhabited by so gallant and generous a people.' (Letter 104.) Their holiday at Weymouth brings a gradual relaxation of claustral constraints. Eminent figures assemble on the green in front of Amelia's sitting room bay window for the king's levee, 'Fitz-rex' among them (Letter 105.)

There is lots of build-up and pathos in the story of Amelia because her death was so recent and the climactic case against the Royal Marriages Act in the minds of The Family and the public at the time that *The Claustral Palace* was written. Amelia's charitable plans in dialogue with Elizabeth give a great deal of detail about the family she is to help (at 15 Beach Street, Weymouth) and their predicament. 'Fitz-rex' is improbably described as 'the most humane as well as the most accomplished nobleman of my father's court'. Her side of the correspondence only makes her seem desperate and him passive and supine. (Letter 106.)

Detail emerges of Fitzroy's involvement as the creditor of the family Amelia is helping; he begs her forgiveness and is revealed to be the author of anonymous verses to her. (Letter 107.) Love grows on the esplanade and on board ship; they match each other's quotations from Dryden witnessed by Elizabeth in person. He rescues the royal party in his yacht when their boat founders. (Letter 108.)

The Family return to the Claustral Palace. There is some relaxation of the regime including 'free use of the gardens at Toadmore'. Elizabeth lends them the use of her cottage. Amelia confers her hand in private; there is the inevitable suspected pregnancy. The shock of the queen's reaction kills her. 'The Old Lady's back is again up, she falls upon Amelia.' (Letter 109.) There is further pathos in Amelia's deathbed scene, 'dying in the arms of a fond and forgiving father'. With the dying words 'Remember me,' She gives her father Fitzroy's wedding ring inscribed with their wedding date. (Letter 110.)

The last act of the book is the evasion of the Royal Marriages Act by a fait accompli just as it claims its youngest and most recent victim. Fitzroy's epitaph for Amelia among may other tributes 'circulating in the Claustral Palace' ends:

> For what more pleasing can she find
> Beneath the regions of the blest
> Than to survey your noble mind
> Of every sorrow dispossessed?

A final unnumbered letter as epilogue summarises the effect of the Royal Marriages Act on the family.

The third volume of *The Claustral Palace* ends with these poems on the death of Amelia and appears complete despite Ashe's boast in his 'Memoirs' that it was a work in four volumes. Elizabeth gives a flourishing 'Finis' from the Claustral Palace on the final page. There were no more siblings' love lives to reveal.

It is difficult to be enthusiastic about the literary quality of this book once the author has told us it deserves to be consigned to the flames, but that remark was to some extent part of an attempt to dramatise his own predicament and hint at the book's malicious power. The Treasury Solicitor after all did not consign it to the flames but had it bound and put it on the shelves of his library.

What is the moral of this extraordinary production? Probably that the royal family and the government could have saved themselves an awful lot of trouble by making Thomas Ashe a Major in the York Rangers in about 1795. It is very specific about people and places, if not always about dates. Where does the information in *The Claustral Palace* come from? Probably from the same source as *The Spirit of the Book*, Caroline, Princess of Wales, since both books emerge at about the same time and it was Caroline who threatened to 'blow the roof off the Nunnery'. Who was her source at Frogmore? The narrative presents Princess Elizabeth as her confidante, but there are other candidates.[9]

The suppression value of *The Spirit of the Book* and *The Claustral Palace* and the sales of the former suggest Ashe is not dealing in common knowledge, though it is difficult to establish who exactly knew what two hundred years ago. Caroline was the most likely source of such gossip. Ashe seems to follow her about without saying so. He is in Brunswick just before she marries, at Blackheath just as she sets up her alternative court, leaving the country as she leaves around 1814. Perhaps he is one of the few Britons (a term Ashe used of himself) actually attached enough to Caroline herself and not to the political causes which fleetingly allied themselves to her. He was sufficiently motivated to continue pursuing the family after her death and well into his own old age.

Ashe's account adds detail about royal relationships only darkly hinted at elsewhere. The circulation of the synopsis of *The Claustral Palace* and negotiations over the manuscript coincided with the revolt of 'the Nunnery' and the petition of the Princesses to their mother to allow them greater freedom, which so horrified her. What is *The Claustral Palace* trying to do? It is sympathetic to Caroline as the recipient of Elizabeth's correspondence, but she is not the centre of attention any more but a sympathetic ear as the established 'wronged woman'. Was it just a set of scurrilous rumours framed for profit, or did it have some broader purpose in highlighting the Greek tragedy of the Royal Marriages Act? Looking back, it has selective targets and coherence of theme, looking for repeal of the Marriages Act but also includes a warning to Charlotte, occasionally addressed directly in a slip of the pen as 'Caroline'. The Nunnery lent itself to gothic treatment; it would be considered very peculiar in any family. There is less vitriol than from the Hunts or Lamb about the Prince Regent, who is not born useless but is systematically made so by the consequences of the Royal Marriages Act. George III emerges as a broadly benign moraliser more humane than his wife, but he cannot escape the charge of being the instigator, gently guiding his family through a sequence of unnecessary tragedies. Though it touches on the early loves of the king there is little hint of George III's madness, or the obscene talk and maid ravishing that shocks and embarrasses Caroline.

Although *The Claustral Palace* seems by its theme and its timing to complement Henry Brougham's policy of keeping Caroline's daughter Charlotte from a foreign 'political' marriage which might weaken her claim to the throne, and remove her from his sphere of influence, Ashe does not emphasise that connection. The book is not political either in that it steers well clear of the causes of the radicals and deplores Wardle's campaign against the Duke of York as Commander in Chief following the Mary Clarke scandal, as well as the machinations of Whitbread and Burdett, not to mention his rival, William Cobbett. Strangely, and perhaps revealingly, Ashe is circumspect on the subject of Ernest, given that eighteen years later he would devote a book to him.

Princess Augusta took the lead in April 1812 when the sisters sent four letters to their mother asking for more freedom. The queen's reaction was one of horror and outrage, and it took all the Prince Regent's tact to effect a reconciliation between mother and daughters, which gave the latter some degree of independence. As her cousins married and otherwise emerged from the Nunnery, Caroline's role as the wronged woman, the focus of opposition attacks on her husband, also diminished, as her true behaviour was revealed and as she seemed increasingly prepared to abandon her daughter and pursue her own freedom overseas. The focus of the Prince Regent's critics shifted to the marriage negotiations around his daughter Princess Charlotte and the attempts to remove her from the succession. Having dealt with the effect of the Royal Marriages Act on her aunts and while his reputation still loomed large with the booksellers and the public, Thomas Ashe also shifted his attention from the mother to the daughter. He now began his murkiest set of negotiations yet, with the many-headed beast that he called 'The Hydra', with Lord Byron and with the Prince Regent himself.

5

The Patriot Princess

As the restrictions on the princesses at Frogmore were being lifted, new ones were being imposed on Caroline's daughter, Charlotte. *The Claustral Palace* had drawn its inspiration from the Nunnery at Frogmore, which confined her aunts, but now Charlotte herself felt imprisoned by the familiar constraints of useless 'goodness', exhorted to good behaviour from the pages of Hannah More while sneakily reading Byron's 'Bride of Abydos'. As usual, the degree of her restraint was bound to induce thoughts of rebellion. Charlotte's escape through Byron's poetry to a world of harems, political marriage and incestuous love brought her back uncomfortably close to the fate of her aunts.

Had the Prince Regent freed his sisters only to imprison his daughter? Under strict confinement and tutelage at Warwick House, Charlotte came to resent her father and her aunts and to bridle at the restrictions set on her access to her mother. As time went on she came to dread her mother's visits, too, and the role she assumed in matchmaking for her. Her education did not appear to be designed to prepare her to be the next queen of England. Therefore, the question arose, as it had for her aunts in the Nunnery; what was Charlotte for? She became the major character in Thomas Ashe's next campaigning epistolary novel, *The Royal Contrast or Patriot Princess*, a book intended to fill the gaps in her political education and make some radical recommendations as to the composition of her future government.

By 1813 Queen Charlotte and Princesses Elizabeth and Mary were able to venture from Windsor to visit Kew. There were still tensions between the freedoms the Regent might grant the sisters and the duty they and in particular their mother felt they still owed to their father, mad and withdrawn from public life though he might be. For example, their attendance at the opening of parliament by their brother the Regent was seen by the Queen as a betrayal of their father. 'The Nunnery' was splitting up just as Ashe came to write of it in *The Claustral Palace*. Now new imperatives had appeared in the form of the Prince Regent's use of Caroline's moral history as revealed by 'The Delicate Investigation' against the interests of their daughter Charlotte. There was a renewed need to expose the hypocrisy of 'The Delicate Investigation' as *The Book* finally came to be published. Then there was the place of Charlotte's proposed marriage in the ongoing war between her parents. Ashe did not focus on the restrictions placed on Charlotte's marriage choices and the absurdities of the wooings of her suitors, as he had done with her aunts, though there was plenty of material. *The Patriot Princess* had a more obvious political purpose, to supplement Charlotte's woefully inadequate education in matters of state, and recommend men who would serve her in the national interest, rather than in their own. Attitudes had hardened since *The Claustral Palace* in which the Prince of Wales had been depicted as almost as helpless a victim of The Royal Marriages Act as his Brunswick bride had been. He was now the enemy and the best way of serving Caroline's cause was to attack him. It was also true that Ashe was no longer Caroline's favoured 'ghost', serving her directly. Caroline was no longer drawing on friends whose acquaintance she had made in Brunswick before her marriage, but was instead surrounded by opposition figures who sought to use her cause for their own political gain. Ashe found himself at one remove, writing for a variety of individuals and agencies who claimed to serve her cause. His patrons seemed to change from one day to the next. They were a colourful and sometimes disreputable lot and his writing for them became less a matter of personal conviction and more an example of political writing for hire. From late 1813 to the spring of the following year, there was a blizzard of correspondence between Thomas Ashe and his patrons, new and established.

It was not to be a smooth, immediate transition for Thomas Ashe to become the champion of the daughter having written on behalf of her mother. The relationship between mother and daughter was too complex for that. For Ashe the experience of the violent reaction to the circulation of the 'Programma' or synopsis of *The Claustral Palace*, the loss of the manuscript and the desertion of his publisher might have convinced him to stop dealing directly with the royal family at all, at least for a while. After all, *The Spirit of the Book* would continue to do its work until *The Book* itself was published.

The outcome of 'The Delicate Investigation' was couched in the language of inference and understatement and the regular leaking of private correspondence by both sides. Charlotte opposed the publication of *The Book* but Caroline was more interested in revenge than political manoeuvring, or the damage its revelations might do to her standing and reputation. By this stage, she was reduced to sticking pins in wax effigies of the Prince Regent. By 1813, the Tories were back in power after Britain's successful Peninsular campaign. The radicals were looking for another plan of attack, and Brougham supported Caroline as a political strategy, leading to a split with loyal Whigs. The implications of 'The Delicate Investigation' were still being debated early in 1813. Was Lady Douglas to be tried for perjury, or were there further proceedings to be undertaken against the Princess of Wales? The lawyer Samuel Romilly expressed surprise that Caroline's advisers pressed for the publication of *The Book*, since this would surely ruin her reputation.

The next stage in the manoeuvring between husband and wife saw the publication in the *The Morning Chronicle* in February 1813 of a letter setting out Caroline's position, carefully drafted by Henry Brougham. It became known as The Regent's Valentine. The circulation of a draft of the letter to the Regent prompted a partial relaxation of the restrictions on Caroline's visits to Charlotte, yet another example of the effectiveness of pre-publication circulation as a blackmailing technique. Caroline was permitted to visit Charlotte on 11 February 1813, but the public protest about access to the daughter went ahead anyway. A Regent open to negotiation and prepared to make concessions was not the opponent Caroline and Brougham wished to be presented, so they took the letter to the press. This prompted the Prince Regent to show Charlotte the still unpublished report of 'The Delicate Investigation', which genuinely shocked her: 'It sinks her so low in my opinion.'[1]

There were now two targets for the literary exploitation of the Royal Marriages Act, the possibility of the publication of *The Book* exposing the miseries of Caroline's political marriage and the prospect of Charlotte being farmed off abroad to weaken her claims and make divorcing her mother easier. A proposed marriage to the Prince of Orange in the summer of 1813 was suspected by the opposition to be part of a plan by the Prince Regent to get

Charlotte out of the country, divorce Caroline and remarry to supplant her with a new (male) heir.

Princess Charlotte was engaged to the Prince of Orange at the end of 1813. There was associated wrangling about how long she should spend in Holland. She wanted to introduce clauses in the marriage contract to prevent her being kept out of England against her will, which infuriated the Prince Regent, who believed it to be part of a move by the Russians to prevent the match. Then the Dutch agreed to her terms, by which time Charlotte had cooled further on the Prince. Her official reason, that she could not leave her mother 'in her present distressed condition' was music to the ears of her father's detractors, but in fact she had her eyes on other possible suitors.

After the breaking off of the engagement Charlotte's servants were dismissed, and she was taken from Warwick House to be supervised even more closely. She ran off to Caroline's house at Connaught Place sending notes to Henry Brougham and others to come and advise her. Brougham counselled that she could not defy the Prince Regent and that she risked becoming a focus for popular demonstration, government reaction and bloodshed. There followed a signed undertaking by Charlotte witnessed by sympathetic members of her family and Whig politicians that she would not marry the Prince of Orange.

Charlotte herself felt a sense of duty to her mother and a sense of fellow feeling in her ill-treatment by the Prince Regent, but she was not impressed by her behaviour or company and came to dread her mother's visits. Visits to her father were marred by the indecent bullying of the Duke of Cumberland, but she came gradually to prefer them. In time, she came to believe her mother had betrayed her by plotting to supplant her with William Austin and conniving in divorce and the possible removal of Charlotte from the succession by agreeing to live abroad, when Charlotte had incurred her father's great displeasure by refusing to do so with the Prince of Orange for her sake. Charlotte had occasional glimpses of the London season, but essentially had to live as a child with no unsupervised contact, money or responsibility, not, as the opposition pointed out, an ideal preparation for a future queen. She was worried that to accept the new situation looked like disloyalty to her mother, but she was too deprived of society not to accept the possibility of some freedom. It must have seemed to Charlotte and to the opposition that the Prince Regent did not intend to allow Caroline's daughter to become queen after his death and that any political education would be superfluous. Thomas Ashe would soon look to supply that defect.

Charlotte had reason to suspect the motives of her mother as well as of her father. Caroline acted as a go-between in Charlotte's relationship with Captain Charles Hesse, reportedly locking them in a bedroom with the words 'I leave you to enjoy yourself.'[2] This was confessed to Princess Mary and passed on to the Regent. Charlotte began to suspect her mother's behaviour stemmed from a desire to disgrace her and supplant her with her adopted heir William Austin, rather than out of concern with her happiness. Charlotte was for a long time concerned that Hesse might have kept her love letters and that her mother might use them in her own marital battle. 'She is quite equal, I am sure, to produce any letters of mine that that might make a breach between the Prince Regent and me...'[3]

The difficulties arising from the circulation and suppression of *The Claustral Palace* may have convinced Ashe that publication on behalf of a commoner who was a victim of the Royal Marriages Act would be more lucrative and less risky than taking part in the ongoing print war between the Prince and Princess of Wales. The next candidate who sought Ashe's services as her 'ghost' was Mary, Countess of Berkeley. The daughter of a local butcher, Mary Cole of Wotton under Edge married Frederick Augustus, fifth Earl of Berkeley in 1796 having previously borne him four sons. After her husband died in 1810, it was rumoured that she received an offer of marriage from the Duke of Cumberland. In 1811, Colonel William Berkeley tried to establish his claim to the earldom. It was held that the earl had falsified the parish register to make Colonel Berkeley appear born in wedlock.

In Thomas Ashe's account of the affair in his *Memoirs and Confessions*[4] the countess offered him the opportunity to write her life as Caroline had done, in order to give her version of events, in a form she could not compose herself. In the case of the countess, there was the added incentive to tell the story of her secret marriage in 1785 and thereby legitimise her children. Their initial session involved five solid hours of confessional conversation supported by documents and correspondence from the royal family, which suggested that she would have married the Duke of Cumberland after her husband's death, but for the objections of the Prince Regent. The book was to be called 'The Persecuted Peeress'.

The countess then withdrew her consent for publication. She had been tempted she confessed by his treatment of Caroline's story in *The Spirit of the Book* into giving a detailed narrative of her passions and her marriage, but she then decided it would be better to wait until the parties involved were dead. Publication, she claimed, would harm her remaining connections and would not be in her interests.

Ashe complained that the change came suddenly and after a laborious and painful process of revision: 'I frequently yielded to her opinion, and altered and mutilated those very passages which I esteemed the brightest ornaments of my work.' Sir Samuel Romilly was brought in to consider 'the Question of your conduct', prompting Ashe to give up the manuscript for £100 to avoid trouble and forestall a possible legal action for extortion. This was not quite the end of the story, for Ashe wrote a second version based on the same material, but with a much less favourable construction on the countess's actions and motivations, to be called 'The Perjured Peeress'. This he sold to a local figure in Gloucestershire almost as notorious as himself, Walter Honyford Yate, Justice of the Peace, political writer and creditor of the Prince Regent. It appears the countess retained the manuscript of 'The Persecuted Peeress' and Yate now offered her 'The 'Perjured Peeress' for the amount he had paid for it. Somewhat unexpectedly, we have corroboration of Ashe's account from Yate's correspondence with the countess and her agents about the 'Perjured Peeress', which emerged in a bookseller's catalogue in 2008.[5]

On 13 November 1813, Yate confided that he had the manuscript and began his attempt to recoup his outlay in buying it from Ashe by selling it to Lady Berkeley and her representatives. He claims to have realised it libelled Lady Berkeley after he acquired it – though presumably he knew exactly what it contained – and offered it to her at the price paid, threatening publication if the money were not forthcoming. In the letter of November 1813, Yate reminded the countess in the third person of

> ...the Difference ... which existed between Lady B: & Captain Ashe & which ended in the abortion of a work composed by that celebrated & ingenious Writer, on purpose, & written under the sanction of Lady B:, & which now Mr. Y conceives is in her possession. The Manuscript Mr. Y: has purchased ... originated from that untoward circumstance, & tho' compiled perhaps under the irritation of conceived ill-usage & disappointed hopes yet Mr. Y: fearlessly asserts it is a classical, interesting, and well-founded work; and which the terrors of the Law cannot suppress.

The implication was that though it was not libellous it was damaging as it referred to 'a public occurrence, the revival of which might be painful to the family' (8th March 1814).

Among Yate's papers were printed notes circulating a 'Syllabus', possibly Ashe's blackmailing note and letters advertising his own work on parliamentary reform; an interesting combination. The work on reform was one Ashe claimed in his 'Memoirs' to have sold to Yate.

Ashe recounted that when 'The Persecuted Peeress' became 'The Perjured Peeress' he was still seeking five hundred guineas for its suppression. He moved from Pangbourne to 11 Park Place, Baker Street, to pursue 'such a life of literary prostitution as is perhaps unparalleled in the annals of letters' and pursued a range of potential patrons to keep him from beggary. One of them was the man who had recently become the most famous poet in England, Lord Byron. While Yate negotiated with the countess and Ashe took refuge from her lawyers including Sir Samuel Romilly, Ashe began his correspondence with Lord Byron. This was before Byron became engaged to Annabella Milbanke. As his marriage collapsed Byron was to have his own problems with Romilly as he would give legal advice to Lady Byron in their divorce case. Her mother Judith Noel Milbanke we have encountered in Ashe's story before, offering £600 for a copy of *The Book* in 1809.

Byron awoke to find himself famous with the publication of 'Childe Harold' in March 1812. In the same month, he wrote 'To a Lady Weeping' about Princess Charlotte's plight anonymously in *The Morning Chronicle*, highlighting her distress at the Prince Regent's outburst against the Whigs at Carlton House. Byron at first found the Prince Regent to be a gentleman with excellent manners and discerning poetical tastes so did not join in the personal attacks on him, but his attitude hardened and he republished it under his own name in 1814, a more reliable indicator of his feelings than 'The Prince of Princes' in 'Don Juan'.

A very brief note among John Murray's letters to Byron is accompanied in an excellent modern edition by a very long footnote and it gives the first hint of a connection between the two writers. The note, conjecturally dated to February or March 1813, is about a copy of *The Book*. This could, the editor suggests, be *The Book* of the 'Delicate Investigation' itself or Ashe's *Spirit of the Book* returned to Murray by Charles Watkin Williams Wynn and passed to Byron.

My Lord

In coming home I found the [that] Mr Wynne had returned me
The Book – when your Lordship has read it do me the kindness
to let me have it again.

Ever yr Lordships
Obliged
JM

The date of the note, and it can scarcely be earlier, suggests
that this volume is a pre-publication copy of *The Book* of The
Delicate Investigation itself, still passing from hand to hand,
just before it was finally published, rather than *The Spirit of
the Book*, which had gone through several editions by then and
was available everywhere. Why would Charles Watkin Williams
Wynn, a prominent and rising figure in the Home Office, the man
who had certified William Austin's birth to Sophia Austin at the
Brownlow Street lying-in hospital as part the evidence of The
Delicate Investigation, need to rely on John Murray for a copy
of *The Book* in its unpublished form? Why would he not have
one of his own? On the other hand, was this Wynn's copy, lent
by him to Murray for repeated onward loan to Caroline's friends
among his clients? Among the Treasury Solicitor's papers is an
anonymous undated note, filed as if it belonged with attempts to
retrieve copies of *The Book* around the time of the assassination
of Spencer Perceval stating 'Lord Byron has lately bought a copy.'
[6] This might be the copy John Murray is referring to, though it
seems unlikely Byron would obtain a copy, presumably at great
expense, wait seven or eight months and then lend it to a member
of the Home Office before reading it. There is another possibility.
If Ashe had saved Sir Watkin's life in the Irish campaign in 1798 as
he claimed in his memoirs, there could be a connection between the
brothers Wynn and Ashe's still circulating synopsis of *The Claustral
Palace*. If Byron had seen Ashe's manuscript at first hand, it would
explain both the tone of his later correspondence and his decision
to support him. The intent and purpose of the manuscripts might
be despicable, but Ashe was desperate, talented and on the side of
the angels against the complacent and callous establishment.

By December of 1813, Ashe had approached Byron directly. To
Thomas Moore, Byron's friend and biographer, Byron's response

was an example of his great magnanimity and generosity, when faced with an appeal most people would have ignored or spurned:

An appeal was, about this time, made to his generosity, which the reputation of the person from whom it proceeded would, in the minds of most people, have justified him in treating with disregard, but which a more enlarged feeling of humanity led him to view in a very different light; for, when expostulated with by Mr. Murray on his generous intentions towards one 'whom nobody else would give a single farthing to' he answered, 'it is for that very reason I give it, because nobody else will.' The person in question was Mr. Thomas Ashe, author of a certain notorious publication called "The Book," which, from the delicate mysteries discussed in its pages, attracted far more notice than its talent, or even mischief, deserved. In a fit, it is to be hoped, of sincere penitence, this man wrote to Lord Byron, alleging poverty as his excuse for the vile uses to which he had hitherto prostituted his pen, and soliciting his Lordship's aid towards enabling him to exist, in future, more reputably.

To this application the following answer, marked, in the highest degree, by good sense, humanity, and honourable sentiment, was returned by Lord Byron:—

TO MR. ASHE.
4. Bennet Street, St. James's, Dec. 14. 1813.
Letter from Lord Byron to Thomas Ashe, 14 December 1813:

"SIR, I leave town for a few days to-morrow: on my return, I will answer your letter more at length. Whatever may be your situation, I cannot but commend your resolution to abjure and abandon the publication and composition of works such as those to which you have alluded. Depend upon it, they amuse few, disgrace both reader and writer, and benefit none. It will be my wish to assist you, as far as my limited means will admit, to break such a bondage. In your answer, inform me what sum you think would enable you to extricate yourself from the hands of your employers, and to regain at least temporary independence, and I shall be glad to contribute my mite towards it. At present, I must conclude. Your name is not unknown to me, and I regret, for your own sake, that you have ever lent it to the works you mention. In saying this, I merely repeat your own words in your letter to me, and have no wish whatever to say a single syllable that may appear to insult your misfortunes. If I have, excuse me; it is unintentional.

Yours, &c.
Byron."

'Your name is not unknown to me.' This again suggests that Byron was aware of *The Spirit of the Book* as well as reading an illicit copy of *The Book* itself and it is no great surprise that Moore elides the two works. Byron was an unlikely source of moral advice, but his was only the estimation of works of blackmail such as *The Claustral Palace* and 'The Perjured Peeress' that Ashe at various times articulated himself.

In answer to this letter, Ashe mentioned, as the sum necessary to extricate him from his difficulties, £150—to be advanced at the rate of ten pounds per month and, some short delay having occurred in the reply to this demand, the modest applicant, in renewing his suit, complained, it appears, of neglect on which, Lord Byron, with a good temper which few, in a similar case, could imitate, answered him as follows:

Letter from Lord Byron to Thomas Ashe, 5 January 1814:

"SIR, When you accuse a stranger of neglect, you forget that it is possible business or absence from London may have interfered to delay his answer, as has actually occurred in the present instance. But to the point. I am willing to do what I can to extricate you from your situation. Your first scheme I was considering; but your own impatience appears to have rendered it abortive, if not irretrievable. I will deposit in Mr. Murray's hands (with his consent) the sum you mentioned, to be advanced for the time at ten pounds per month.

P.S. I write in the greatest hurry, which may make my letter a little abrupt; but, as I said before. I have no wish to distress your feelings."

The service thus humanely proffered was no less punctually performed; and the following is one of the many acknowledgments of payment which I find in Ashe's letters to Mr. Murray: 'I have the honour to enclose you another memorandum for the sum of ten pounds, in compliance with the munificent instructions of Lord Byron.'[7] Thus, we find the great John Murray, Byron's publisher, correspondent and confidant acting as banker and source for Ashe's £10 a month, the same scheme he advances to Lord Perceval and later to the government.

Rowland Prothero in *The Letters and Works of Lord Byron* gives us Ashe's letter to John Murray applying for his £10 from Byron a couple of weeks after Byron's second letter, on 21 January 1814, from the Rainbow Coffee House, Covent Garden.

> I am engaged upon a work which will occupy me about a Month. After that time, I shall be happy to assist in any Literary Undertaking of which you may have the Conduct. Although reduced to the state of Beggar in the Streets, there is no department of Literature, no range of Science, but what my pen has visited with success.[8]

This work of a month was presumably *The Patriot Princess,* which survives in manuscript at the National Library of Scotland,[9] now also the home of the archive of John Murray. Another set of correspondence, which again emerged only in 2008, this acquired by The Bodleian Library in Oxford,[10] gives some insight into the gestation of this work as part of the campaign of an opposition group advocating Caroline and Charlotte's cause, or at least attacking the Prince Regent. Ashe called them The Hydra. At the time of Byron's letters, Ashe is negotiating with this many-headed creature camped around the Princess of Wales, which led to the composition of the *The Patriot Princess* and to the possibility of Ashe going to Australia in a civilian or penal capacity. Why was he in correspondence with Lord and Lady Perceval at this point? From his point of view, perhaps, ten pounds per month from a sufficient number of patrons would be a tidy sum, though there must be a risk that they would eventually talk to one another and realise that they were not his sole sponsor and saviour as they had previously imagined. Ashe had plainly not learned his lesson, or thought it was worth the risk, to play both sides off against the other, despite Spencer Perceval's reaction to discovering that Ashe was both 'Sydney' and 'Albion' in 1809.

Ashe's letters to Viscount Perceval and his agents include the original first letter but are otherwise copies. Lord Perceval obviously felt they were worth copying and keeping. Perhaps because they were interesting in themselves. Possibly because it was wise to keep a written record of your dealings with Thomas Ashe to guard against any future action or accusation he might make. Ashe's first approach was to Viscount Perceval directly on 10 December 1813. Given that Byron replied to him on 14 December, it is possible he wrote to both men at the same time in very similar terms. Here as he often did he set out to make a good impression, keeping up highbrow literary appearances with Latin tags. The envelope was marked 'Dum spiro, spero' another epigram from his favourite poet Horace 'while I breathe I hope.' There followed a familiar litany of failure to benefit from his serious works; then a recitation of his journalistic career, which would later be reproduced in his letter to the Regent in the following May, and which was published in his *Memoirs and Confessions*. Respectable publishers flee him, he said, which had left him living at the mercy of those who 'poison the public mind'. He was, he says, compelled to write *The Claustral Palace* or 'Memoirs of the Family' a work *now in the Press*, but which merits to be cast into the flames'. There still seems to be am intimation that *The Claustral Palace* would be published. His threat if Perceval and his wife did not support him was to become a loyal writer again 'to conciliate myself with the State'. With both sides, he used his possible defection to the other as a reason to be bribed with a pension. 'A small fund to keep me independent of the booksellers for a twelvemonth', to compose his own memoirs.

Did Ashe really want to cast *The Claustral Palace* into the flames with the moral repugnance at his own work that he pretended? Or was this simply a tribute to its incendiary power? 'Now in the press': it was obviously well worth someone's while to prevent it being published. By the time he reproduced his plea to the Regent in May 1814 *The Claustral Palace* was no longer 'in the press' but out of his hands.

Ashe wrote to Viscount Perceval at Blackheath on 10 December 1813 from Ryde, Isle of Wight, apparently awaiting, or avoiding, a ship to take him to Australia, self-imposed exile being another possible course if the Percevals failed him. Harriette Wilson was reported by Lady Bessborough to have been living at Ryde in September 1812 waiting for the Marquis of Worcester's ship. For them both the island was a place to wait for news, passage and developments in security, a bit beyond the reach of London society and the agents of the court and government. 'Never more shall I be the poor deluded Votary of absurd fiction,' Ashe claimed. The style of his letters of repentance is very like the style of his absurd fiction, which suggests it was natural to him. He repeated this resolution in the Preface to his 'Memoirs', but it was not true. He retold the story 'eight months ago' of his abortive passage to New South Wales on the *General Hewitt*, now renewed by The Home Department with possibility of passage at Christmas 1813 on the *Broxburnbury*, but he now feels no position will be found for him in Botany Bay. He was not to be trusted with money – or at least only in instalments of £10 a month.

Next, Ashe wrote from the Isle of Wight to an unnamed agent of Lord Perceval, probably Mr Templeman again, in response to 'your letter of yesterday', 19 December 1813. This letter did not have the desired effect so Ashe resorted quickly to his dramatic desperation tactic in a letter of 4 January 1814: 'I write with a razor at my throat.' He was still looking for money to cover the expenses of a voyage to New South Wales. It must have been difficult to write a letter with a razor in his other hand, held to his throat. Byron's second letter and promise of £10 a month via John Murray was written on 5 January. When Thomas Moore reported that he supported Ashe because no one else would, he was certainly entitled to think so, but it was not quite true.

Passage to Australia on the *Broxburnbury* had been 'provided by the Secretary of State', Ashe wrote on 8 January, so the government retained an interest in his going into exile. Ashe was of course using the Home Department's interest in him as a lever, designed to persuade Lord Perceval to retain him to write for Caroline and naturally represents this to him as his own natural inclination. Ashe gives as his reason for rejecting the Home Department's offer that his 'redemption' should be in the country where he has committed his sins.

By 14 January 1814, he had decided to set off for London on intimations of assistance via Mr Bradley of Portsea. A week later, he was writing his coffee house letter offering his services to John Murray and claiming the first instalment of his stipend from Lord Byron. Perhaps that accounts for his better spirits in this letter to Perceval's agent, Mr Templeman. He has put his razor down and the greater part of the letter is an essay on 'The Liberty of the Press', avowing loyalty and eschewing calumny – though it does not sound genuine. He notes, incredibly for a dedicated satirist, that the French Revolution was caused by the toleration of calumny. As a loyal writer, 'Albion' in Blagdon's *Register*, Ashe reports, he barely kept body and soul together, only 'want' turned him. His professions to Caroline's party in 1820 that his natural loyalty was to her, sound more genuine. He acknowledges the 'Opposition Schools' have a more exciting style, 'impenetrable mists and dazzling exaltations', than loyal writing, again much like his own style. Apparently now in receipt of £10 a month from both Byron and Lord Perceval, Ashe wrote again from Grove House, Highgate, on 25 January 1814. There now appeared for the first time a figure who would assume great importance in Ashe's life in the months to come, the man Ashe describes at this stage as 'the agent of your humanity', Mr Charles Crandon. 'I resigned all my claims upon the Secretary of State' (Henry Addington, Lord Sidmouth). Ashe provoked the displeasure of the Home Department and, reasonably enough, tthey did not give him clothes bought for his passage to New South Wales by the government. These were given instead to the ship's Captain, Captain Stedman. This led to Ashe's announcement, on 12 February, of the gestation of another work 'on the subject of the conduct of the Home Department towards me'. Sir Nathaniel Conant and Lord Sidmouth maintained their interest and the former secured him some of his Portsmouth property being a 'humane man' but Ashe remained at liberty to expose others' 'infirmities'.

By 20 February 1814, Ashe admitted that he had been 'among the booksellers ... but had met disappointment from them all'. He was again angling for the payment of his allowance from Perceval or he would have to go to back to his brother in Bristol, the implication being that he would then be an independent writer again, available for hire by the Home Department.

Perhaps the disappointment at the booksellers related to *The Royal Contrast, or Patriot Princess*, since Ashe's next move was to take it to Lady Perceval directly. This was a very poor piece of timing on Ashe's part as he visited her the day after she had been disgraced in court and no one would trust a work from her in print again. Lady Perceval had supplied forged letters to *The News* in Caroline's cause, then denied doing so when the forgery was discovered. The newspaper editor in his own defence published letters from her agent proving she had done so. The Percevals sued him for breaching confidentiality. She then blamed and prosecuted for perjury her own agent and relative, John Mitford, a caricaturist and author described as 'feeble-minded', whom she had released from Hoxton asylum so he could act for her. In the first case in June 1813 Thomas Adderley Phipps, editor of *The News*, wished to publish letters from her agent in his own defence against her charge of publishing untruths without her knowledge. The Percevals had claimed these letters were confidential and should not be published. Since the letters were not published for profit and Lady Perceval did not have 'clean hands', the case went against her. Judgement was given by Sir Thomas Plumer, one of the lawyers who gave legal opinion on *The Claustral Palace* in 1812. She then had Mitford tried for perjury at Guildhall on 24 February 1814. Baron Ellenborough, the judge in that case, also found against her. Phipps confessed he 'gave too hasty confidence to persons whose rank in life formed their only title to credit'.

Caroline was implicated in Lady Perceval's deceptions, but she knew of too many similar forgeries by the prince's party in *The Courier* and *The Herald* for them to risk accusing her directly of complicity. No one in her party in the Commons was minded to defend her. It was a discreditable incident not worth associating with, even for her sake. It rather proved the point that her supporters valued the cause above her personal reputation. Thus, as Ashe recounts in his 'Memoirs', his latest work, *The Royal Contrast or Patriot Princess*, designed to inspire the Prince Regent with 'sentiments worthy of the character of a British ruler', would have no chance to do any such thing. Ashe visited her with his manuscript the day after the perjury trial as the scandal hit the papers:

It was the day after Lord Ellenborough did this ungracious kindness to the Hydra, that I called upon Lady [Perceval] , with my "Royal Contrast, or Patriot Princess," under my arm. She was reclining on a sofa, and the Morning Post was in her hand. I was announced by name; yet, as I entered the apartment, it seemed that I. was entirely unobserved.

'But,' continued her Ladyship, 'leave your "Royal Contrast" with me; I will revise it at leisure, and furnish you with the means of giving it a grand and effective publicity, and of enabling the Princess of Wales, in spite of judges and juries, to THROW THE HEART of HER LIEGE HUSBAND to The Dogs'[11]

Shocked at this vehemence, Ashe changed the title from *The Royal Contrast or The Patriot Princess* to *The Patriot Princess or Political Monitor*. The criticism of her father the Prince Regent becoming less explicit, though still implied. It was no longer about comparing the two, though still about avoiding the mistakes of his ministers.

The Hydra could no longer publish in the existing press after Lady Perceval's disgrace. In Ashe's account, their contributions ended up with the Crandons and with Ashe at Catherine Court. They decide they need their own paper, Ashe was offered the editorship at £600 a year and a chance to serialise *The Royal Contrast* weekly but with his output strictly supervised and controlled:

> The restrictions were, to alter my prospectus and 'Contrast', according to the presumed amendations, to insert my 'Royal Contrast' in weekly numbers, and on no account to publish any original matter without first submitting it to a censorship, which was to be formed out of the Hydra members, whose office it would be to meet me, for the purpose of revision, every Thursday, at Mr. Crandon's house.
>
> After studying under those lamps, which Pitt, Fox, Sheridan, Wyndham, and Burke had lighted up, these conditions and restrictions could not fail to be highly disgusting and offensive to me.

Ashe's first letter to Charles Crandon after Lady Perceval's disgrace survives in the Bodleian's correspondence. It came from 43 Dorset Square, Baker Street on 6 March 1814, an address he describes, with no great accuracy, as a 'humble retreat between Primrose Hill and Hampstead'.[12] They do not read like the letters of a valued writer who has just turned down a £600 editorship on a matter of principle, though it is just possible. Once again, he had fallen back on the help of his friends. A gentleman 'of some influence' would, he said, visit his creditors at his brother's house, and another gentleman had placed 'the annexed advertisement' (not present) in *The Morning Advertiser* for any honourable position for Ashe, on condition he applied to none of them directly for financial aid. Despite these efforts, his rent was still to be paid on the quarter day, so he held out the hope of further support from Crandon 'a five pound note to meet the expenses of the 21st Inst.'. Here Ashe sounds rather like Mr Micawber or Dickens's father in the tone and style of his begging letters and it is tempting to see him in Southsea in the 1810s or Bath in the 1830s as a model for a shabby genteel character from that author's favourite age and milieu. A note of 8 March confirms that 'silence' greeted his latest application. Then the note of urgency returned on 20 March 1814: 'I have not this morning one shilling.' His next letter was from a new address on a quarter day, presumably after a flit to avoid the rent, though not a long-distance one. This was from Park St, Baker Street, the location of Ashe's ultimate literary prostitution recorded in his memoirs. Perhaps wisely, Ashe starts to suggest that he might produce some useful literary work in return for the support he was seeking. 'I am not a man who cuts the hand of Benevolence with Cold heart and folded arms.' Ashe suggested himself as the editor of a worthy weekly paper to preserve him 'from the forums of the factions and the palaces of the venal' with detailed chimerical profits calculated in a Prospectus, and a fanciful plea to come and live with his protector. He was soon rebuffed, but on 26 March 1814 he renewed his plea for a monthly allowance. Then at the end of the month came the familiar threat to apply to the other side through Sir Nathaniel Conant and the Home Department for the rest of his Portsmouth things and additional funds.

There was a month, a month of indifference, before the next letter from Ashe to 'Dear Sir', addressing Crandon on colder terms from yet another address, 6 Diane Place, Fitzroy Square, still chasing an allowance and resorting to 'the language of ingratitude'. On the same day (28 April), we have a copy of a letter from Ashe to H. C. Litchfield, the Treasury Solicitor. How did this copy come to be in Perceval's possession? Did Ashe sent it to him as evidence of his overtures to the government? It is possible that Litchfield was the man with the manuscript of *The Claustral Palace* in his cupboard and presumably, the one who paid for its removal from Ashe's house. Did Ashe know this? Possibly not, since he is addressed as 'My Dear Sir'. Equally, the letter could be prompted precisely by the knowledge of what the Treasury Solicitor had done with his manuscript. There is no mention of *The Claustral Palace*, but the letter is worded as if to a worthy opponent who has won the latest battle, but has no hope of beating Ashe in the ongoing war. In the letter, Ashe claimed to have given up political writing and to have been threatened by a Treasury official with possible action over his conduct as Deputy Commissary General (at Kilmainham). Was this a genuine error in accounts or a trumped-up charge, designed to ensure his loyalty? The negotiations around this supposed offence certainly suggest that both sides regard him as a valuable commodity as a writer, or at least someone not be crossed. Ashe mentions that the Treasury Solicitor regarded him as being in a conspiracy against the Prince of Wales, but was now convinced of Ashe's loyalty. He revived his Botany Bay scheme, receiving letters giving him free passage and a civil or military place from the governor, but not the price of his passage to Portsmouth. Transportation was, Ashe told the government's chief briber of writers, preferable to writing for money. The last line of the letter was a confession of his journalistic career too sordid to be confided to the Treasury official who 'menaced him: 'I wrote for Lady Perceval in *The Independent Whig.*'

Again, Ashe seems to be playing off both sides simultaneously, discussing the mechanics of his passage to Australia or founding a school in Somerset, which would leave him free to write independently. In a postscript to the Treasury Solicitor, he confides that he was leaving behind his manuscript called the 'Shield of Innocence', the letter belonging to it and the Prospectus for the intended paper for the Hydra. 'Be so good as to put all into the purple bag left in Mr Crandon's little back room.' This seems an odd thing to write to the Treasury Solicitor, unless, as seems possible, Ashe had sent these offending items to the government for information and expected Litchfield or his agents to return them to Crandon, the secretary of the Hydra, in secret, while Ashe made good his escape to Australia. Perhaps Litchfield sent Charles Crandon Ashe's letter to him, or a copy of it, in order to destroy his credibility with the Hydra and to show Ashe's duplicity.

It was at this point, on 1 May 1814, that Ashe wrote his letter seeking the patronage of the Prince Regent himself. Perhaps the direct patronage of the Crown would secure him a more agreeable post in Australia. [13] With a few subtle changes the wording of the letter was the same as that sent to Viscount Perceval in December of the previous year: For example in the opening paragraph of his letter to Perceval he had admitted that his own character flaws 'an ungovernable spirit of extravagance' had barred his way to military glory. In his letter to the Regent, he became the victim of misfortune. Perhaps the Prince was the wrong person to talk to about extravagance. In another major change, *The Claustral Palace* was no longer 'a work now in the press but which merits to be cast into the flames.' It had become a 'work partly printed, but finally suppressed'. It was characteristic of Ashe that he made no attempt to conceal *The Claustral Palace* from his authorial CV though it blackmailed the royal family and the prince's government had suppressed it. To Lord Perceval he had proposed the 'one mode' to extricate Ashe from his predicament was to establish a 'small fund' to keep him out of the hands of the booksellers for a year so that he could write his memoirs. The Regent was presented with the opportunity to give him an appointment in Australia, 'should other places be deemed too important for me'. The fact that this long letter in May so closely resembled the letter sent to Perceval five months earlier suggests that Ashe kept his drafts or copies of his letters. There is an element of standard practice in this, but the thought of Ashe retaining copies and his correspondents retaining copies too, adds to our sense of the vulnerability of letters at this time and particularly in this blackmailing milieu; letters could be stolen, traduced and used against you.

His own valentine to the Regent is prefaced by another quotation from his favourite classical author, the Roman poet Horace. It was not 'While I breathe I hope' as it had been for Perceval. It seemed an innocent enough line about it being worthwhile to listen 'Audire est operae pretium', an obvious enough sentiment for a humble petitioner, except that this came from the 'Satires' and prefaced remarks of the perils of adultery and the corruption of pleasure.

> It is worth your while, you who wish no straightforward progress for adulterers, to hear how they struggle on all sides:
> To His Royal Highness George Prince Regent, &c. &c. -
> Audire est operae pretium.—Horace.

> SIR,
> If you do not shrink back at the idea of descending to the unfortunate; if a being of my description do not lie beyond the observation of a Prince, grant, I beseech you, a gracious attention to the following narrative. I am the son of an old officer, and I pursued myself the profession of arms, till a variety of misfortunes, and an absurd day-dreaming cast of mind, obstructed my way to glory, and caused me to forfeit one civil appointment, and four commissions in the army, two of which I had the honour of having conferred upon me while serving as a volunteer in the field. The loss of my civil and military professions was quickly followed with the loss of fame; of that fame, which is as the beams about the sun, or the glory around a picture that shews it to be a saint. The cry of the world was now raised up against me. The world looked into the volume of my follies, and not into the principles of my heart; it regarded me as

a lost character, and treated me with a contempt and severity too painful for your Royal Highness to hear, or for me to describe. Being yet young, my pride revolted at the premature cruelty of such conduct: I abandoned my country altogether; and, during an absence of several years, I subsisted myself on the continents of Europe and America, at one time as a soldier, and at other times as a civilian, minister, and diplomatist, but more frequently as a man of letters, and professor of languages, living and dead. Flattered by the estimation in which I was held, both in the old and in the new world, I returned to England, and fondly thought, that, by the exertion of talent, the display of experience, and the power of industry, I should be able to veil over the errors of my youth, and finally recover the affection of my friends, and the good opinion of my countrymen. Vain, delusive hopes of man!— It was in vain that I endeavoured to fan, with the refreshing wings of genius, the frigid bosom of exasperation and prejudice. It was in vain that I wrote my "Belville and Julia," my "Travels in America," my "Liberal Critic," my "History of the Azores," &c. &c.; for the appearance of poverty, and the absence of fame, clouded over the coruscations of my mind, dimmed the lustre of all my compositions, and compelled me to take for them, one with another, a price too contemptible to be named; and without the advantage of redeeming either public or individual esteem. A galling sense of want, joined to injured pride, poverty, and vanity combined, now broke in upon my sensibility, and held so supreme a dominion over me, that I was constrained to abandon the higher chambers of literature, and to sink into the slough of private scandal and political reproach. In short, I was driven to the necessity of considering, not what ought to be written, but what was likely to be read. Hence, I became the Sidney of "The Phoenix," the Publicola of "The Times," the * * of "The Register," and the author of the "Spirit of the Book." "It is with an author as it is with a woman—when she once falls from virtue, she exceeds man in the flagrancy of her crimes. I had advanced but a few steps in the mazes of this perverted literature, before I found a return to honour and to reason as impracticable as unsafe. All the virtuous portion of the booksellers fled at my approach, and left me solely at the mercy of those infamous publishers who haunt the avenues of literature, and who subsist by poisoning the springs and rivers that supply the public thirst. Under the tyranny of such traitorous taskmasters, I was condemned to write the "Mask Removed," the

"Book of Books," and the "Claustral Palace," which were partly printed, but ultimately suppressed. Sir! I abhor, as every honest man must, this nauseous compound of drudgery and prostitution, of disloyalty and slavery.

And believe me, my Prince, I am not acting from free choice, or for pleasure. I am transgressing from necessity; and my only hope is, that your Royal Highness will be of opinion with the Roman (Petronius Aribiter) who says—Quisquis inops peccat, minor est reus—he is less guilty who offends from necessity. And, again, Quem paenitet peccasse paene est innocens—a penitent sinner is nearly as good as an innocent man. Sir! I am penitent. I do repent. I do wish, with tears, to recall the past; to compensate for the past; to conciliate myself with the state; and to devote myself once again to the true interests of my country. It may reasonably be asked, where is the effect of this contrition? Where are the fruits of this repentance Sir, the great see the world but upon one side only, and are ignorant of those springs and principles which control, the conduct of the indigent; therefore they can with difficulty form a real judgment of the cause of my continuance in so degenerate and lamentable a condition. I presume to repeat it; I have fallen too immensely low to rise by the means of my own individual struggles; and the booksellers, like the keepers of wild beasts, take care to keep me upon a diet so low, that I never can, from my own immediate exertion, emancipate myself from so disgraceful and dangerous a bondage. There is but one mode which can possibly extricate me from this treacherous and degrading compromise of honour for subsistence, and that mode manifests itself in this last effort of expiring genius; in this last and deep appeal to the humanity of your Royal Highness; yes, Sir, I dare to beg some small appointment, civil or military, in any one of His Majesty's distant colonies, even in New South Wales, should other places be deemed too important for me. Sir! It would be superfluous to say more. Should this appeal awaken your sensibility; should it excite, in the smallest degree, the exercise of those precepts of generosity and mercy which govern your actions, I shall ever gratefully remain, &c. &c. -

Thomas Ashe No. 11, Park Place, 1st May, 1814.

Ashe's letter to Lord Perceval had ended with lines from Ovid about his loyalty. He did not think it worthwhile to reproduce them for the Regent.

What had happened to his loyalty to Caroline at that point? Was he really so careless about advertising himself as the author of works, which the Regent must have known, either attacking him or championing his wife? It seems unlikely that the author of *The Spirit of the Book*, designed to rescue Caroline's reputation after 'The Delicate Investigation', would be popular with her estranged husband. Was the begging letter also a threat, reminding him of the power Ashe could wield with his pen, if he were not bribed sufficiently by the Crown? Perhaps your CV as a writer indicated your worth whichever side you were on and provided evidence that it would be worthwhile for the Regent to employ him to keep him from the clutches of the opposition.

Evidently, Ashe was still taken seriously enough for his letter to be passed on via Lord Yarmouth to Lord Sidmouth. 'Towards the end of May,' Ashe recalled, he received a note: 'Mr Conant wishes to see Mr Ashe any morning before 11 o'clock at 14 Portland Place.' Nathaniel Conant, the bookseller magistrate involved in tracking down trade copies of *The Book,* was the man the government felt best able to deal with Thomas Ashe in a firm but friendly way. He took the humane view that Ashe had been corrupted by want and misfortune, and he offered him free passage and a letter to Governor Macquarie. Once more, bound for Botany Bay, Ashe again lost his ship, the East Indiaman *General Hewett*, through a misunderstanding over what authority was sending him and about the documentation required. Instead, according to the 'Memoirs' he answered what he thinks is Caroline's cause to be 'the object of her esteem and patronage' again. He turns on his patrons as designing men who had tried to exile him for political reasons.

'Returned to my patroness after an absence of three years' (he implies by this perhaps she was his source for both the *Spirit of the Book* and *The Claustral Palace*) he is compelled to write insolently to Sir Nathaniel Conant and Lord Sidmouth, who respond to his defection with sadness and mild rebuke. He reproduces a wistful letter by Conant as proof:

> I shall always rejoice in your well-doing. I never approved of your New South Wales scheme, and have yet hopes you may prosper in your own country. Although it is an invariable rule with me never to meddle in the affairs of public writers, I cannot help wishing that you may avoid the necessity of plunging into that literary slough in which I found you, and out of which you once evinced so much laudable ambition to be extricated. This is saying more than I ought.[14]

In the version of events Ashe gives in his memoirs, he comes to think more highly of the humane Conant and Sidmouth, thinking them less venal than the Hydra. The sequence of events as it appears in the memoirs implies that he only turned to the Hydra after his correspondence with the Regent (1 May 1814) had led to his temporary patronage by the Home Office, ending in the failure of his New South Wales scheme. In fact, his correspondence with Viscount Perceval, which began in December 1813, shows he chose the opposition first and was fleeing the Hydra by the time he wrote to the Prince Regent. Perhaps there was simply a cycle of patronage, beginning with a failed attempt to be sent to Australia by the government in the autumn of 1813, followed by the courting of Byron and the Percevals in 1813-14, followed by a return to the Home Department and another failed attempt to be voluntarily transported in the summer of 1814. The chronology of the *Memoirs and Confessions* appears to be muddled, placing Lady Perceval's fall from grace in February 1814 seventy pages after his letter to the Regent in May of that year, but it is still remarkable how much of the correspondence Ashe reproduces in it seems to have survived to support his account. All the while, he tried to maximise his return on the *The Claustral Palace* and bring *The Patriot Princess* to light in uncensored form. Despite his stipend from Byron to keep him from writing political scandal, he kept his options open. His final letters to Perceval's agents confirmed his defection.

While the Treasury Solicitor dealt with the evidence of Thomas Ashe's defection from the Hydra and the problem of finding him something to do, preferably on the other side of the world, he was still facing calls on his funds from 'The Delicate Investigation', even though *The Book* was now published. Lady Douglas wrote on 19 May 1814 pleading poverty from Maize Hill Greenwich.[15] Those who had served the government's cause expected payment if not a pension. It is difficult not to feel some sympathy for the Treasury Solicitor, though perhaps he had brought it on himself and his office by his practice of suborning hostile writers and supporting loyal ones. His postbag had in quick succession demands for support from the author of *The Spirit of the Book* and the principal source of *The Book* itself. It must have been difficult to remember at various times who he was subsidising, who he was threatening and why.

From Portsmouth on 1 June 1814, Ashe made his last appeal and threat to the Hydra. This confirmed this intention to 'avoid publicity and noise'. He would reapply to Mr Bradley (to whom he had addressed his appeals in January). If that course failed he would apply to Lord Perceval directly again. If he was ignored, he threatened, 'I will prefer a charge against him in Parliament.' He claimed to have lost £2000 in literary earnings and to have had only £45 of his £120 yearly stipend. 'I will seek redress in a manner which will clothe your friends in sackcloth. I have three certain means of redress: I can indict for a Conspiracy, I can appeal to Parliament and I can make the parties debtor for all the losses I have sustained by their means.' All these options seemed fantastical and the sequel suggests a very small sum was sufficient to get Ashe to stop the correspondence and allay his threats. His final note to Crandon on 15 June 1814 showed the menace had had some effect where the pleas had not. 'I am satisfied and silent – Perhaps pitiful – Thomas Ashe' I allude to a letter received this day from my Brother.'[16]

What is Ashe's course? Certainly not to New South Wales. Possibly to Bristol and Somerset in the company of his brother who was similarly taking refuge after a chequered career at Kilmainham. While Thomas was menaced by treasury officials for irregularities in his accounts, Jonathan had problems of his own with his role there as chaplain. Jonathan was always described by his brother Thomas (in contrast to his own moral lapses) as a deserving cleric, too honest and busy to hunt for position and so continually passed over for preferment. A chance survival of his letters show a different side to him.[17] In Ashe's narrative, Jonathan recommended him to the Commissary General at Kilmainham. He did not mention, perhaps because the events coincided with or post-dated the publication of the memoirs rather than because they were too out of character for the narrative, Jonathan's loss of the chaplaincy there and his threatened duel with one of the governors, Colonel Littlehales. Letters from him at this time suggests a fierce desire for preferment in Jonathan and a temperament which was just as disreputable as anything recorded in the *Memoirs and Confessions*. He was just as prone to career-ending financial embarrassments. Jonathan was a prominent freemason and co-founder of a masonic charity, the Society for the Schooling of the Orphan Female Children of Distressed Masons, in 1795. He was capable of his own literary productions or at least partially his own. He was the author of an apparently plagiarised work on freemasonry, which he dedicated to the Duke of Sussex. His 'masonic manual' and affiliation proved that being a freemason was not a guarantee of professional preferment. As summarised in the auction catalogue, Jonathan wrote:

Being prevented by some pecuniary difficulties from personally discharging the duties attached to me, as Chaplain to the King's Military Infirmary, I obtained ... leave of absence 'till Christmas last ... his Excellency [the Governor of the Infirmary] had allowed no succession to take place in my disfavour with respect to the Military Chaplaincy, though solicited by Mrs. Latouche in favour of a Mr. Campbell. Notwithstanding this ... I find that you, Colonel Littlehales, had a full month previous to the expiration of my leave of absence, disposed of my chaplaincy to Mr. Campbell. From all these proceedings of yours, I conceive I am warranted, in the fullest extent, to pronounce your conduct towards me to be that of a confirmed Rascal and Scoundrel.

A subsequent letter to the Colonel was taken by him to be a challenge and a provocation to fight a duel. Bloomsbury Auctions in cataloguing the letters speculated that Jonathan Ashe might have died at the point of Colonel Littlehales' sword or run away to die in obscurity. It is possibly fortunate for his reputation that we cannot trace his career beyond that point, through his brother's memoirs and the records of the Church of England suggest he followed his curacy at St. John the Baptist parish, Bristol, with a stipendiary curacy at Stogumber in Somerset, followed by another at Pilton ten years later. They also suggest he had become a Doctor of Divinity by 1815. There was perhaps a move towards a retired country life away from the bright lights of Bristol. His lack of preferment despite his qualifications, bemoaned by his brother in 1815, continued, and his gradually devaluing stipend of £50 a year remained unchanged ten years later. He did at least have his accommodation thrown in, so unlike his brother he was never reduced to beggary in the streets.

Withdrawn from the censoring committee of the Hydra, *The Royal Contrast*, subtly re-titled as *The Patriot Princess or Political Monitor*, was recast as an inspiration to Charlotte rather than an attack on her father. In its full title, it proclaimed a lofty ambition:

The Patriot Princess or Political Monitor, calculated to rouse the reflection, invigorate the spiritual health and fortify the mind of Her Royal Highness Charlotte, the Princess of Wales, previously to her approach to the sovereignty of the British Empire.[18]

Even this title, was subject to Ashe's characteristic revisions and hatched crossings out. One of these seems to conceal an intention of 'restoring' or perhaps 'restraining' the Princess's passions', which was probably a bit presumptuous and intimate, even for Ashe, in a book addressed to a teenaged princess who might soon become queen. After revealing the plight of her aunts in *The Claustral Palace* the time was right for Thomas Ashe to prepare Charlotte for sovereignty, revealing the bad examples of her own family and their designing ministers, and the upright men, men like Byron who were also his patrons, who should form the government in her reign.

The book still in the epistolary tradition but this time the letters come from Ashe directly. Charlotte is not confiding in him as Caroline and Elizabeth did in *The Spirit of the Book* and *The Claustral Palace*. It has Latin tags and the outward signs of one of those Renaissance instruction manuals, which set out the qualities of a good Christian Prince, but gradually it unfolds as a revelation and a warning of the failings of her father and his ministers. We begin with an epigram from the Roman poet Claudian rather than Horace for once: 'Fallitur, egregio quisquis sub principe credit servitium. Nunquam libertas gratior extat quam sub rege pio.' Ashe renders this as 'He knows no bondage who a good king sways/For freedom never shines with clearer rays/Than when good Princes reign.'

Needless to say, this is a hope for Charlotte's reign, not a description of her father's government in 1814. The true state of the country, Ashe claims, is concealed from her by the ministry. 'You must know from this hour that the Estate which you are to inherit is an entailed Estate deadly deteriorated and deeply mortgaged ... 900 million pounds in debt, with three million paupers to be maintained in workhouses .' (Letter III.) Ashe has some serious and radical policy suggestions: to eliminate the national debt by the sale of foreign possessions and to rely on trade instead of conquest. 'To a commercial intercourse with foreign nations we may justly attribute the stability of Empire and the opulence of a people, because it encourages an Universal spirit of industry, removes local prejudice and elevates the mind to magnanimity and wisdom.' (Letter IV.) This openness is contrasted to the claustral gloom of George III's reign, characterised by the building of barriers, 'barracks and walls', fortifying the state against the people. (Letter V.)

The description of George III – 'in peaceful times he would have made a good king' – in Letter VI echoes Elizabeth's sentiments about her father in *The Claustral Palace*. The description of the Regent, whose virtues are turned to vices by dissipation, as suffering from 'florid weakness' again uses the same language as *The Claustral Palace*. (Letter VII.) There is a heartfelt letter on the evils of imprisoning debtors, without trial on another man's word, presumably based on his own experiences in King's Bench prison. (Letter X.) There are a plenty of observations on the oddity of the king's political position. 'The King can do no wrong... The King is the passive instrument of the ministry.' In making these observations, Ashe gets a bit passionate and his handwriting gets larger. In conclusion he reminds Charlotte of her constitutional eminence, 'in fine, raised above your fellow citizens, not sunk beneath them'. (Letter XI.)

> It is the hard destiny of the political monitor, that he cannot submit to weave his lessons with romantic fiction, he cannot consent to become the pander of passions, that, by soothing, he may allay them, nor can he bribe the senses that he may permit his access to the reason or to the heart.

The 'monitor' encourages Charlotte to tour the country to see the state of the nation for herself: 'you will be astonished by the appalled looks of your premier.' There follows a tirade on the false presentation by the ministry to the monarch of a prosperous nation, when Britain faced enormous social problems. 'Three million in workhouses, two million more staring famine in the face'. (Letter XII.)

The period of neglect of the people and economic decline of the nation is the same as that covered in *The Claustral Palace*. The government building walls and barracks to secure and separate itself from the people was the same regime which imprisoned the royal princesses at Frogmore. This ran in parallel with the swelling of the workhouse population, with paupers imprisoned for their own good: 'Every administration from the time of Bute to the present'. (Letter XIII.)

There is then an essay on the virtues and effects of piety. I think Charlotte would probably have picked the book up and thrown it at 'the monitor' at this point. Would she recognise the description of her mother?

> What was the first sorrow that assailed your bosom? Was it the cruel stroke that separated you from your illustrious and beloved

mother? Do you shed the sweetest tears of gratitude and pleasure when beholding that suffering saint?

There is a serious risk that the Princess might answer no to all those questions and scoff at the idea of her mother being a saint, but the 'political monitor' has a clear agenda. He sets out a loyal letter she might have written saying she had written to that effect, 'in the dawn of adolescence'. Being a patriot princess and 'the saviour of a sinking state' depends on Charlotte retaining her mother's pure religious convictions! (Letter the Fifteenth)

Ashe described the moment of the conception of the Royal Marriages Act in similar terms to that of the 'Delicate Investigation' as reported in *The Phoenix* in 1810. Instead of Caroline's ruin alone, all the royal children are snared by a designing ministry. Ashe could not say, of course, that the prime mover behind both was the Crown itself and not conspiring politicians:

> In a moment of dark mystery and bold imposition the Minister of the day proposed a law to Parliament, the tendency of which was to deprive the children of the crown of their rights and birthdom, by compelling them to form foreign alliances, or else pass their lives in the slough of domestic celibacy, illicit enjoyment and ignominious ease. When the Minister proposed the enactment of this law, he knew it to be a law both unnatural and unrighteous. Blessed be the Patriot Princess who will consign it to the flames and again revive the hopes and golden dreams of the children of the throne of England! (Letter the Sixteenth.)

There is naturally a letter on the state of Ireland since the act of union and a plea to repeal it. (Letter the Seventeenth.)

Ashe's most substantial letter to Charlotte looks critically at the established political factions of Whig and Tory and identifies The Duke of Northumberland as the head of party of patriots outside those factions. No doubt, it was coincidence that these figures were all patrons or potential patrons of Captain Thomas Ashe:

> In speaking of just and independent men the name of Lord Perceval is not to be forgotten. It has been often and justly remarked that the most brilliant characters in society are by no means the most respectable; that they glitter but to deceive and shine but to mislead. That abilities and eloquence and genius

are frequently accompanied by such meanness of mind and such profligacy of principle as depreciate their worth and tarnish their lustre, whilst rectitude of soul and integrity of intention exalt the humblest of talents and dignify the weakest exertions.

Perceval, he reveals is not an orator either but 'the honest and upright senator' who captures the heart and understanding. 'Not as an in and out man but a character whose foundations are much deeper laid.' This seems rather faint and mixed praise for his intermittent patron and rather a dull form of goodness. He had no such doubts about Lord Byron whose £10 a month was still rolling in:

In a sketch of men of extraordinary virtues or endowments, Lord Byron is not to be omitted. This noble Lord from his early youth hath been seriously engaged in endeavours to become an ornament to his country and an acquisition to Literature: His life is a passing scene of active utility and severe study. To the most extensive research, the most ardent zeal for knowledge, His Lordship adds a very brilliant imagination and the most ready and rapid pen. Others may possess the same correctness of drawing, but the colouring is his own. Others reason, but it is Byron only who captivates, he alone conveys his images through the medium of the heart, he alone knows how to affect, to rouse, to soothe, at the same time, that from the plenitude of knowledge, he arms his arguments and his high classical attainments, have taught him to adorn them and conduct them with unerring force, through every avenue to the breast of the Reader.

By toiling in the mines of literature Lord Byron has grafted knowledge upon genius, so great is his proficiency in this art, such is the splendour of his sophisms, in views so infinitely varied, he has the magic power of displaying his subjects and his episodes and illustrating his principles, that a prism is necessary to distinguish his colouring and mark his true stream of life light from his fancy. His conceptions are vigorous and his poetical arrangements are excellent and by a happy union of all the sister sciences, he is equally able to inforce persuasion and charm the fancy. His lordship joins strength to delicacy, precision to copiousness, justness to elegance and symmetry to variety. His winged expressions aptly represent his thoughts, which often have a boldness that were they uttered in a certain Assembly would fall upon a guilty minister with the impetuosity of the Thunderbolt. Like Scott his ideas are abundant and his language copious and flowing; it animates and irradiates the Reader. And his flowing thoughts are exhibited in so pleasing a light, that he plays with the feelings of the heart as the wind with the waves of the watery element. His powers of delusion are unequalled, his sources of knowledge are great, his memory is comprehensive and faithful, while his mind teems with the most luxuriant imagery clothed in the most elegant language and strengthened by the most fortunate and brilliant figures. The splendour of his fancy is unrivalled. From science, from history, from Parnassus, from the passing moment, as well as that which is gone forever, it collects and commands the most apt, varied and beautiful images to decorate his compositions. In the very tumult of eloquence, they instantaneously present themselves from the general miscellany of nature and things, like the soldiers of Cadmus, in complete armour and array to support the cause of their Creator.

Lord Byron is yet young and politics have not the charms to attract his attention, but I nonetheless venture to assert that no member of the Cabinet knows better how to unfold with dignity the operations of a patriot soul, or to record with truth, the duties and privileges of a society. Princess! May your hearty approbation wait on him, and may he look for confirmation of his honour of obtaining under your government, the means of promoting the prosperity of his country.

There was an element of a fellow author's wishful thinking in placing Byron at the centre of the legislature on the strength of his imagination and vocabulary, but in 1814 it was not impossible. It soon would be. The chief ornament of Ashe's fantasy patriotic government, Byron was soon to leave his native country never to return, chased by marital scandal worthy of Ashe's fiction. Fortunately, Ashe was not solely reliant on young men like Byron to form a cabinet for the future 'Queen Charlotte'. William Wilberforce was already reducing his constituency obligations on the grounds of ill health when Ashe wrote to recommend him to her:

Nor is the Commons without a galaxy of great men. Mr Wilberforce is a man with the greatest legislative capacity I ever knew and the most comprehensive reach of understanding I ever saw, with a deep engraven impression of public care, accompanied by a temper which is tranquillity itself, a personal firmness that is adamant, in his train is every private virtue than can adorn human nature. It is impious to disrespect such a man.

His last two recommendations were rather less well known but were connected to Wilberforce and evidently part of a group sympathetic to Caroline's cause and the Hydra. William Astell, formerly Thornton, changed his name in 1807 because of a family inheritance. His disinterested patriotism took the form of maintaining the interests of the East India Company, for whom he served as a director for 47 years. 'Mr Astell is also a character singularly gifted. With sound talent, he has great experience and the pride of genius. When he rises, he will raise the country along with himself, at least I pledge myself, he will never seek to build his elevation on the degradation of England.'

The second was Samuel Thornton, a cousin of William Wilberforce returned for Hull by by-election in 1813 to the House of Commons Thornton was an informed, and often influential, speaker on commercial and business affairs. They were both independently wealthy through inheritance and their business interests and to that extent were not beholden to the aristocracy or the government, though Thornton had not sought re-election to the House of Commons in 1812 after the failure of some of his financial ventures.

> Mr Thornton too, is a name I shall ever regard. Enlightened, sensible, laborious and useful; proud of the city and patriotic he would prefer death a tyranny exercised over a venal courtier. Formed to unite aristocracy and the people with the manner of a court and the principles of a patriot, the flame of liberty and the love of order, unassailable to the approaching of power, of profit or of titles, to be annexes of the love of freedom, a veneration of sovereignty and casts on his fellow citizens that admire him, the gracious shade of his own accomplishments. (Letter the Eighteenth.)

I suspect the prospect of Byron her cabinet might have excited Charlotte's interest, the others rather less so. Well-meaning though the desire to supplement Charlotte's political education might be, she might well have skipped the final essay on 'the origin and progress of the British Commons since the Norman Conquest'.

Having extolled the constitution as the guide of the monarch and the protection of the subject Ashe ends with a flourish:

> The concluding wish is I trust not misplaced, when delivered within this philosophic Island. The sciences ever flourish in the train of liberty. The soul of a slave could never have expanded itself, like Newton's over infinite space and would have sighed in captivity at the utmost barriers of Creation. In no other country under heaven could Locke have unfolded with dignity, the operations of an immortal soul or recorded with truth the duties and privileges of society.

These flights of rhetoric designed to work on Charlotte's conscience to usher in a new age of virtue and liberty are somewhat undermined by Ashe's confessional postscript:

> I, Thomas Ashe, make oath that the foregoing work was written by the desire of persons professing to be the friends of Her Royal Highness the Princess of Wales and that I received the sum of forty pounds and upwards while employed by such persons. The person who actually employed and paid me was Mr Charles Crandon of no. 4 Catherine Court, Tower Hill, and that he, the said Crandon, informed me that he was an agent of Lord and Lady Perceval, who were the friends of the Princess of Wales. I further make oath that the said Crandon mentioned the names of Mr Thornton and Mr Astell and gave me clearly to understand that he was the agent of an association formed for the express purpose of elevating the Princess or the ruin of the Prince of Wales. 8 July 1814 [Signed] Thomas Ashe: The Author under the above instructions.
>
> Sworn before me at Chichester, Thomas Trew Mayor.

The Chichester connection suggests the hand of Captain Henry Bell of Fishbourne who puts Ashe back on the path of loyalty and buys him off in a series of impressive-looking but probably spurious bonds in the Treasury Solicitor's papers. The Treasury Solicitor's file about Ashe's threatening letter to the Duke of Cumberland after he sent him the manuscript of 'Osphia: Or the Victim of Unnatural Affections' in 1830 also contains material relating to *The Claustral Palace* and 'The Patriot Princess in 1815'. Bell evidently renewed his petition for compensation for his supposed purchases of Ashe's manuscripts in 1815, when his friend was notorious again in 1830. Here Ashe's rescuer from debtors' prison, as recorded in 'The Memoirs and Confessions' first sought recompense for suppression of Ashe's manuscript of the Patriot Princess and Claustral Palace poems written after the suppression of the novel in January 1815.

Bell sent a petition dated 5 January 1815 to the Prince Regent claiming expenses for suppressing libels on the royal family. He was, he says, 'nurtured in the lap of loyalty and devotedly attached to my Sainted Monarch and his illustrious family'. Surely, the Treasury Solicitor, with his keen eye for satire, must have recognised that as parody!

Then, rather as Joseph Haydn had done in relation to *The Claustral Palace*, Bell constructed a backstory for Ashe's financial obligations to him. He says he met Ashe four years earlier as a fellow inmate of King's Bench with Bell's brother, for a bill drawn on Honeywood Yate (Presumably the Walter Honeyford Yate we have already encountered in relation to 'The Perjured Peeress'). A year later he met Ashe and was offered the manuscript of the Claustral Palace poems, 'an obscene and traitorous attack on every branch of your ... family' founded on a work of a similar title, that had been he said surreptitiously obtained from him at Bath. He obtained it for 50 guineas and the cancellation of the £110 original bill against him! He then bound Ashe in a bond of £2000 not to publish and got 50 guineas compensation from the Duke of Cambridge. 'Last Spring I ascertained the fact that Mr Ashe was in the pay of a party inimical to the Peace of Your Royal Highness and adverse to government.'

Later, 'by great good fortune' he finds Ashe employed by the above party. He obtained *The Patriot Princess* under the terms of the bond and then, he says forwarded it to Lord Castlereagh. (Presumably, this is the manuscript now in the National Library of Scotland.) He had, he says, now lost property to the value of £10,000 thanks to a decision in the Court of King's Bench. There is a nice touch at the end of the petition. Bell says he would be happy to settle for a job in the royal household as a 'Gentleman Usher' or in the post of Commissioner of Hackney coaches, 'in the event of the Decease of Mr Douglas who I understand is dangerously ill'. It could of course all be true, or approximately so. The documentary evidence supporting his story looks suspicious though. He enclosed an impressive-looking but unlikely bond signed by Ashe on 7 April 1813. Ashe gives his address as 2 Little Rider Street, St James at the bottom of a bond in £2000 not to publish anything to the prejudice of the royal family. This fashionable address was his briefly when he came into his inheritance in 1805 and presumably it was used to give an air of respectability to the bond. Subsequent correspondence suggests he had left it for much less fashionable addresses long before this date. Bell also enclosed equally impressive looking but probably fictitious receipts signed by Ashe:

> London 7 Apr 1813 for the 'Claustral Palace' poems 50 guineas and one hundred guineas for copyright.
>
> Chichester 14 July 1814, Received from Mr Henry Bell esq. the sum of one hundred and fifty pounds in full for my manuscript entitled 'the Patriot Princess, or Political Monitor' and which I composed under the instructions of the Agents of Her Royal Highness The Princess of Wales. Thomas Ashe the author.

The whole thing was annotated by the Treasury Solicitor on 20 January 1815 'Mr Bell inclosing a Petition (supported by certain vouchers) praying for some remuneration in consequence of having ...expended various sums of money in suppressing libellous and abusive works against various Branches of the Royal Family'. This was accompanied by a covering note from Bell of the same date observing the proper form in sending his petition to the Prince Regent via Lord Sidmouth on the advice of the Privy Purse, Colonel McMahon.

The Treasury Solicitor saw through Bell, as a man 'formerly connected with Ashe and probably playing some game of his now' but still it was evidence worth keeping. 'These papers to lay by until occasion arises'. They were passed by Lord Sidmouth to Sir Nathaniel Conant, as if they might be of some active use in negotiation with the man himself, some indication that Ashe had not yet gone abroad yet, despite the intention expressed in *Memoirs and Confessions* to go to France 'forever' in 1815.

The memoirs suggest Ashe met Henry Bell his friend from the King's Bench prison who had summed up The Hydra in detached fashion and decried the use to which Ashe has put his talent. 'In your dealings with the world you are negligent and unprincipled.' Bell presents the Crown, somewhat improbably, as the defender of the poor. At this point Ashe realised or at least acted on the notion that 'The Princess is misled' by the Hydra. After Lady Perceval's disgrace, Caroline withdrew from the Hydra and went abroad, at least in part to escape their influence following Ashe's letter to her exposing them. Byron and Northumberland clear his debts and he sells 'a Latin manuscript' for enough to go to France 'for the remainder of my days', to write his memoirs and to reflect on the bad party which has gathered itself around 'the lovely suffering Princess of Wales'.

Did *The Patriot Princess* have any effect? It does not read like a normal Ashe work of scandal designed to be circulated and suppressed. It does not say anything defamatory about the Prince Regent, beyond the general assumption that government by him and his father since the ministry of the Earl of Bute had been self-serving and misguided. It reads much more like a genuine book of instruction for Charlotte in the interests of the the Hydra, promoting a small group of Ashe's current patrons, with the added lure of painting her mother in the unlikely colours of a suffering saint. Did Charlotte ever see it? Would she have read it if she had? Even though she read 'The Bride of Abydos' in her seclusion at Warwick House, it seemed an unlikely manoeuvre to recommend its author as a member of her Cabinet.

Charlotte's refusal to be sent abroad because of her mother's 'distressed state' had been a gift to the radicals. Brougham convinced Charlotte, not without reason, that Caroline going abroad would jeopardise Charlotte's claim to the throne, as it would make divorce and new heirs more of a possibility. Caroline, though, began to feel bullied and controlled by her allies as well as by her enemies. Whether or not prompted by Thomas Ashe's letter exposing the Hydra, she accepted her husband's offer of £50,000 to live abroad. On 1 July 1814 Brougham wrote to Thomas Creevey, 'I suppose you have heard of Mother P bitching the thing so completely in snapping so eagerly at the cash ... though she deserves death we must not abandon her.' Brougham spread the rumour that the Prince Regent was jealous of Charlotte's claim to the throne 'to the point of insanity'. Certainly Charlotte reminds him too much of her mother, coarse and immodest.

Underneath the cynicism, Brougham in the *Edinburgh Review* in 1814 attacked The Royal Marriages Act in principled terms familiar to the readers of the works of Thomas Ashe. 'The members of a Royal as compared with those of a private family are by law debarred from feelings common to humanity and from all free action. They cannot fall in love without the consent of The Crown.'

As Ashe reported in his memoirs, he was not rewarded for past services but set to do more unprincipled drudgery composing libels of his own, 'writing down' the Prince Regent for the Hydra. Ashe's job was 'to compose Parliamentary orations and to hire vagabonds to hoot the Prince'. Despite his sustained correspondence with Charles Crandon, he claimed never to have been commissioned by the same person twice, though Lady Perceval was the chief mover. There is some evidence from the Egmont Papers at The British Library that Ashe circulated his *Memoirs and Confessions* to Lady Perceval before they were published.[21]

Ashe was presumably starting to write the memoirs during and after the disgrace of Lady Perceval and Caroline's withdrawal from the clutches of the Hydra; why then would he circulate the book to Lady Perceval before publication? He is not very complimentary about her in them. Is he looking for approval, pitching to have elements suppressed, or offering to re-write? His negotiations, both with Lady Perceval and with Lady Berkeley, hinge on sudden changes in their characters from fragrant and obliging to vile and violent. This is to some extent explained by the souring of his relationship with them detailed in the narrative but it may also be evidence of rewriting in the light of his attempts to negotiate with his most recent female patrons how these raw and still potentially embarrassing episodes should appear.

Thomas Ashe concluded his memoirs in 1815 with a resolution to write his next book, another political romance called 'The Tyrant' which probably became his *roman a clef* set in old Spain eventually titled *The Soldier of Fortune*. Ashe was apparently positioning himself as the man who would rescue Caroline from the amoral party that had gathered around her for political gain and, as Caroline had always wanted, would write for her personally. His movements seemed designed to shadow hers as they had done in Brunswick and Blackheath.

The memoirs acknowledge Ashe's obligations to Byron and the Duke of Northumberland and they are dedicated to them. 'Upwards of £300' received from them proceeded, Ashe says, from their 'independence of principle and fixed horror of oppression'.

The introduction to his own history contained a denunciation of his own life's work:

> It is even poor deluded votaries, the promiscuous worshippers of absurd fiction, whom I now call upon to forsake the flimsy decorations and outward glare of a fabric that contains nought but pollution of every kind, and endeavour to gain the Temple of Virtue, on whose high altar the pure and everlasting flame of knowledge and truth burns with ethereal splendour and never-fading lustre.[22]

As Byron could, Ashe might contest that an inability to live life according to the standards he set others was an acknowledged human weakness rather than hypocrisy and indeed, there are broad parallels in the lives of lives of the two men whose lives crossed at crucial points. Both seemed outside the pale of English society, Byron with his bear in Venice, Ashe as a kind of wild animal in his own right: 'It became fashionable to think that I was a sort of wild beast which could neither be dragooned nor caressed into tameness.'[23]

An epigram he wrote in 1814 in a letter to Lady Melbourne conveys Byron's view of that society with devastating clarity:

Tis said Indifference marks the present time,
Then hear the reason—though 'tis told in rhyme—
A King who can't—a Prince of Wales who don't—
Patriots who shan't, and Ministers who won't—
What matters who are in or out of place
The Mad—the Bad—the Useless—or the Base?[24]

It seemed that Shelley, Byron, Caroline and Ashe were all fleeing abroad at about the same time to escape the indignation and hypocrisy of the British public. *Glenarvon*, Caroline Lamb's 1816 roman a clef, about her relationship with Byron, skewered the poet in the Ashe style. Lady Holland noted in a letter to Thomas Creevey of 21 May 1816 that the book was 'published by Lady C Lamb against her family and friends' and that 'the work has a prodigious sale as all libellous matters have.'

On August 9, 1814, Princess Caroline sailed to the Continent in the frigate *Jason* as the Countess Wolfenbuettel but with a large case marked 'The Princess of Wales to be always with her'. Did this contain documents incriminating to herself or others, or her still unfinished memoirs? Caroline's biographer Joseph Nightingale notes that she was seen off at Worthing by agents of Bow Street, perhaps the Conants, to make sure she went.[25]

Caroline wrote to Charlotte from Athens on 28 April 1816 having been brought the news of Charlotte's impending marriage to Prince Leopold by none other than the brave and loyal Captain Browne:

It was in the harbour of Malta also, my, dear Charlotte, that
I heard that your nuptials with the Prince of Cobourg were

positively fixed to take place next month. Yes, my love, Capt. B, that brave and worthy officer, whom I have so long had cause to rank in my list of friends, was in the harbour, and with tears of joy in his eyes came alongside my crazy bark to cheer the heart of your wandering mother with the joyful tidings.[26]

The year 1817 saw the death of Ashe's nemesis, the Privy Purse Colonel Sir John McMahon, leaving his widow the proud possessor of drawers full of cash and incriminating documents. There seemed to be little security around those in whom the Crown had reposed its trust. John Aubrey's *Brief Lives* is full of fears that the manuscripts of eminent people will fall into the hands of illiterate servants at their deaths and be use used as firelighters before anyone can rescue them. By the late Georgian age, the fear was that they would fall into the hands of blackmailers. McMahon's death left the Duke of York worried about his papers, 'which it is highly desirable should not fall into improper hands'. [27]

The death of Princess Charlotte in complications following childbirth in the same year ended whatever prospect there had been of a cabinet with Lords Northumberland and Byron in it. An alternative government of enlightened men under the patriot princess dissolved as the chimera it probably always was, even had she survived. Byron's scandalous relationships and self-imposed exile had debarred him from political office in Britain long before her death. Her demise had a galvanising effect on her uncles. There was sudden pressure on the royal brothers again, for the Dukes of Clarence, Cambridge and Kent to give up their mistresses and produce a legitimate heir to the throne. The Duke of Kent gloomily considering marrying for the succession and giving up his long-term mistress. The apparent counter-productiveness of the Royal Marriages Act haunted The Family once more. Could none of the many children of George III produce a viable child in wedlock? The fact that dynastic marriage and ensuring the succession was their central purpose and a matter of legislation didn't seem to help.

Charlotte's death also freed the Prince Regent of any obligation to her mother. The prospect of divorce loomed again and it became clear that his agents had been gathering evidence against Caroline as part of another investigation into her character and conduct ever since her departure. Was Thomas Ashe one of these agents? Was he still the faithful 'ghost' of the *Spirit of the Book*, ready to rescue Caroline again? Or was he both?

BOOK III

'Ashe is in town'

6

Her Majesty's Saviour

With the death of her daughter Princess Charlotte in 1817, Caroline lost her strongest advocate at home and for the moment, any reason to return to Britain either on her own account or as someone politically useful to the opposition. That all changed with the death of King George III in January 1820, for Caroline was now, nominally at least, and much to her husband's annoyance, Queen of England. Henry Brougham, her brilliant but wary advocate noted that 'Mother P's change of name' (Caroline becoming queen) had made her popular.

The long reign of George III might have been followed by a very short one, as the new king marked his long-awaited accession by falling seriously ill. Thomas Creevey, the diarist and sociable politician, was back in England for the death of the old king and was seriously alarmed by this dangerous illness, though he disliked the son. There was a sudden fear in opposition circles of an ultra-Tory regime under the Duke of York given backbone and malevolent purpose by his wicked brother Ernest, Duke of Cumberland.

As always, the new king's principal affliction, other than his own lifestyle and its effect on his health, was his wife. On his recovery, his main concern was not so much taking up the reins of state as removing his wife from his life entirely. His deliberate slights in instructing diplomats not to accord her any new dignities on his accession became her motivation for claiming those rights, thus driving her back into his path. The king raged at his Cabinet, insisting that Caroline must be removed from the liturgy. Praying for the queen was seen by many as a civil convention, and the attempt to exclude her a sign of petty vindictiveness on the part of her husband. Then it was pointed out that if Caroline was recognised as queen before God she must therefore be queen before men as well, a possibility which seems to have occurred to nobody initially, but which logically made her exclusion absolutely necessary.

Henry Brougham met Caroline at St Omer and urged her to claim her rights and dignities from abroad rather than coming to England, perhaps taking on the style of 'the Duchess of Cornwall' and petitioning the government with quiet dignity. That was not Caroline's way. Brougham was wary of the forces of popular sentiment and disorder that Caroline's return might unleash. Surely, like all members of it, she should have been aware of 'the manifold evils of a public enquiry into the most delicate matters connected to the royal family'.[1]

Now, however, both sides of the marriage seemed more intent on revenge than on upholding the dignity of the monarchy, just as they had been in the wake of the Delicate Investigation in 1806. Brougham's reference to 'delicate matters' seemed to point to that earlier enquiry, so perhaps he should have known better what Caroline's attitude would be.

Brougham had good reason to prefer the queen to remain abroad. He wanted her as a threat, but doubted she could succeed in claiming her rights given her husband's implacable opposition. Brougham's description of her character in 1819 strongly echoed the assessment of her by James Harris, Earl of Malmesbury in 1794:

> There was great ground for alarm at the carelessness with which she suffered strangers to make her acquaintance, and of her gaiety and love of amusement leading her into the society of foreigners, and those exposing her to the constant risk of false reports being sent to England by the spies set about her.[2]

Brougham's language again clearly evoked the 'Delicate Investigation' of 1806 and with it the political turbulence of the rise and fall of Spencer Perceval and the literary game that had been won by writers like Thomas Ashe. Did the government really want to risk going through all that again with a fresh enquiry? Could Caroline's reputation survive another investigation, could her husband or the monarchy itself? Both sides seemed minded to overlook the damage to themselves as long as the other side suffered more. What about the status and repute of the Crown itself at home and abroad? That was the concern of private diaries of worried commentators but not, it seemed, of the parties themselves. The so-called Milan

Commission brought fresh allegations of adultery against Caroline focussed on her relationship with her major domo and companion Baron Bergami. It seemed as if the investigation which reported in 1806 had never really stopped.

For a while, in the years after Caroline's departure from England in 1814, the European continent seemed to be full of disaffected Britons including elements of its royal family, writers, politicians, spies and gentleman blackmailers. If they were not actively following Caroline, they were avoiding her husband and Home Secretary Henry Addington's repressive laws at home. Some few trusted Britons remained in her entourage; others enjoyed the gossip about her at a discreet distance. Thomas Ashe said he would leave for the continent when his *Memoirs and Confessions* were published in 1815, and he did travel, but not in her entourage. By his own later admission, he was lured into the service of the agents of the Regent to track down evidence of Caroline's misbehaviour in Brunswick before her marriage. We can be sure that he was already back in England in 1820 when Caroline returned. He wrote and published another book quite unlike his others and made further applications to the Literary Fund. He was there making a nuisance of himself with her lawyers in the amazing summer of the Queen's return and 'trial' in 1820. By December, Ashe was in a trial of his own.

It was thought that the Regent and the Foreign Secretary Lord Castlereagh had been so glad to be rid of Caroline that they gave little thought as to how she might behave, or to the diplomatic havoc which this might cause. Arguably, though, the biggest threat to the reputation of the king and his government was not Caroline herself, but the underhand and vindictive way they persecuted her. Her biographer Joseph Nightingale detailed allegations about the role of government agents in Caroline's departure and in fomenting and buying the evidence of the Milan Commission, including attempts to bribe the object of its accusations, Baron Bergami himself.

In his *Memoirs of the Public and Private Life of Caroline* Nightingale gave the Baron a rare chance to give his own account to an English readership. Bergami's narrative included the appearance of the Earl of Oxford and Lord Byron in the queen's box at the opera. His account included an episode in which he disguised himself and found himself being offered bribes by agents of the Milan Commission to come up with incriminating evidence against himself and her.

The close attentions of the agents of the Commission made Caroline's life intolerable and she became more inclined to return. An air of corruption and perjury hung about the evidence of the Milan Commission, though the sheer weight of evidence was difficult to explain away. By the summer of 1818, the Commission had begun to investigate Caroline's behaviour on the continent and in particular her relations with Bergami. As early as November of that year, the commissioners felt they had sufficient evidence of adultery. Forty-eight people had been interviewed by the Commission by July 1819. Henry Brougham's brother James provided independent evidence of Caroline's extravagance, sufficient he thought for divorce, He thought it better for her to sue for divorce first on the grounds of the undoubted adultery by her husband, since at that point she seemed to have no ambition to be queen. Divorce proceedings were bound to bring out distasteful revelations on both sides, as adultery had to be proved but 'could not be instituted without serious hazard to the peace of the kingdom', an oblique way of referring to revelations of the Prince's affairs. There were also some doubts, social and xenophobic, about the value of the Commission's findings, being based on 'the evidence of foreigners not above the rank of menial servants'. This doubt was shared by the cabinet as early as June 1819, which wondered if the evidence of 'foreigners' would be considered credible by Parliament or the public. One benefit of the foreignness of her supposed sins was that she could not be tried for high treason since Bergami and the countries in which he and she had lived together owed the British Crown no allegiance.

When Caroline returned to England in June 1820, she consciously allied herself with the radicals. Brougham's equivocations convinced her finally of his political motives. He wanted her near enough to be a millstone to the government but not in London where events might take on a momentum even he could not control. Once she had defied Brougham, Caroline became a focus for those opposed to her husband and those who did not share Brougham's fear of disorder, The 'Bill of Pains and Penalties' as the parliamentary proceeding against her was called, became the talking point of the summer. Newspapers covering the sensational events were read aloud in taverns, making twenty-five readers for every paper.

The Milan Commission's findings were made known to parliament, presented in 'the green bag', a gift for caricaturists. A reasonably coherent kernel of solid evidence of the Queen's misbehaviour, albeit from witnesses the British public were unlikely to credit, was overlaid with hearsay. Material amassed in preparation for the trial included evidence from Mary Anne Clarke's suppressed diary that Frederick, Duke of York, had met Caroline in Germany in 1791 and found her pregnant. Thus, the government suppressed Mrs Clarke's evidence and then exploited it.

To meet the public demand for stories of girls behaving badly, 1819 had also seen the emergence of 'Olivia Moreland', the putative author of *The Charms of Dandyism or Living in Style, edited by Thomas Ashe*. It was perhaps his most unexpected and uncharacteristic publication. It appeared in a list of 'Books Published this Day' advertised in *The Times* on 12 February 1819. The list of novels at the end of volume three of *The Charms of Dandyism* would have been enough to make Wordsworth tear his thinning hair, three pages of 'idle romances' mostly by, or purporting to be by, women. Ashe had something slightly more serious in mind. The 'living in style' of the subtitle was a phrase Ashe had used to describe his own extravagant lifestyle when bribing Mrs Clarke after coming in to his inheritance in 1805. The book was a moral tale based on his own experience, Olivia's not so fashionable addresses and privations were clearly based on Ashe's own. His female narrator had a disconcertingly Ashe-like voice: 'Bath is the paradise of women, not the school of reflection.'[3] Narrator Olivia revisits the sights of Ashe's literary prostitution as recounted in his *Memoirs and Confessions* living first in Pangbourne then in Park Place, North Baker Street as the kept woman of Mr Townley. Her vicissitudes mirror Ashe's own, brutalised by misfortune. He transposes his rather self-inflicted miseries on to a woman who has them inflicted on her, though both are culpable in their addiction to living in a style beyond their means. Ashe was never quite as grand as Olivia's many lovers, so the autobiographical elements jar a little as not being quite the right setting for her. For all the characteristic smoothness of Ashe's prose, we are often made to feel as uncomfortable as his heroine does: 'A young woman, elegantly dressed and without any friend or attendant was not a subject to be treated with neglect or inattention in a Margate packet boat.'[4]

As the narrative progresses though, it becomes clear that Ashe identifies strongly with his heroine in her powerlessness, she as a kept woman, he the plaything of the booksellers and the Hydra. Why did he not just write another tranche of autobiography to take up from where his memoirs finish? Instead, there is a touch of Harriette Wilson, the great courtesan's memoir, though Olivia is much more given to self-doubt and reflection. Olivia was not taking revenge on great men, though the names of her paramours hint at aristocratic families. It was not a sensational or erotic book, even by the standards of some of the competing titles on the back cover. Could it really be a moral tale warning the reader of the pitfalls of his own extravagant lifestyle? It certainly was a departure from the rollicking, candid style of the memoirs. It was perhaps therapeutic to make himself the victim rather than the author of misfortune.

Another indication that Ashe was already in England at the beginning of 1820 came in his final application to the Literary Fund. Perhaps he hoped the Fund would not have kept records of his previous applications or its investigation into his character. He applied twice in March 1820.The Fund also received his printed petition, 'The Martyred Scholar an author of 40 year's standing'.[5] This was something of an exaggeration since it supposed Ashe had been writing in 1780 at the age of ten. He was again unsuccessful. Perhaps they were wary of writers who dabbled in political controversies and the memoirs of notorious women in any case, as the Committee dealt as circumspectly with Joseph Nightingale[6] and Harriette Wilson's publisher John Joseph Stockdale.[7]

The government kept its own detailed records of literature worth supporting or suppressing. The Treasury solicitor kept a file on pamphlets and popular demonstrations of support for the queen.[8] Another file retained samples of caricatures[9] for this period including ninety-one considered for prosecution as 'abominations'. Once again, the government faced the problem that no jury would convict and publicity would make things worse. They included Thomas Dolby's 'Hum IVth and his ministers going to play the devil with the satirists'. They ridiculed instruments of suppression including special juries. Some depicted the deposition of the king in favour of Caroline or Frederick Duke of York. There were only 28 prosecutions for seditious libel in 1820 compared with 63 in 1819, though many more satires were produced. This was partly because of the risk of disorder associated with prosecution, but also because radical opinions had become mainstream; Caroline was a middle class cause. Stupendous sums were offered through the Privy Purse for the suppression of cartoons injurious to the king. As soon as it became clear that Carlton House would pay more for suppression than could be got by publication, threatened cartoons against him burgeoned. Captured in the official documents is the repeated popular sentiment that the conduct of the investigation was more questionable than the conduct of the queen herself, involving bribery, theft, threats and deception.

Captain Browne was still appearing in popular cartoons at the time of Caroline's return to England. In August 1820, the 'The Royal Bruiser or Bloomy Floor'd' showed the queen's return heralded by her handsome hussar, Captain Browne, whose courage would add to the shame of the panicked figures depicted. The Duke of Wellington is depicted fearing her return more than Napoleon. Benjamin Bloomfield as Privy Purse is thrown to the floor. Captain Browne, if it is he, is taken from memory, not from the life, as he, like Ashe himself, would be 50 years old by now. The queen herself, naturally in pro-Caroline prints, often appeared younger and more attractive than the slightly comical figure who put ashore in England in 1820.

What about the still genuinely young guardsmen who toasted the queen's health and damned the king's eyes in their barracks in Chelsea? Could the army pawns really be divided between queen side and king side and therefore refuse to quell disorder on partisan lines? Wellington's note to Lord Liverpool on the loyalty of the Guards regiments following mutiny in one battalion of the third Regiment of Guards, suggested they might be:

> We and the public have reason to doubt in the fidelity of the troops, the only security we have, not only against revolution, but the property and life of every individual in the country who has anything to lose. In my opinion the Government ought, without the loss of a moment's time, to adopt measures either to form a police in London, or military corps, which should be of a different description from a regular military force, or both.[10]

Thus, some of the impetus for a Metropolitan police force came from the military. Partly this followed the Peterloo massacre and the difficulty of deploying the yeomanry against civilians, but it also reflected a fear of armed men turning on the government in a political cause. Fear of the effect of the summer's events on public opinion and public order were everywhere. Byron's supplier of *The Book* and the man who had witnessed Willy Austin's birth certificate for it, Charles Williams Wynn, wrote from Barmouth on 27 July 1820 to the Marquis of Buckingham after having been asked questions about the queen's 'trial' by local fishermen.

When William Wilberforce brought forward a motion urging the queen to relinquish having her name restored to the liturgy in return for a stay to the proceedings against her, which 'whatever its results must prove derogatory to the Crown and injurious to the best interests of the country', government ministers were among those who voted for it. This suggested to at least one observer that this was tantamount to the government admitting that its own measure was damaging to both the Crown and the country.[11]

The queen should accept the offer on the same grounds but does not, so both sides were prepared to risk the damage to the institution of monarchy in their own personal cause. What of public opinion after the Peterloo massacre and threat to the government of the Cato Street Conspiracy? Was not the risk now higher than in 1806? What would happen if the Bill passed the Lords but not the Commons? Could it provoke a constitutional crisis, even a revolution?

The man who would bring about the Duke of Wellington's desired police force in London as his Home Secretary, Robert Peel, confided to J. W. Croker on 10 August 1820 that the government was to blame for undermining the respect in which monarchy was held:

> I do think the Queen's affair very formidable, it is a famous ingredient in a cauldron which has been bubbling for a long time, and upon which, as it always seemed to me, the Government never could discern the least simmering. They applied a blow-pipe, however, when they omitted the Queen's name in the Liturgy: when they established a precedent for dethronement for imputed personal misconduct. Surely, this was not the time for robbing Royalty of the exterior marks of respect and for preaching up the anti-divine right doctrines. If she be worse than Messalina, nothing but the united voice of King, Lords and Commons should have degraded her. I certainly would have tried her the moment she set foot in England, but I would have prayed for her as Queen till she had been tried.[12]

If the queen could be deprived of her rights and privileges because of her reputed actions, why should not the king be, who was manifestly as guilty as his wife was, if not more so? Once again, it was the government itself which seemed to be undermining public confidence in the monarchy and fanning the flames of revolution. However much they might deplore the king's intransigence and fear the consequences for law and order, no one in the government would dare put the clear logic of that argument to the king himself, for fear of committing treason by the mere suggestion.

No wonder it is so difficult for us at such a remove to gauge a contemporary view of the power and importance of monarchy, when the king and queen seemed indifferent to it as an institution in their eagerness for personal victory. Meanwhile, crowds flocked to Caroline at Hammersmith. There was no thought or possibility of suppressing them. Respectable ladies and gentlemen and sober tradespeople were alongside the 'mob', whoever they might be, in saluting the queen. Members of the Royal and Merchant Navies marched and sailed to Hammersmith in support of the queen. The guardians of British liberties against Napoleon thus found themselves ranged against the government. Eight hundred loyal addresses were received by Caroline at Brandenburg House, amounting to a million signatures. Caroline moved to St James's Square for the duration of her trial, next door to Lord Castlereagh, who promptly moved out.

While the Bill of Pains and Penalties made its uncomfortable way through Parliament, the Duke of Wellington was hissed and booed in the streets. The trial ebbed and flowed especially on the damning evidence of Teodoro Majocchi, who, under examination from Brougham, affected not to remember ('non mi recordo') much of the detail he was asked about. This famous phrase stayed with Ashe, who would recall it in his own Old Bailey trial ten years later. His evidence and the queen's staged shock exit at his betrayal of her on 21 August began to lose her popularity. As he did in Ashe's mind when comparing him with the Hydra, Lord Sidmouth and others seemed to retain a certain amount of dignity in the eyes of the public in comparison with the Italian circus with which the queen was associated.

Many Italian witnesses were put off giving evidence at all by tales of mistreatment by the mob, sometimes this being elaborated into lynching or even rumours that Caroline had assumed power and was arresting her opponents. Brougham asked the witnesses against her for the name of 'their employer' emphasising the widely held assumption that they had been paid to testify. Many witnesses were on a daily retainer, which only cast further doubt on their evidence.

While reliable testimony was hard to come by in the queen's 'trial' the government found it could not depend on a jury to convict the authors of the many satires and cartoons generated by the proceedings in Parliament, however weighty the evidence against them. Satires flowed. William Hone produced a pamphlet that made the king the subject of 'Non mi recordo'.

Gradually the government lost confidence in the Bill. The divorce clause was removed in the House of Lords, a move designed to make the bill less difficult to pass, but it also took away one of its central purposes. What, now, was the point of it? The *True Briton* carried a sceptical line of argument often echoed by the modern press. It calculated the cost of the queen's 'trial' as being equivalent to the endowment of fifty hospitals.[13] An account published in March 1821 shows £130,000 had been spent in proceedings against the queen since 1817, including £46,000 by the long-suffering George Maule, Treasury Solicitor from the Civil Contingencies Fund.[14]

Even without the divorce clause, the progress of the bill through Parliament was slow and uncertain given the character of the witnesses against the queen and the skilfulness of her defence conducted by Henry Brougham and Thomas Denman. Public opinion was ranged against it and this made the government nervous. What disorder might follow the successful passage of the bill – who was controlling government business and the country? The proceedings against the queen threatened to set Parliament against the People.

Her 'trial' had begun on Thursday on 17 August and prompted Thomas Creevey's famous comparison of the queen with a Dutch doll weighted with lead, which would spring upright from any position. His eyewitness account is all the more entertaining and believable as Creevey was sympathetic to her cause and did not aim at satire:

> To describe to you her appearance and manner is far beyond my powers. I had been taught to believe she was as much improved in appearance as in dignity of manners; it is therefore with much pain I am obliged to observe that the nearest resemblance I can recollect to this much injured Princess is a toy you used to call Fanny Royds. There is another toy, of a rabbit or a cat, whose tail you squeeze under its body, and then out it jumps in half a minute off the ground into the air. The first of these toys, you must suppose to represent the person of the Queen; the latter the manner by which she popped all at once into the House, made a *duck* at the throne, another to the Peers and a concluding jump into the chair which was placed for her.[15]

Though written for comic effect to a trusted correspondent, Creevey's description captured a fundamental truth at the heart of the public perception of the queen, which was at once her strength and her undoing. She was undoubtedly 'much injured' and more sympathetic and likeable than her husband, but she was not regal enough to be supported as a cause in her own right, only as a means of opposing and annoying the king. Caroline's progress in a state barge drew a crowd of 200,000. The sentiment of the crowd was as much anti-king as pro-queen, but Caroline treated it as her personal following that might 'blow him off his throne'.

On 4 September, when the initial tide of evidence threatened to overwhelm the queen, Thomas Ashe returned to the scene in an impassioned letter to her attorney William Vizard, claiming a unique ability to serve her cause despite a recent history of accepting bribes from the Crown. The letter was addressed, warily, care of 'Lendall, York', a forwarding address, since he feared the interception of his correspondence (the letter makes clear he was unhappy with the security of Vizard's seal on a previous letter) and discovery of his location. His letter was prompted by Vizard's previously expressed, understandable hesitation to employ Ashe on the queen's behalf when he was known to have worked for the king's party. Ashe was very worried about the fate of his letter, Vizard's previous letter and any future correspondence. With reason, it seems, for it found its way into the standard edition of the king's letters despite being neither from nor to him. Presumably, it was felt to be important enough to be forwarded alongside other intercepted letters following the Milan Commission, for the preparation of the case against the queen and the hindering of her defence. Did it ever reach Vizard?

I am truly sorry that the considerations you are pleased to mention should have made you hesitate to employ my agency in the cause of her persecuted Majesty and I am equally sorry to find that you know so little of my capacity, and late connection with the Government as not instantly to feel that I am the most powerful lever that could possibly be placed in your hands for raising your Royal client to the high station on which her own merit and the laws of your country give her a title to stand.. You might, Sir, have easily learned that I was seduced, at a time of deep distress to abandon the interests of the then Princess of Wales; that I was retained in the service of my seducers for upwards of four years, and that my sole employment during that long period was to traduce HRH and to elevate the husband at the expense of the wife. Hence, it can be proved that I received upwards of 1000 guineas through the medium of Sir Nathaniel Conant and Sir Benjamin Bloomfield for the distinct purpose of preparing the public mind for 'a divorce'. And I can also prove that Mr. Croker of the Admiralty *at this moment* pays 50 pounds per week to certain persons whose duty is confined to the vilification of the Queen and flattery of His Majesty. And should you doubt even my recent connection with the Government, I refer you to Mr. Jayes, solicitor, Charlotte St. Rathbone Place and he will prove to you that Sir Benjamin Bloomfield has conferred on a rascal of the name of Bull, £500 a year because he was the cause of suppressing a work written by me in favour of the Queen. Mr. Jayes can also tell you that I instituted a suit with the view of bringing the conduct of the King with the Queen into Court – and that to stop such suit Government interposed all the influence ministers possessed. I beg you to call Mr. Jayes and to look at the copy of his proceedings – the work suppressed was called 'Curtain Lectures'. But it is utterly impossible to go into detail of the extent of the services I can render her Majesty. I can bring Mr. Croker before the Lords and make him confess he not only writes against the Queen himself*, but that he pays 50 pounds a week to others to degrade and defame Her Majesty. I can give you the address of a clergyman and one dozen other characters to substantiate all that I have here asserted, and much more which I can put into your brief to state before the Lords. And what is the object of all I can prove and get proven? The object is to shew to the Lords, that for a series of years a number of persons have been employed and suborned *to write the Queen down:* for I can also prove that a person (myself) was sent to Paris there to procure a published pamphlet taxing the Queen with licentious habits previously to her having left her father's Court! The effect of such evidence as mine, corroborated by persons of unquestionable character, is incalculable! [It would be confirmed by Sir Benj. Bloomfield, Sir Nathaniel Conant, Mr. Watson, Lord Yarmouth, Mrs. Coutts, the Marchioness of Hertford, Mr. Croker, Lord Howden, &c &c ALL of WHOM WERE PRIVY TO MY CONNECTION WITH THE KING and TO THE EMPLOYMENT *imposed on me by His Majesty's desire.*] I shall only further observe Sir, that I shall sincerely trust that you will no longer suffer any consideration to deprive the Queen of my faithful services: but I must beg of you to be more cautious – your letter was not directed according to my instructions and reached me open – the WAFER had never adhered to the paper. Direct to Capt. Ashe care of Mr Sidney Lendall, York. I have great reason to believe that the proceedings against the Queen would be suffered to drop sooner than MY evidence should appear before the Lords.

[PS] I beg of you not to take any step respecting me in a public manner, till I have the honour of seeing you. My expenses to town and the means of getting a suit of clothes are all I require to repair to town the instant I hear from you. And you may rely on my punctuality as I desire nothing more in the world that the author of *The Spirit of the Book*, notwithstanding the prostitution of his principles by the servants of the King, is the most faithful defender and advocate of Her Majesty.

I candidly avow that I alone can serve and save her Majesty. But I require no kind of terms: I never appealed to Her Majesty – even when reduced to the necessity of selling my talents to Sir B Bloomfield &c &c &c. Have faith! I can serve and save the Queen!!! and I can be relied on.

* I can shew his handwriting.[16]

The great epistolary blackmailer suddenly feared the vulnerability of his own letters. In the hands of a nervous and driven government, his own modus operandi was coming to find him out. There is something manic about this letter, breathless and desperate, full of emphatic capital letters italics, underlinings and exclamations. Ashe was relying on the willingness to testify to the veracity of his statements of people who would thereby be condemning themselves and their own cause and who have the power simply to ignore Ashe or crush him.

It is difficult to present yourself as a reliable witness of criminal endeavour when you are one of the perpetrators. Ashe gave his poverty as an excuse for taking part in the campaign to 'write down' the queen and named others who had been similarly bribed, as well as those who offered the bribes. Ashe claimed he got his 'upwards of 1000 guineas through Sir Nathaniel Conant and Benjamin Bloomfield. Mr Croker of the Admiralty pays £50 a week to people to vilify the Queen.' Croker wrote the review of 'Endymion' in the *Quarterly Review*, which Byron supposed killed Keats, as well as criticism of Byron as a betrayer of his class in letters to John Murray.

There were dark hints by Ashe that he was employed by the king's party to go to Paris to find a copy of a pamphlet about Caroline's love life at the court of Brunswick before her marriage, part of the programme of state-funded dirt dishing associated with the Milan Commission. Presumably, his knowledge of Caroline's life in Brunswick and the whole business of producing scandalous pamphlets made him well qualified for the job and the recipient of largesse from another government slush fund. Even Ashe's determination to distance himself from the battles of a corrupt government with the unscrupulous Hydra culminating in his determination to retire to France to write 'The Soldier of Fortune' was predicated upon his continuing engagement in this sordid trade.

As well as the letter itself, Aspinall's edition of the king's letters contains a further deposition from Mary Crandon about Ashe dated 1 November 1820. Her deposition was sworn before the Mayor, George Bridges, at the Mansion House. The Crandons were as we have seen the chief agents of the Hydra, as revealed in the letters of Ashe to Viscount Perceval.

> The deponent Mary Crandon of East Ham in the County of Essex deposes that in the year 1814 she saw Thomas Ashe, commonly called Captain Ashe who informed said deponent that he was under confinement in the King's Bench prison for heavy debts. He, the said Thomas Ashe, further stated to deponent that he was employed to write a certain work called *The Spirit of the Book*, and that some person belonging to the Home Department paid the debts of the same Thomas Ashe, for writing the said book, and he was forthwith liberated from prison.[17]

Since *The Spirit of the Book* was written in 1811 with the aim of rescuing Caroline's reputation this seems unlikely, but it does show that some suspected that the government rather than the opposition were behind Ashe's work. Presumably, the Crandons wanted revenge; Ashe had betrayed them so now they wished to destroy his credibility as Caroline's saviour by suggesting his bestselling work in her favour had been subsidised by the government. Ashe's memoirs suggested his imprisonment in King's Bench came after the composition of *The Spirit of the Book* and his release came in negotiations around a work called 'The Legal Vulture'. There is no explanation in Mary Crandon's evidence as to why the government would pay Ashe to write *The Spirit of the Book*. Surely Vizard, as Caroline's solicitor, must have known that *The Spirit of the Book* was a pro-Caroline work; why would he suddenly have made this confession, three years after the event? Not surprisingly, Vizard, like Perceval before him, decided he could not trust a man who had written for both sides, and did not take up Ashe's offer. He need not have investigated too deeply to discover Ashe was not to be relied upon and had written for the king's party.

The role of Caroline's literary ghost was instead taken up by Ashe's despised and deadly rival, William Cobbett. She describes the wrongs she has suffered in an open letter to the king (which she is holding in the Lonsdale portrait) almost certainly composed and published by Cobbett on 7 August 1820. He reckoned to have sold two million copies in Britain and five million in America. Like Ashe's versions of her, it presented a purer and more restrained picture of Caroline than she would have produced had she written the letter herself. There was no scandal in it, no accusations about her husband's relationships, which Caroline would surely have alluded to herself. The threat of 'the stability of your throne' is thinly veiled.

> I cannot refrain from laying my grievous wrongs once more before your Majesty, in the hope that the justice which your Majesty may, by evil-minded counsellors, be still disposed to refuse to the claims of a dutiful, faithful, and injured wife, you may be induced to yield to considerations connected with the honour and dignity of your crown, the stability of your throne, the tranquillity of your dominions, the happiness and safety of your just and loyal people, whose generous hearts revolt at oppression and cruelty, and especially when perpetrated by a perversion and a mockery of the laws.

Through the summer of her notorious 'trial' Thomas Ashe emerged as something other than Caroline's creature, though he shared in her moment and its passing, carrying on an increasingly lonely and desperate campaign on her behalf, which it appeared she no longer wanted. Other, stronger forces were at work,. William Cobbett emerged as her letter writer and as the author of both popular supportive addresses to her and of her replies. Ashe actually views the king's party with respectful regret compared to the unscrupulous Hydra and the radical opposition. He felt no more warmly about Cobbett as a fellow writer in Caroline's cause than he had as his journalistic opponent in America and London. Caroline no longer looked to her old Brunswick allies to turn her letters into fiction, leaving it to a different political faction to compose them from scratch.

Not everyone was swept up in Caroline fever. Princess Lieven wrote to her favourite correspondent Prince Metternich on 6 September 1820, two days after Ashe's letter to William Vizard, to give a very different view of Ashe's suffering saint:

Anyway the queen is quite mad, and what surprises me is that they don't question the witnesses about that, or at least ask her doctor. If they pronounced her mad they would avoid all this scandal and be nearer the truth besides.[18]

Byron thought 'there is not the slightest doubt about the Queen and Bergami' but that the King's own affairs gave him no right to punish her. The proceedings were adjourned on 11 September until 3 October.

As late as October, evidence was still emerging about the venality of the evidence and the tactics of the government in obtaining it, which exposed the continuing vulnerability of, and trade in, private letters. Lady Charlotte Lindsay was one of the most widely believed and respectable of the witnesses in the queen's favour, a companion of her travels and one whose evidence might be expected to carry considerable weight. She had been cross-examined with a ferocity that reduced her to tears and surprised many observers. Lady Cowper wrote to Frederick Lamb on 11 October 1820:

> The most shameful thing that has appeared in the whole transaction is Col. Lindsay having sold to the Govern[men]t L[ad]y Charlotte's letters written to him from Naples, and it was upon these that her cross-examination was founded. Did you ever hear such a thing?[19]

The attitude of the members of The Family to the proceedings was much discussed, not just what they thought but why. Lady Cowper wrote again to Frederick Lamb on 26 October 1820 that, unusually, the Duke of Gloucester, husband of that least passionate former inmate of the Nunnery, Princess Mary, supported the queen, but the motive was familiar, the possibility of Caroline spilling the beans and besmirching the royal family.

> The Duke of Gloucester [is] for her stoutly; this is not so much believed to be his generosity as he pretends for former friendship, as the Duchess is doing to prevent the Queen fulfilling her threat of Publishing Memoirs of herself and the rest of the Princesses. By the way, such a threat as that shows what a degraded person the Queen is, yet people are so blinded now [that] if she were to do such a thing they would reckon it all fair...[20]

Perhaps, even now, the service Ashe could do the queen was not, as he presented it to her solicitor William Vizard, as the man who could demonstrate the lengths and expense the government had gone to in order to denigrate her, but instead as The Blackmailer of Frogmore. The Bill was voted on in November and passed by a narrow government majority, down to nine on third reading in the Lords, which in a matter of state was tantamount to defeat. The throne had been degraded but revolution, if one was indeed imminent, had been averted. The king was reported to be delighted that the bill was 'lost'. After all the effort, expense and chicanery to bring the bill and its supporting evidence to Parliament, he had avoided the possibility of being toppled from his throne had the bill been passed. What reliance could be placed on him? Could the ministers responsible for the fiasco survive in office? Would the king, as the satirists suggested, flee to Hanover? The queen greeted the abandonment of the bill with 'I am lost.' The government had saved itself by throwing out its own bill. The queen could only gain her full rights on the back of a revolution, which would not now happen.

The popular reception of the queen's victory was nonetheless uproarious with bonfires and breaking of windows. Sir Richard Birnie, a magistrate later directly involved with Ashe at the time of his trial in 1830, sounded sympathetic to the 'rioters' brought before him. He felt they should mourn the queen being found guilty by a majority in the Lords rather than in pretending a triumph. The Tories feared for their safety if they left office and the Whigs risked disappointing the public appetite for vengeance and reform if they came in. There were further reports that if the Bill went to the Commons Caroline would carry out her blackmailing threat against The Family:

> They [the Opposition] meant it to go to the Commons to give the Queen an opportunity of recriminating – at least so I have heard. She was prepared to do so to the widest extent including the Women as well as the Men of the Royal Family.[21]

How right Spencer Perceval's senior law officers had been to point out that suppressing *The Claustral Palace* would achieve little if the source material was still extant. Might she turn again to Thomas Ashe to produce a new bumper edition with fresh revelations since 1811?

Henry Brougham's trial summing up shook the country and wowed the clubs, but most people on reflection thought Caroline's witnesses were even more unreliable than the king's. Defensive evidence, of those attesting to what they had not seen, is in any case always a little flat.

Thomas Denman's summing up was intended to be sympathetic but in calling on the queen to 'sin no more' confirmed the sense, at the moment of Caroline's triumph, that she was in no fit state to be queen of England. It gave rise to a popular rhyme:

Most gracious Queen, we thee implore
To go away and sin no more
Or if that effort be too great
To go away at any rate

The constitution, against all the odds, had worked, after a fashion, and by leaving months of abuse directed at the king largely unchecked had preserved the monarchy more surely than heavy-handed suppression would have done.

Brougham and Denman rose to some of the highest offices of the law under William IV having called him a slanderer to his face as Duke of Clarence during the queen's trial.

Brougham's memoirs touched on his alarm at the troops being on the side of the queen. Any threat of violence and revolution would undermine his case in Parliament if he or the queen had any contact with them. Like Lady Erne, he talked in terms of 'recrimination' and the surprisingly widespread assumption that he and the queen's party would use new blackmailing revelations against The Family in retaliation if the Bill went to the Commons. He says all he intended was to make more widely known what was already known in society about the king's mistresses. Brougham by this time had a copy of the king's will as Prince of Wales, referring to Mrs Fitzherbert as 'my dear wife'. This will in Mrs Fitzherbert's favour might have been enough to support the king's forfeiture of the Crown under the terms of the Act of Settlement, but Brougham had no intention of provoking the disorder which might result. There were violent celebrations but the trial had been cathartic and people had had enough of all the parties involved.

The king's agents at Carlton House slandered those who visited the queen, gave patronage to those who refused and the programme of state literary blackmail continued. Scandals in the newspapers were brought to her knowledge in the hope of wearing her out and driving her abroad again. 'Among other tricks practised, there were thefts of her papers and letters, as well as letters in other people's possession.'

After the bill was thrown out, November saw a service of thanksgiving at St Paul's Cathedral for her deliverance from conspiracy, a congregation of gentlemen and people with no aristocrats, huge crowds and no disorder. The queen's popularity fell thereafter as the reality of her person replaced the idea of the injured woman. She got no concessions with regard to the liturgy, allowance or residences, so had no money and nowhere to go, and became ridiculous. She was still petitioning to be restored to the liturgy in March 1821 and there were cabinet minutes on procedures to ensure there would be no disorder if the queen decided to present the petition in person at Buckingham House. Her petition was silly and misspelt. It was always clear when she has written on her own account and when someone with a greater command of English had done it for her. The king's right to exclude her from the Coronation was personal rather than based on precedent. She was popular when attached to a popular cause, but her behaviour showed that she was not politically engaged, rather acting in what she considered her own personal interest. The means of her temporary success, the popular press, had profited. With its pro-Caroline coverage of her 'trial', *The Times* doubled its circulation.

At the end of it, the paper covered another trial, that of Dobson versus Ashe. Once again, Thomas Ashe did not exactly cut a revolutionary figure, this time trading on spurious aristocratic connections to defraud a tradesman. Dobson brought his action for work done in preparing the defendant's cottage and garden in Hollyhill, Kent. Ashe is described as a 'gentleman of fortune' who supervises and comments on the work being done but then denies liability for any of the cost. Ashe, as he so often did, behaved badly but won the case. It was judged that credit had not been extended to him directly so he was not liable. Notwithstanding the contract, it was not reasonable to expect Ashe to bear half the cost of redecoration on the expectation of a pound a week in rent, merely half the cost of 'necessary repair'. There is no doubt that Ashe encouraged the expense and something of his character comes across in his reported speech. The wallpaper he described as 'cursed handsome' and the cost was justified: 'it was a pity that the ship should be spoiled for a ha'porth of tar.'[22]

The Times described Ashe as being 'Between 60 and 70 years of age' (though he was exactly fifty). The other party, Mr Leslie, 'Lord Newark' had recently been declared an insolvent debtor, so the plaintiff had recourse to Ashe. This was very much Ashe's style, still using the veneer of aristocracy to fleece credulous tradesmen; for all his poverty, he was still plausible and well connected 'William John Leslie, commonly Lord Newark, late of Erith' was perhaps a step down from thye princesses and countesses of his prime. The right of the Leslies to style themselves 'Lord Newark' was disputed. In 1793, the House of Lords declared that the 1672 charter by which the peerage was claimed was a forgery but it carried on being used. The last claimant is recorded as Lt-Col John Leslie who died in 1818. Despite the notoriety of the Perceval versus Phipps case, there were still those who felt their rank entitled them to credit and there were others prepared to extend it to them. Despite the popular fervour and the degradation of monarchy in the eyes of the people during Caroline's 'trial', poor Dobson seemed to bear out Brougham's obervations as to the innate conservative temperament of the British.

Without this conservatism, it can be quite difficult to explain how, given the public feeling against him the previous summer, George IV's coronation in July 1821 managed to restore his image and popularity, or how Caroline became so unpopular so quickly after it. The king enjoyed and spared no expense in producing the theatre of monarchy and in doing so restored a sense of majesty which allowed his subjects, temporarily at least, to forget his personal failings and the sordid revelations of Caroline's 'trial'. On her side, even her lawyers could not represent the proceedings against her as being anything other than damaging to her reputation, and tramping round the abbey on foot seeking admission to her husband's coronation made her appear absurd. Ultimately, she was not interested in the popular causes that had attached themselves to her. Many of those who had campaigned with the slogan 'The Queen Forever' had realised that she was, after all, an unsuitable person to be queen. Her reception at Westminster Abbey was reported differently by both sides, some saying she was cheered, others that she was booed. Presumably it was both. Even Brougham noted the great contrast with her reception at St Paul's in November.

Caroline was reported ill soon afterwards with daily bulletins about her health coming from Brandenburg House. Within weeks, she was dead. With her death came the end of the possibility of 'recrimination' from Caroline either directly or through Thomas Ashe. The only possibility now from the revelations lovingly recorded in her manuscripts was further damage to her own reputation and to The Family from which she could no longer benefit. Soon afterwards came reports from her staunch friend and companion Lady Anne Hamilton on the burning of Caroline's manuscripts at Brandenburg House, so that they should not to fall into the hands of the king. These manuscripts included her account of 'the whole history of her life since she came into this country together with the characters of all the different persons she had been intimate with'.[23] What a loss that volume was, the life's work of that consummate mimic, not a regal trait but a useful one for a writer. The closest things we have are the novels of her 'ghost', Thomas Ashe.

Even after her death, Caroline was the cause of dissension. The route of her funeral procession was hotly debated, the authorities fearing 'the mob' would be provoked to further offences if her body passed through London. Sir Richard Birnie and Sir Nathaniel Conant, who both suffered as magistrates from being Thomas Ashe's intermediaries with the government, were involved in maintaining order at the funeral. There were also involved in the investigation into the circumstances of the deaths of two men killed when fighting broke out over the funeral route. Conant had written to the Home Office, resigning as a magistrate in the spring of 1820 due to ill health. He died in 1822.[24] His son succeeded him at Bow Street and would have his own correspondence with Ashe. The queen's cortège passed through Kensington where 'Johnson', one of the central characters in 'The Charms of Dandyism' lives and possibly where Ashe was living at the time, since he returned there on his fateful journey to the capital in the summer of 1830. Perhaps he could have paid his last respects to her without straying too far. No one who hoped for preferment under the king could risk being seen there. Major General Sir Robert Wilson was removed from the king's service for attending Caroline's funeral.

There was an outpouring of literature commemorating the queen's life and capitalising on her death. *The Memoirs of Queen Caroline* (1820) by the Reverend Joseph Nightingale went into twenty-two editions in that year and spawned several follow-up volumes after her death. In it, readers were reminded of 'the handsome Irishman' relationship ended by the Duke of Brunswick for political reasons, when the prospect of marriage to the Prince of Wales appeared.

Just as the threat of Caroline's recriminations died, another blackmailing threat to the establishment emerged. In 1824 the serialisation of Harriette Wilson's *Memoirs* began and with it, the sending of letters to those involved, with an offer to buy themselves out of its pages for £200. As Ashe did in his circulated synopsis to *The Claustral Palace*, Harriette Wilson's notorious publisher John Joseph Stockdale circulated, in order of rank, a list of the illustrious people who were to feature in the forthcoming volumes, including the Duke of Wellington, but hers was a more general blackmailing campaign than any undertaken by Ashe. For she had been wronged personally and in love by whole swathes of the establishment. For good measure, she also had also retained letters of one of her lovers to Lady Conyngham, George IV's latest mistress, which the king paid handsomely to suppress. Stockdale took on the costs of publishing Harriette's memoirs and the liabilities of libel in return for half the profits. Though the memoirs were immensely successful, Stockdale risked bankruptcy, for the libel actions were directed at him while the profits were undermined by piracy, as immoral works could not claim copyright.[25]

Fresh from the profits and pitfalls of publishing Harriette Wilson, Stockdale was linked to the next phase of Captain Ashe's own blackmailing campaign. They shared legal representatives Mounsey & Gray, solicitors of Carlisle, and the long-suffering Duke of Wellington and his government feared that Stockdale was the man to publish Ashe's most scandalous novel yet. By this time, Ashe was living what he called his 'savage' life in rural Cumberland, not as a romantic poet but as a prose blackmailer, or what the local bishop was pleased to call 'library pursuits'. Caroline could no longer be saved, but the career of her 'ghost' continued after her death. Her confidences of murder and incest within The Family would inform his most notorious manuscript and use the power of her secrets in the cause of Irish liberty and Catholic toleration against their greatest opponent, Ernest, Duke of Cumberland. The Duke of Wellington famously is supposed to have met the threat of Harriette Wilson's memoirs to his own reputation with 'Publish and be damned', but as Prime Minister he could not allow the publication or even the exhibition to a jury, of Thomas Ashe's 'Osphia, or the Victim of Unnatural Affections'.

7

The Victim of Unnatural Affections

With Queen Caroline's death, the purpose and patronage of Thomas Ashe's writing might seem to have disappeared but he was not so easily defeated. The Dobson versus Ashe case showed that even after the disgrace of Lady Perceval and the public exposure of the dangers of trusting those whose 'rank was their only title to credit', Ashe was using dubious aristocratic connections to dupe honest tradesmen, rather, it seemed, for the fun of it, than for any great personal gain. He needed a campaign after the death of the queen and that meant finding a new inspiration from among the princesses of *The Claustral Palace*.

He admitted in his *Memoirs and Confessions* that he had learnt by experience not to expect greatness in high places, but he was compelled to seek patronage to support himself, and could see no other system than the one he attacked. His adoption of the Regent's or Caroline's party seemed to depend on his adherence to or abhorrence of individuals and his personal circumstances, rather than points of principle. As Ben Wilson says of William Hone, a great humane writer characterised by his opponents as an unprincipled ruffian hack, there are not separate tribes of writers inhabiting a literary overworld or underworld, only individuals with flexible skills writing for the occasion. One might have thought, given his own reliance on these skills, that Ashe ought to have been consistently in the party of those who 'do' rather than those who 'have', but he was too well connected to side with the have-nots. He half expected to be, and often was, rescued by well-placed friends. He is also ready to claim his political work is done out of necessity or against his will. In fact, his *Memoirs and*

Confessions show this specially commissioned writing for a cause is his natural mode and produces his best prose. Ashe complained to his potential patrons that his more virtuous books did not sell, but it is also clear that writing improving literary works in relative comfort bored him.

His periodic evocation of some kind of Arcadian idyll as his ideal life is shallow, unconvincing and always rapidly disposed of in the chaos of his personal narrative. *The Claustral Palace* shows this, even in his description of the genuinely happily rustic Princess Elizabeth. Despite her determination to find contentment in her constrained circumstances and in her farm, human nature and heightened passion get in the way. Without it, life becomes just too good and boring to write about. He writes of the rural life as good in principle in a classical way, but not as something anyone with ambition and ability would want to stick at for long. He was quickly bored of the horticultural delights of Chelsea, never mind the rural isolation of Cumberland. While Romantic poets went there to find inspiration from nature, Ashe was there on the run from the Carlton House gang, or whomever else he had offended, or threatened to offend. His appreciation of poverty, if not of poetry, was as profound and personal as Wordsworth's was. It could be argued that Ashe found real happiness in the backwoods of Maryland, but even there, the temptations of the newly founded political mire of Washington proved, temporarily at least, to be too great.

The *Memoirs and Confessions*, published in 1815, mention a brief stay in another rural idyll, the Isle of Man, in the 1790s, when, after the restoration of his half pay he wished to live a quiet independent existence. There he composed his 'tale of illicit love in undisguised realism', *The Manks Monastery of Memoirs of Belville and Julia*, described as the 'earliest Manx novel', which restored his finances after a characteristic series of failed ventures. Back again in the 1820s he was again publisher of literary works, including those of Elizabeth Craven, the author of *Ellan Vannin*, briefly the anthem of the island. Her poem 'A Dream of Glenmay' was included in the collection edited by Ashe. 'The Pier and Bay of Douglas, or, Forget Me Not from the Isle of Man' was published in 1825. He was also an early editor of the *Manx Sun*, founded to defend the constitutional rights of the Manx and the House of Keys against the powerful Duke of Atholl and later the landed interest against reformers urging public elections and the rising influence of trade.

Lady Sarah Murray, wife of the Bishop of Sodor and Man, adorned his Manx Sketchbook (also 1825) with lithographs. Among the illustrations was the Nunnery near Douglas, a real one this time. His life on the island as George Goodwin reported it in his 'Manx Annals' followed the familiar pattern of personal animosities and financial disaster punctuated by literary production.

In May 1823, Mr Ashe announced that the appearance of his new illustrated magazine would be on the first of the following month. He said the views for the first twelve numbers were then ready: Douglas Bay, Castle Mona, Castle Rushen, Dalby. Peel Castle, Falls of Rhenass and Glenmaye, Bishop's Court, prospect from Bishop's Court, Sulby Glen, Ramsey Bay, and Laxey Glen. Amongst the, monthly articles was to be 'The Hermit in Douglas, or Delineations of Manx Society'. Subscriptions 20s a year. Orders to be left at his study, Athol-street, Douglas.

Mr Ashe had previously started a museum; and got hard up. Then the magazine; but was still hard up. Then a lottery; and was floored. In October he laid his case before the public, thusly; 'Soon after my arrival in the Island last year, I had occasion to announce myself as a man sold to no side. It was a matter of indifference to me whether I took dinner at Castle Mona, Kirby House, Bishop's Court, or Ballagawne. But this independence as a politician was a death blow to me as a public writer and director of a museum. A dinner with the ex-deemster cost me one third of the Island, and my visits to the Lord Bishop lost me the other two-thirds. Goaded by claimants; and firmly convinced that any further struggles of mine to barter literature or talent for bread in the Island could answer no good purpose, I have to solicit my creditors to accept of my all — the contents of the museum, in lieu of their claims.'

Mr Ashe's plates for his intended magazine, I believe. came afterwards into the hands of Geo. Jefferson. At any rate, the latter published in 1826, for 7s 6d., 'The Manx Sketch Book or Beauties of the Isle of Man in a series of Lithographic Engravings', and the list, with the exception of one picture, was the same as that of the magazine.

As early as 1825 Douglas resident Mr T Ashe's A Manx Sketchbook [a] tourist guide, with illustrations by bishop's wife Lady Sarah Murray, extolled the delights of Sulby Glen to early tourists: 'This region, on the borders of the road from

Kirk Michael and Ramsey, is the most enchanting spot on the Island, and a singularly rich one... The scenery here is highly diversified. The ground is well covered with trees and shrubs, apparently all planted. The valley winds considerably... Swelling grounds, cultivated hills, naked rocks, variegated groves and falling waters, present themselves to view in stages rising above each other, till mountains clustering together in the background shut up the scene.'[1]

His connection to the Bishop would have unexpected results in the next chapter of his career.

When he returned to mainland Britain, perhaps becalmed by his idyllic sojourn despite his latest set of financial disasters, his pace was slowing and the powers opposing him were strengthening and becoming more recognisably those of a modern state. At last, he began lose the ability to keep a step ahead of the impending disaster that had threatened him from the beginning of his adventures. The masterly control of the *Memoirs and Confessions* which allowed him to skip merrily along in his own narrative, narrowly avoiding the full consequences of his own actions finally deserted him and he was overtaken by events. His world of gentlemanly blackmail as the ghost of his royal patron ended in the moral quagmire and conflicted loyalties of Caroline's trial. Her cause had lost its personal connection to her Irish friendships made at the court of Brunswick before her marriage, to be taken up instead by an opposition who found her politically useful as a tool with which to attack her husband, but who had little time for her as an individual. For all its sordidness this was a comparatively good-natured episode compared to what followed, the bitter conflict around the bills for Catholic relief and parliamentary reform, which saw the rise of the ultra-Tories against a renewed fear of revolution across the monarchies of Europe. Even darker forces were now at work. There was time for one last 'hurrah'.

Ashe's political and literary focus after the liberation of the Frogmore nunnery and the death of Caroline and her daughter Charlotte was to be Princess Sophia, 'one of the most lovely women that was ever condemned to a life of stagnant celibacy and Claustral sloth' as Ashe described her in *The Claustral Palace*. Happily for Ashe, she too traded in confidences and she had confided in her cousin Caroline the circumstances of her mysterious pregnancy in 1800. The equerry Thomas Garth, 'Tharg' in the gothic horror of

'Toadmore' in *The Claustral Palace* had been identified by Ashe as being the father in 1811. There was also gossip naming Sophia's own brother, Ernest, Duke of Cumberland, as the father. This had either been unknown or ignored by Ashe in 1811. Perhaps Ashe had been unwilling to credit the rumours, even if they came from Caroline directly, when he still remembered Cumberland as the valiant soldier of their shared campaign against France in the 1790s, the man who had assisted him when he returned from that conflict wounded and destitute. Even as late as 1811, Ernest was a man Ashe might have hoped for more from. Now the evidence presented by the younger Thomas Garth in the Court of Chancery provided new insight into the 'unnatural affections' to which Sophia had been subjected and Caroline's view of the child's paternity seemed more likely. It was politically opportune too, to attack the duke, since Cumberland was the most strident critic of the bill for Catholic relief. The case was altered.

Scarcely in modern history has someone so prominent in British public life, let alone a senior member of the royal family, had so many ugly rumours attached to their name as George IV's brother Ernest Augustus, Duke of Cumberland. Aside from the allegations in relation to Sophia's child, there was a more general suspicion on the part of the Prince of Wales and others that none of his sisters was safe alone in Ernest's company. Then there was the mysterious and bloody death of his servant Joseph Sellis in 1810. A commission of inquiry at the time found the death to be suicide brought on by remorse after Sellis had attacked the duke as he slept. The evidence of the inquiry, published in Cobbett's *Register* in July, was copious, meticulous and contradictory. Moreover, since many giving evidence were dependent on the duke and a verdict against a prince of the blood was in any case unlikely, the possibility remained that he had murdered Sellis and contrived his own wounds to lend credence to his own version of events. More recently came still more rumours of a 'Cumberland Plot' that he planned to have Princess Victoria murdered, to divert the succession from his brother Edward's child to his own. Cumberland it was said began a rumour that the Duchess of Kent was Sir John Conroy's mistress and planned to have Princess Victoria removed from her care, put away and even quietly disposed of on a pretext of accident or illness.

True or not, the nastiness and persistence of the rumours were testament to the level of animosity the duke generated and to his political importance. *The Claustral Palace* had dwelled on the unwilling uselessness of the royal brothers and sisters, debarred from employment and happy marriage. Cumberland, the 'tea table General', had in his youth in fact been closer to military action and more conspicuously valiant than his brother Frederick, the Commander in Chief had. Like Ashe, the wounds he sustained in the campaigns against Napoleon in the 1790s did him lasting harm and were said to have soured his character. Since his father's death, he had taken it upon himself to remind the new king, his brother George, of the obligations of his coronation oath, and to uphold the Protestant succession. Ernest took this convinced Protestantism a stage further than his father had done, as head of the Orange order.

The duke had returned to England in 1828 after years of self-imposed exile to stiffen the resolve of king against moves to Catholic emancipation. The Irish Catholic party tempted Ashe back to undermine the power of the duke by blackmailing him from the comparative safety of Cumbria. Again, our source for what happened next comes from the case files of the Treasury Solicitor. Rex versus Thomas Ashe 'for sending a threatening letter to HRH the Duke of Cumberland'.[2]

Characteristically, the legal action relates to Ashe's letter threatening the duke if the manuscript is not returned to him, but not the writing or the sending of the novel itself, the contents of which are too terrible to be mentioned and the return of which seem to be a matter of honour between gentlemen, rather than criminality.

The file begins with an undated covering note, headed by Ashe 'Important Revelation'. This was sent by Ashe to the duke, with the manuscript of 'Osphia'. It was retained in the Treasury Solicitor's papers as it gives an account of the composition of his extraordinary book.

No sooner had the Duke of Cumberland raised the Protestant standard than the leaders of the Catholics traduced and impeached him and this with the purpose of diverting public attention from their own crimes and designs.

With this in view Mr O'Connell announced his intention of causing the Cumberland question to be early investigated in Parliament and with the same view he and his associates collected materials and caused to be composed the annexed Manuscript entitled 'Osphia or the Victim of Unnatural Affections'.

Ashe then wrote of himself in the third person:

> The public writer they employed is one of those unfortunate Men of Letters who are reduced by poverty to barter their principles for bread. If you are a physician and want practice, turn atheist and be talked about, if you are an unpopular parson, preach mysticism and paradox and you will be rewarded, and if you are a Man of Letters in distress write slander...

Ashe claimed that he was duping his employers in sending the full manuscript rather than a synopsis to the duke. Was he acting out of old loyalty to Cumberland (for assisting him when he returned home from hospital in Bremen having been reported dead and deprived of his army pay), or because he thought he could get more for suppressing it than by publishing it? On balance, it looks more likely that Ashe was 'playing the Perceval game' again. He may have been commissioned by O'Connell's friends, as he claimed or simply have taken the opportunity to write on his own account when the political situation pushed up the costs of suppression. He told the Duke of Cumberland that he is withholding his address until he is sure of the duke's favourable reaction, because he fears he will return it unread. He chooses to send it through the police magistrate John Conant, presumably because of his long-standing connection with his father Nathaniel Conant, who had impressed him with his uprightness while trying to negotiate him away from the clutches of the Hydra. 'The author is no vulgar character... a remarkable man well-known to every branch of the Royal Family.'

If his father had indeed chosen to ignore John Bellingham's threatening notes to Spencer Perceval as the work of a crank, could his son John now ignore Ashe's threatening letters to the Duke of Cumberland? The Conants were a link between the magistracy and Ashe's world of bookselling. They barely needed Ashe's letters to remind them of the parallels with Perceval.

Ashe remained in hiding and in penury in Cumberland, his address given with deliberate vagueness as 'Rickerby cottage near Carlisle'. From there he sent a note asking Cumberland to reconsider before taking legal action against him. He asks him to recall a conversation '16 years ago' with the Countess of Berkeley (the Persecuted or perhaps Perjured Peeress) about 'Captain Ashe'. Is this a plea for compassion based on their shared experience of a woman who, in Ashe's account could turn suddenly vindictive and vengeful, or another threat, that the countess had confided in Ashe the details of Cumberland's marriage proposal to her and that he therefore had further blackmailing material at his fingertips?

He was definitely looking for compassion (and possibly for a longer memory than the duke possessed), when he took him twenty years further back in recounting his woes. Then, he recalled, the duke 'took him by the hand and sent him on his way rejoicing' when 'returning naked thro' Hanover from Gibraltar 36 years ago'. Or perhaps again he was looking to portray himself as a sinister figure, who had known the duke a long time, had been close to him on several occasions and had the knowledge and character to do him genuine harm. Ashe disputed John Conant's assertion that no one would publish 'Osphia' since he knows, he says, that J. J. Stockdale (the publisher of the blackmailing memoirs of Harriette Wilson) would. Ashe ended by asking his persecutors to pay postage if they returned the manuscript. These three instances of credit and threat when Ashe returned to England wounded in 1794, when he negotiated with The Family over the 'Perjured Peeress' and now in his connection with Stockdale were an odd cocktail of power and pleading. Even to someone more level-headed than the Duke of Cumberland, it would have been a confusing and disturbing letter, trading on his connections, their past association and confidences.

This must in some ways have been familiar if unwelcome territory for the Duke of Wellington too. Ashe employed the same law firm Mounsey and Gray of Carlisle used by the publisher of the memoirs of Harriette Wilson. John Joseph Stockdale had written to Wellington on 16 December 1824:

> In Harriette Wilson's 'Memoirs' which I am about to publish are various anecdotes of your Grace which it would be most desirable to withhold, at least such is my opinion. I have stopped the press for the moment, but as publication will take place next week, little delay can necessarily take place.[3]

This and an approach from the author herself prompted Wellington's furious 'publish and be damned' but he still threatened Stockdale with court action. In the end, Wellington neither paid for suppression nor took legal action and the passages relating to him appeared in the published version. They made him look doting and ridiculous, but did little lasting damage to his reputation.

The relief bill for Catholics also presented a threat to Wellington and to his relationship with the Duke of Cumberland, since Wellington came to regard it as a political necessity and Cumberland opposed it on principle regardless of the consequences. Tory opposition to the relief bill led to a duel between Wellington and Lord Winchelsea on 21 March 1829. Robert 'Orange' Peel piloted the relief bill through Parliament despite his religious convictions, in the belief that the potential for civil unrest in Ireland if it were not passed would be worse. Some Ultra Tories believed the government used the rotten boroughs to get the bill through in the teeth of popular anti-Catholic sentiment and that a more representative House of Commons would not have passed it, so they began to initiate moves for reform, essentially splitting the Tories as the anti-reform party.

The Catholic Relief Bill received royal assent on 13 April 1829 so any political purpose 'Osphia' may have had in blackmailing the Duke of Cumberland by O'Connell's party had evaporated by the time it came to the attention of the Duke of Wellington. O'Connell then switched his attention to the Union between Britain and Ireland, which Ashe also opposed.

There were signs of strain in the relationship between Wellington's tired government and the royal family over Catholic relief and electoral reform. Ashe's threat and the need to spend long, urgent meetings with the Duke of Cumberland was the last thing all of them needed. The Tory government was committed to bringing in legislation it disliked in order to avoid unrest. Fear of civil war on Ireland and revolution at home drove Wellington's government towards relief and reform, driving ultra-Tories into alliance with the Whigs. In the wake of Thomas Ashe's threat, Cumberland was compelled to consult Wellington and his senior law officers, but there was mistrust on both sides.

It was on 3 October 1829, that the Duke of Wellington became involved in the unsavoury business of Captain Thomas Ashe. He summoned Edward Drummond, clerk to the Treasury and private secretary to Sir Robert Peel, and the Treasury Solicitor George Maule to come and see him the following day at Downing Street to discuss the threat posed by Thomas Ashe. Drummond was to become famous in death when a would-be assassin mistook him for Peel as he approached his house and shot him. The possibility of political assassination is ever present in our story, and it is ironic that a man consulted by the Prime Minister about Ashe's

threatening letters to the Duke of Cumberland should himself have
been a victim. Drummond was to be buried in the same church as
Spencer Perceval, St. Luke's Charlton. Drummond's killer escaped
execution on the grounds of insanity. His insanity took the form
of a persecution mania about the Tories and their agents, a defence
Thomas Ashe, and many others could have advanced since.

Did Drummond and Maule only see Ashe's threatening letter, or
were they shown the dreadful manuscript of 'Osphia' itself, with
its claims of incest and murder? Perhaps Wellington thought it too
great a risk even to show it to private secretaries or to the Treasury
Solicitor himself, since on the following day he described it to
George Maule in a letter as being

> ...an atrocious libel upon the King and the whole Royal Family,
> particularly the Princess Sophia and the Duke of Cumberland.
> The letters show who the writer of the book is. There are some
> questions of law and others of discretion arising out of this case
> in its existing state. The first is whether this Captain Ashe could
> now be prosecuted for sending a letter to the Duke of Cumberland
> threatening to publish this libel if he did not pay him £100. If he
> can, it would it be prudent to bring the case forward as I conclude
> that the book threatened to be published must be produced in
> evidence. The next question is what we should do with the book?
> Shall we send it back to him leaving him to publish it at his peril,
> or shall we pay him the £100?[4]

On the same day the manuscript of 'Osphia' and papers relating
to its author were placed by Wellington in the 'Strong Closet' at
Downing Street. This was definitely not a case of 'publish and be
damned'. The threat was not just to one man's personal reputation
but a wider one to the state, at least in the mind of the Duke of
Cumberland, who was most directly concerned. The author himself
was still in hiding in his Cumbrian bolthole, and wrote on the same
day, 5 October 1829, to raise the temperature and concentrate the
minds of the Prime Minister and the government on the question of
his manuscript, when they should perhaps have been concentrating
on other things:

> Captain Ashe has advanced too far in the slough of desperation
> to think of Retreat. He must take refuge in the arms of his
> employers if repulsed by the Duke of Cumberland. At all events,

the Duke will have to treat him with humanity and generosity or send him back his manuscript. Should the manuscript be detained in contemptuous silence, as at present, Captain Ashe will be forced to seek its recovery by legal process. Any step of this nature would multiply the value of the manuscript to an immense degree.

There was a further gap of eight days to consider these legal questions before the next correspondence. Even letters about the case were sensitive and vulnerable, never mind the manuscript itself. There was a slightly furtive and uncertain note 'Can the papers be sent in the normal post to (The Duke of) Cumberland at Walmer Castle or should they go by messenger?'

Wellington had recently been appointed Lord Warden of the Cinque Ports and lived at Walmer Castle, spending August to November there most years. He died there in 1852.

There is another undated copy of a letter from Ashe, which declares his intention of coming to London to put his case to the Lord Mayor. As in his letters to the Duke of Cumberland, his claim of his connection with the Conants came with a veiled threat. He boasted to J. E. Conant that he held 'upwards of 100 letters of his (father's) in testimony of his respect for me'. Nathaniel Conant was always polite, but since their correspondence was likely to have been about negotiations for Ashe going to New South Wales or writing for the king's party in 1814, they were more likely to provide evidence of wariness, humanity and pity rather than respect. Perhaps these letters of respect were in fact intended as a reminder and a threat that he had retained evidence of official attempts to 'write the Queen down' at the time of her 'trial' in 1820.

The Duke of Wellington in the security of Walmer Castle still felt the threat of the prospect of Thomas Ashe coming to London. He wrote to John Singleton Copley, first Baron Lyndhurst, the Lord Chancellor, sending Ashe's note to John Conant for his legal opinion. It was obviously something to be discussed in person since Wellington told Lyndhurst he would be in London on Saturday.[5]

The Duke of Wellington also consulted Sir William Draper Best, Lord Wynford on Ashe's manuscript and the threat it posed. As a judge, Wynford, the Dictionary of National Biography tells us was notorious for bias and political prejudice. He recently given up his post as Chief Justice of the Common Pleas on the grounds of ill health. The legal advisers to the Duke of Wellington as Prime Minister were largely an unhappy, unhealthy and unpopular group of men, though not as incompetent and ineffectual as the group advising Spencer Perceval on the eve of his assassination in 1812. Lord Lyndurst did not believe Captain Ashe could be prosecuted for threatening to publish the libel unless paid a sum of money. However, sending the libel to the Duke of Cumberland counted as publication and Ashe could be prosecuted for that. Lyndhurst did not advise prosecuting Ashe and suggested that Cumberland should be told to take no notice of the letter.

The duke and Lyndhurst gave the king this advice; the king was not inclined to accept it and wanted something done. Then the temperature was raised again. The Treasury Solicitor Maule sent a second threatening letter from Ashe. Perhaps articulating a confidence he did not feel on 19 October 1829 J. E. Conant wrote a note from Great Marlborough Street police office to Ashe denying any knowledge of the whereabouts of 'Osphia'. 'I know nothing of the fate of your manuscript and must decidedly decline any further correspondence with you on the subject.' A note of the same day from Conant to George Maule complained of Ashe: 'his correspondence seems interminable.' Being his intermediary could be a tiring business. His letters and perhaps the novel itself were sent to Maule to be copied and filed, the originals were returned to Conant. Ashe was wearing the authorities down with the volume of his correspondence, rather than being worn down by them.

Lord Wynford in a copy letter to the Duke of Wellington agreed with Lord Lyndhurst and advised Cumberland not to prosecute for sending the 'libel' or for extortion 'threatening to publish a book charging him with murder' but only if published. 'I should be obliged to Captain Ashe if he would bring an action for his papers, that would give us an opportunity of letting the world know what a villain he is without disclosing more of the book than would answer that purpose.' This is the first and perhaps only indication in the correspondence that 'Osphia' contains reference to the murder of Joseph Sellis. Documents relating to the inquiry into the assault on the duke and the death of Sellis had been published by Cobbett in his *Register* in July 1810, the alternative scenario that Sellis had been murdered was well-known – but did Ashe have details to add from his own royal sources?

Wellington seemed to be outside London a lot, as if he would like to have left his responsibilities in London for others to deal with. Neither the duke nor Thomas Ashe would let him. This time he wrote from Sudbourne Hall in Suffolk. He sent Lord Wynford the latest instalment in the Ashe saga. Despite telling Wynford that the latest papers did not alter the case and were not worth sending to the Lord Chancellor, on the following day he did so, together with Wynford's reply. Wellington believed that on receiving Conant's reply Ashe might act as he had threatened and come to London to retrieve his manuscript and that the government should be prepared. Wellington asked if the papers should be laid before the Attorney General to enable him to take the necessary steps.[6]

On that day the Treasury Solicitor's file recorded that the Duke of Cumberland was 'not yet keen' to return Ashe's papers to the Treasury Solicitor. Four days later, he had done so, because by then the Treasury Solicitor had delivered both the manuscript of the novel and the related papers by hand to Wellington and had them returned to him by Wellington with the latest legal opinion:

> The Lord Chancellor has since answered ... that the whole should be laid before the attorney general in order that he may have a knowledge of the case and that he may be prepared to act at once in case Captain Ashe should put in execution his last threat or should take any other step to recover his work. Ever dear sir yours most faithfully Wellington.[7]

The apparent copying of 'Osphia' and related papers for ease of circulation within the government might have been necessary given the number of people being consulted about it. It was potentially a rather hazardous procedure, which risked the contents of the manuscript becoming more widely known.

While the government deliberated, Ashe changed tack, sending a threatening note via Wellington to Cumberland, presumably in the knowledge of the legislation relating to threatening letters, which offered a measure of protection if the letter were not sent directly:

> HRH The Duke of Cumberland is most respectfully informed through the medium of the Duke of Wellington that it is to his honour and interest to restore to a certain individual his property or to explain the motive of its detention. Were injustice and contumely not amongst the Vices of Mankind [George] Villiers, Duke of Buckingham and Spencer Perceval had never been assassinated.[8]

This threatening note, picked up by the Receiver of Letters at Kew, came with a General Post Office covering note from Francis Freeling, secretary of the Post Office to The Duke of Cumberland. The Duke of Wellington sent a copy of it to Lord Wynford, asking the Treasury Solicitor to lay it before the law officers of the Crown.[9]

Wellington gave his opinion to Wynford with the copy letter 'which I think goes as near the wind as possible'. This suggested that it came as close to being actionable in itself as Ashe could dare. Wellington told Wynford he had not troubled the Duke of Cumberland with the letter but asked him to mention the contents of it to the duke.[10]

On 29 October 1829, John Conant sent George Maule a letter from Captain Bell, presumably Ashe's friend Henry Bell who rescued him from the Hydra and acted in the murky negotiations around *The Patriot Princess*. His sensible friend of *The Memoirs and Confessions* was evidently still seeking money for his suppression of Ashe's earlier works, though in Conant's opinion the 'subject (was) so stale that the profit would hardly be worth the risk'. He enclosed the bonds we have already seen for the suppression of *The Patriot Princess* and *The Claustral Palace* poems, witnessed in Maule's chambers in Stone Buildings, Lincoln's Inn, an august legal setting for a lot of shady goings on. Presumably Bell thought it worth trying his luck to get his reward as a public-spirited citizen, now that Captain Ashe was notorious again. Or perhaps they were working together again and this was a timely reminder of Ashe's credentials as a writer.

On the last day of October came a letter from Ashe's solicitors Mounsey and Gray of Staple Inn (though with Carlisle connections) requiring the return of the manuscript of 'Osphia'. While it contemplated whether legal action could be taken against Ashe as a threat to the state, the government now faced the possibility of legal action from the man himself. With this letter came the only detailed description we have of the manuscript. 'Bound in green with yellow edges, contains 321 royal octavo pages and has the name of Colonel Hoffman on it'. This last was possibly a misnomer for Colonel Poten, the Duke of Cumberland's ADC. 'Captain Ashe has however been seconded by information from a quarter which leaves us no other alternative than the course we have adopted.' Could this mean that the revelations came from Sophia herself? This is a long book, not just a pamphlet hinting at a couple of disreputable incidents, but rather a level of detail as in *The Claustral Palace* likely to include 'dangerous sofas' and dresses of flame coloured taffeta decorated with Indian figures.

With perfect timing, on the same day, the Attorney General gave his opinion that the prosecution of Ashe could not proceed without the contents of the manuscript becoming known. This confidential legal opinion then made its way via Edward Drummond to the Duke of Cumberland.

Lord Wynford sent the latest from the Duke of Cumberland to the Treasury Solicitor. 'The Duke of Wellington informs me that he has put some papers in your hands relating to Mr Ashe of Cumberland.' Wynford confirmed Ashe's solicitors as being those who acted for Stockdale in publishing Mrs Wilson and that there were several actions against Stockdale in Common Pleas 'when I was in that court'.[11]

On the day after the Attorney General gave his opinion, the Duke of Wellington asked his Lord Chancellor if the government should prosecute, thereby risking the possibility of some of the 'libel' being printed, and enquired what the penalty for writing the letter would be.[12]

The question became whether it was worth prosecuting Ashe, and to punish him with transportation, if it meant the 'libel' would then be bruited. Wellington considered that 'if the Duke of Cumberland's life were in danger or if Ashe attempted to carry out his threat, he would have no doubts on the question. However, considering the persons at whom the libel was aimed, it was not expedient to take a step which would bring the libel to the notice of the public,' a clear indication that 'Osphia' was considered to be incendiary. Wellington enclosed a paper giving the Lord Chancellor's view of the subject. Wellington now wondered if the Duke of Cumberland's view of it had now changed.[13]

On 7 November 1829 another letter from Mounsey and Gray threatened a bill in Chancery or damages at common law in pursuit of the recovery of the manuscript of 'Osphia'. This was the route chosen by the younger Thomas Garth, bringing a bill in Court of Chancery to assert his royal paternity and associated rights. Ashe followed this note from his solicitors with a renewed threat of his own, addressed through Colonel Poten, indirectly again, it is to be 'as close to the wind as possible' without laying him open to prosecution. This note is annotated by the Duke showing it was delivered.

Silence is the policy of Sir Herbert Taylor [Private Secretary to the Duke of York and his go-between with Mary Anne Clarke] believe me it will answer no good purpose – besides those who despise the man should dread the dagger. The Duke of Buckingham and the Minister Perceval have taught the world this lesson.

Again, your silence gives publicity and you cannot be so darkly ignorant as to suppose that I can ever consent to leave my property without explanation in the hands of the Duke of Cumberland.

I am not disposed to say anything in the way of menace, but though it appears, from the annexed letter that your silence has weight with my London solicitors it has none whatever with me. I know how to break that silence without incurring the cost of Law and I consider it at once candid and honourable to tell you that should this note not be replied to in due course, I will proceed up to London and personally demand my property, my book, from the hands of the Royal Duke. This step, into which further silence must drive me, will lead to a breach of the peace and then the charm of the silence is broken at once.[14]

Thanks to Edward Law, Earl of Ellenborough's political diary, we know that the problem of Thomas Ashe was a repeated preoccupation of the cabinet meetings of the Duke of Wellington's government. Ashe was the only private individual recorded as having been discussed on 14 November 1829, alongside weighty matters of state:

Dined at the Duke's. A man of the name of Ashe is writing letters threatening the Duke's [Cumberland's] life if he does not give up a book in manuscript.

This book of Ashe's is a romance detailing all sorts of scandals of the Royal Family and of horrors of the Duke of Cumberland. The book is actually in the possession of Duke of Wellington.[15]

There are a couple of interesting hints here about 'Osphia' and its contents. First, that it ranged more widely than revelations about the Duke of Cumberland and secondly, that the 'horrors' of Cumberland were not a surprise to Ellenborough, though apparently, still unknown to the public. Ellenborough was a rising young man in a government of elderly men, still in his thirties he had been Lord Privy Seal since January 1828 and President of the

India Board since September of the same year. He had already had time to acquire his own whiff of scandal following his second marriage in 1825, which would lead to divorce in 1830.

Then Ashe's connections on the Isle of Man brought unexpected benefit in the form of a character reference from a bishop. Hugh Percy, Bishop of Carlisle, previously Bishop of Rochester, was on the face of it an odd man to testify to Ashe's blameless retired life in Cumberland. Percy had presumably responded to official enquiries about Ashe's recent movements and activities. He was definitely part of 'The Thing', William Cobbett's name for the corrupt self-interested nepotistic establishment. His ecclesiastical preferment came under the patronage of his father-in-law Charles Manners Sutton, Archbishop of Canterbury, who died in 1828, at which point his career stalled. He was an opponent of church reform and the best judge of a horse in the district, a High Churchman attacked by Chartists, a man who could presumably could be relied on to keep the authorities informed of the activities of dangerous disturbers of the status quo.

His note to Sir Robert Peel must have made disappointing reading for Peel, who had identified Ashe as a potential royal assassin. Ashe, Percy said, had come to reside in the neighbourhood of Carlisle early in the year, having previously been resident on the Isle of Man and acquainted with the present Bishop of Rochester (George Murray, whose wife had supplied lithographs for Ashe's *Manx Sketchbook*). Percy had moved from the see of Rochester to Carlisle so may have had this intelligence from his successor or from Ashe directly. Ashe, the bishop assured the authorities 'lives very retired occupied in Library pursuits'. Peel at the Home Office could go back to developing his new police force with a sense of reduced threat to the nation's law and order from Captain Ashe of Cumberland. Although, since Ashe's most recent substantial 'library pursuit' had been a 300-page book accusing a royal duke of incest and murder, perhaps this witness statement was not as anodyne as it appeared.[16]

On the same day that the bishop wrote his well-meaning assessment of Thomas Ashe's character, 16 November 1829, the Earl of Ellenborough's journal recorded a discussion about Ashe in Cabinet:

A long talk about Ashe who has written a libel on the Duke of Cumberland, which the Duke gave to the Duke of Wellington.

Ashe wants it back, and threatens if he has it not returned to him; but in a letter and in such terms that the Attorney General does not think him liable to prosecution. He might be held to bail perhaps, but that would bring out the case. It was decided to do nothing, but to take precautions against his doing mischief. The Duke of Cumberland has been cautioned.[17]

The Cabinet's discussion, probably coincidentally, introduced a debate about the administration of Ireland, but there may be a connection given the roots of 'Osphia' in the Irish Catholic interest. Ellenborough was not a lawyer like his father, but was clearly involved in the legal question of what to do about Ashe. This is further evidence of the seriousness with which the threat of Thomas Ashe was taken and the political risks involved in the various possible courses of action. No one wanted to commit himself to prosecute or say 'publish and be damned'

Robert Peel, keen to try out his new police force, bypassed the ditherings of the Cabinet. Ashe was a state matter to be dealt with by a trained executive, not just a personal nuisance to a member of the royal family. He had Ashe watched in Cumberland.[18]

Before correspondence about Ashe began again in the spring, there was time for another Duke of Cumberland scandal to blow up. Thomas North Graves committed suicide on 9 February 1830, the cause his wife's affair with the duke. So one of the men sent by the Prince Regent to treat with Thomas Ashe for the manuscript of *The Claustral Palace* had died following the machinations of the subject of his latest book. The Privy Purse William Knighton noted: 'Whatever might be his innocence to intrigue with Lady Graves, the public were in a state of mind not to believe it.'

It became necessary politically to distance the king from his brother. Knighton's diary at this time also gave this assessment of Wellington's character:

The Duke has strong sense, great resolution, but being wrong he has no power of setting himself right, either from the advice of his friends, or the contemplation of his own reflections. In this respect, he is Irish. There is much to admire in him, but a great deal to wish different. I mean as the Governor of a Kingdom. He has no humanity – no knowledge or power of judging that a man should be rewarded for civil service.[19]

Given this attitude, it was difficult for Wellington to manage scandals involving the king and his brothers, particularly Cumberland. Were they pillars of the state or a threat to law and order? Naturally, Cumberland had his own view of who was to blame for his predicament. He wrote to John Scott, first Earl of Eldon, a fellow opponent of reform, on the scandals alleged against him and the obstacles to his interests within the government:

> But really I am sick of boring you with such trash, the invention of malice and what is worse, if not encouraged, then at least countenanced by the papers in Downing Street, which that immaculate nest has been crying so much against in their own case; but I am determined positively not to follow the example of the Duke of Wellington and his double-faced Lord Chancellor [Lyndhurst] and put myself in the hands of Scarlett, never, for I should only raise a host of newspaper writers against me.[20]

So many scandals attached themselves to the Duke of Cumberland that it sometimes difficult to tell in the official correspondence which scandal is being talked about. The letters cited by Arthur Aspinall as referring to the Lady Graves scandal might just as well refer to 'Osphia' and the letters about Ashe in the strong closet at Downing Street. They show the tension in the relationship between the Dukes of Cumberland and Wellington and Ernest's reluctance to take the advice of Wellington, not to mention his distrust of the tactics of the other law officers including James Scarlett, the Attorney General since June 1829. There follows the suggestion by Cumberland that a statement of his innocence be made in the House of Lords. 'For in times of violent political feelings as we have been living in for the past two years, there is none among us who is not liable to such attacks.' Characteristically he blames the times and not his own behaviour, recognising the antipathy to him but not his own role in its cause.

Ashe meanwhile was composing his final letter before deciding to end his campaign of correspondence and come to London in person. Given their other preoccupations, it is understandable that the government was content to leave Ashe in his cold Cumbrian cottage. Finally in May came the letter that failed to sail close to the wind and landed Ashe in court:

Carlisle, May 27, 1830.

SIR, - I am an unfortunate public writer by profession, and after wasting a rather lengthened career in the uses and abuses of the press, I find myself a solitary individual of the world, a vagabond in appearance, and a beggar, in fact.

While smarting under this mortifying condition last summer, I composed a work allied to the honour and interest of H. R. H., the Duke of Cumberland, and I refused from the booksellers one hundred guineas for the work. I confided the work to the hands of H. R. H., on the strict condition that he should return it to me, or explain to me the motives of its detention. H. R. H. has detained it in his possession ever since last summer, and has resolutely refused to give me any explanation whatever on the subject. I have wrote to every person attached to the honour and interest of H. R. H.; many remain silent, while others assert that they have been enjoined by H. R. H. by no means to enter into any explanation with me about the work in question. I begged of Mr. Conant, the Magistrate, to apply to H. R. H.; his interposition is interdicted. I caused Messrs. Mounsey and Gray, the Solicitors, to institute legal proceedings against H. R. H. for the recovery of my work; they wrote to the private secretary of H. R. H.; he made no reply, and they refused to proceed further without I advanced the cost of proceeding by action of trover. I have not, Sir, the wherewithal to meet the exigencies of the day, much less to go to law with a Prince of the Blood Royal. What am I to do? Am I submissively to lose the subject and fruit of my labour, or am I to recover them, and to repel cruelty and contumely by such means as Fenton and Bellingham were driven to employ? I am doomed, and determined to recover them, or to perish in the attempt, and I now swear by the faith and honour of a man, and by that God who witnesses my distress, arising out of the Duke of Cumberland's conduct towards me, that if H. R. H. persists in detaining my property without explanation, that I will proceed up to London, and make the matter a personal question between us. This must make the question a question of Police, one that must fall within your jurisdiction, but as "prevention of crime" is said to be a marked feature of the New Police, I would implore you, Sir, to communicate with H. R. H., and to see that I recover my property from him without having recourse to measures that appal and horrify the mind. Bellingham wrote a letter of this nature to the late Sir Nathaniel Conant, the letter was regarded as an imbecile threat, and it cost Mr. Perceval his life. I want nothing of H. R. H. but my work; my property which he detains in his hands, and in proof that I wish to recover my work through legal agency, I invoke your interposition. If you refuse me that interposition, and regard this letter as an idle menace, you will act after the manner of Sir N. Conant, and invite the commission, in place of preventing crime. I have the honour to be, Sir, your obedient Servant, THOMAS ASHE.[21]

Ashe had alluded to the assassination of the Duke of Buckingham in 1628 and of Spencer Perceval in 1812 in his letter of 26 October 1829, but now the threat was more direct. Before he had suggested the same forces that had compelled John Fenton (usually Felton) and John Bellingham to acts of murder were at work on him. Now he was on his way.

The king was clearly dying, Wellington was looking to retire to allow Robert Peel the management of the House of Commons, and the government was described as 'peevish and disillusioned'. Still Wellington's papers show him corresponding with his law officers about the new evidence supplied by Thomas Ashe and the need to keep him under surveillance.[22]

The Earl of Ellenborough's diary confirms that Ashe's latest letter had tipped the balance and legal action against him had been agreed. 'One Ashe, who has libelled the Duke of Cumberland or written a threatening letter, will be prosecuted as if he had done the same thing against any private individual.'[23]

The Cabinet was also considering Lord Combermere's conduct in the government of India and the 'trouble brought upon us by Astell'. Presumably, this was William Astell, recommended by the Hydra and suggested by Ashe in *The Patriot Princess* for Princess Charlotte's Cabinet when she became Queen. Ellenborough suggests Astell's dangerous letter is ghost-written and he only signed it. Presumably, this was no longer a job for Ashe but some unfortunate successor 'ghost', writing for a new Hydra against the government. After his bitter experience with them, Ashe now preferred to operate alone from his hiding place in Cumbria. Astell had obviously become a significant figure, albeit it in the government of India rather than of Britain, without Ashe's help.

On 9 June 1830 Sir Robert Peel gave the Treasury Solicitor George Maule his not very profound but entirely accurate thoughts about Ashe's letter of 27 May. 'It appears to Sir Robert Peel that the writer holds out in this letter the threat of assassination.' Maule replied on 10 June that a course binding Ashe to keep the peace and indicting him for the letter might be pursued.

When on 26 June 1830 George IV finally died, naturally there was a break in the correspondence. It was a tumultuous time in Europe with the July revolution in France. On 13 July a letter arrived addressed to the chief of Police, marked post office Kensington, which announced that Ashe had abandoned his 'library pursuits' and had acted on his resolution to come to London in pursuit of his manuscript and the royal duke who kept it from him:

> Sir- I am so averse to a measure that is of a nature to plunge the Royal Family into a state of unqualified mortification and sorrow, that I again invoke you to see that HRH The Duke of Cumberland either returns to me my manuscript volume entitled 'Osphia' or accords to me an explanation respecting the detention of the same.
>
> I have travelled 300 miles on foot to obtain my manuscript or an explanation, and you sir have sufficient experience of crime and misery I know, that when a man with famine in his heart and blood upon his mouth is treated with injustice and contumely, justice should be rendered him before he is goaded into acts of desperation and illegality.

This latest note caused a tremor around the Prime Minister's office and Treasury Solicitor's department. Their correspondence becomes increasingly urgent and petulant in tone. It implied that they would soon have to deal with the man himself rather than just his messages. His claim to have walked to London was confirmed by agents following his movements and the correspondence carries the panicked annotation, 'Ashe is in town,'

On 15 July 1830, his sixtieth birthday, Ashe wrote again, still convinced that a combination of his importance and his poverty would win him some sort of special consideration from the Prince or his agents.

> I am a remarkable but not a common or a vulgar character, if the Duke of York had not deprived me of my half pay I might have been an honourable one… O'Connell &c suspecting my defection dared not attack the Prince in Parliament. Though the Prince has, for 12 months, kept me in a continual state of suffering and excitement, I never appealed to the Press.

He claimed to have had 'one answer to 50 letters'. His poverty rendered him unfit for London society, ill-equipped for the course of action the Prince's treatment had compelled him to take: 'I have no black coat – I wish anxiously to enjoy my accustomed savage and rural life.'[24]

Does this mean O'Connell's party intended to retain the manuscript to blackmail the duke and try and restrain his opposition to the relief bill, and that Ashe sending the manuscript to the duke 'on approval' broke his trust with them and that the party lost its lever over the duke?

On the same day Sir Robert Peel wrote to Wellington enclosing reports on Ashe's arrival in London and with the news that, despite Cabinet discussions of the possibility, the Duke of Cumberland had refused to exhibit articles of the peace against Ashe, so there was no direct action to be taken against him. Evidently Cumberland was still anxious to avoid an arrest and trial which might give a platform for Ashe's revelations about him. Peel assured Wellington that Ashe would be watched to prevent mischief.[25] The next day came the first report of Ashe's movements as he closed in on the duke's house on Kew Green. He was 'seen about the premises at Kew yesterday loitering'. When Ashe ventured to call on the duke the following day, the reports became more detailed.

This morning about 9 o'clock, he went to Kew, enquired for Colonel Poten at the Duke's House and was referred to Colonel Poten's house and went there, was informed that he was not at home. – [He] replied that [it] would not do, he must see him, [and] waited for some hours on the green about the house. – Then Colonel Poten went out to him and addressed him and took him in to the house and [Ashe] demanded the book and was told that the Duke had it not – he complained that he had had no dinner for five days. He said he must speak to the Duke about money, Colonel Poten said he could not speak to the Duke then. He replied it is very easy for you who dine every day to wait but I have not eaten for five days, Col. Poten then said as you are in such distress I'll give you five shillings, which he did and then went away.[26]

On the same day, James Scarlett, the Attorney General whom Cumberland had scorned in his letter to Lord Eldon, gave his opinion that Ashe could be bound over to keep the peace but not indicted. As Sam Phillips, Home Office Under-Secretary of State, put it to the Treasury Solicitor, 'He [Ashe] is become a serious annoyance to the Duke and something must be done without delay.' 'Something must be done', the war cry of every failing government since, was being used two hundred years ago.

Ashe was the first agenda point at a cabinet meeting later that day, recorded in the Earl of Ellenborough's diary:

> Cabinet. First, a question about what should be done about Ashe, the man who wrote a libel on the Duke of Cumberland, which he sent to him and now reclaims. He has written many letters indicative of an intention to assassinate, and has now come up from Carlisle on foot and has been walking opposite the Duke's house for three hours, having first written another letter of a threatening nature.
>
> Lord Wynford wrote to Peel on the Duke of Cumberland's part, but the Duke will not exhibit articles of the peace. Colonel Peter [Poten] gave Ashe 5s. and he went away.
>
> The question was what could be done with him? I suggested, as in a case of an expected duel, a magistrate on mere information that a breach of the peace was apprehended would take persons into custody and hold them to bail; so here the same thing might be done, one of the letters distinctly threatening a breach of the peace. This would secure the man, till it could be discovered whether there was legal ground to indict him for the letters. This will be done.[27]

On 18 July Lord Eldon wrote to Sir Robert Peel, primarily about Thomas Garth's Chancery case, but it was also a chance to review other current legal problem cases including Thomas Ashe. It must have seemed as if they all involved the Duke of Cumberland and that he had a habit of making the government's job difficult. At the back of their minds was the possibility that 'the libel' might be based in truth and legally defensible. 'Ashe might be able to argue he had been provoked by the matters of alleged misconduct in the several parties alluded to.'[28] Thomas Garth the younger was looking to blackmail the duke with incriminating letters of the elder Thomas Garth after the latter's death in 1829, Ashe exploited the renewed topicality which the proceedings brought. [29]

Thanks to the prompt actions of Thomas Quick of J Division and his colleagues in the New Police, with which this book began,

Thomas Ashe found himself bound over to keep the peace and under suspicion of having written a threatening letter to the Duke of Cumberland. There in the House of Correction for Middlesex in Cold Bath Fields, he kept himself busy doing what he did best, writing. By 22 July, he had drafted a petition and a covering note to the magistrate Sir Richard Birnie:

Sir Richard, The annexed is honest but not commonplace, I hope you will not object to it, but that you will employ it, as to release me if possible by Tuesday, when the 'Tourist' steamer starts for Newcastle from Blackwall, this would serve me most materially as Newcastle is but 56 miles from Carlisle.

I have now, Sir Richard, only to beseech you to mention my destitute condition to some high quarter or to take such measures as your humanity may suggest for making me ... a small purse to meet the exigency of my situation and allow me time to look around me in Cumberland and see, having a little time afforded me, whether I cannot produce a good in place of a bad book.

Could I get back to the maintaining myself 4 months, I could engage to redeem myself and become, instead of a mere slave in the mine of literature, a rich merchant and dealer in its wealth.

I do believe you will, Sir Richard, endeavour to give me this one fair trial, to prove the purity of my views and intention. I would not want the necessary funds in hand, but sent to me to Carlisle monthly. Say £10 in hand to relieve me here and convey me down and £10 monthly for 4 months; that is £50 in all and this would effectually serve to save me and stand between me and those miserable characters who subsist by the abuse of the press.

I declare I shake and tremble at the idea of going destitute out of this prison and being compelled to prostitute my pen. I absolutely would prefer to remain in prison. To pursue and yet to abhor crime is a fearful destiny! A destiny ever mine.

Do, Sir Richard, mention these things to the barrister I saw at your offices and such others as might by the expension of £50 to save reform and regenerate a sinking man. One thing is certain; I am not a lost character. I possess the materials of reformation and only want the fashioning hand of humanity to receive the sterling and obtain currency. Stand by me Sir Richard on this occasion and you will never have cause to regret and I ever will be the most grateful of men THOMAS ASHE

I beg the great favour of Sir Richard to forward the letter of
Capt. Clowes and to add a recommendation to it. It is necessary to
pay the inland postage and Mrs Ashe who enjoys under the Irish
Government a considerable pension, lives with him. Has she not
a right to make me some allowance, seeing that she prefers living
separate from me. While our daughter was unmarried I never
looked for a shilling, I think I now may. Without Sir Richard
recommends the measure it never will be attended to, nor would
the letter be answered.

I wish to strain every nerve to get out of London.[30]

Almost lost in this flood of requests comes the revelation that
Ashe has a daughter of marriageable age. His *Memoirs and
Confessions* do not mention a marriage apart from to Fauveen,
the 'woman of colour' in America in 1799, let alone a family.
Ashe is obviously separated from his wife and from his daughter,
who if old enough to marry in 1822 was certainly old enough to
have figured in the memoirs, which took his life to 1815, but she
does not. Despite her father's reputation and continual absence,
Elizabeth married well and reputably. It was perhaps not a
surprise, given his aversion to domesticity and his ceaseless high
wire adventuring, that his wife preferred to live separate from
him. His failure to make any mention of them in his memoirs is
presumably an indication that his behaviour towards them would
have lowered him in the esteem of his readers to a level even he
could not risk.

Perhaps the separation and peculiar financial arrangements
explain why they do not appear in his frequent petitions of poverty.
He is not out to highlight his domesticity in the memoirs, but his
treatment of them would probably have been in keeping with what
we know from other sources.

Ashe's daughter Elizabeth's marriage was at Smyrna in July
1822 to Captain (later Admiral) Thomas Ball Clowes. Was Ashe
there to give her away? Or was that left to her mother? Admiral
Clowes left a 'poetical commonplace book' and naval journals
covering this period, now at the National Maritime Museum. If
Clowes had a literary side he might not be as hostile to his father-
in-law as all that. Eight years after the marriage, his father-in-law
was in the House of Correction sending, as usual, a petition to the
authorities.

22 July 1830

To His Royal Highness The Duke of Cumberland &c

The Petition of Thomas Ashe, Paria[h] and Prisoner in the House of Correction, Middlesex

Humbly sheweth: That in all that relates to the MS entitled 'Osphia' his 'poverty not his will consented'. That he implores HRH to employ the Roman adage 'The Gods, willing to ruin him, first make him mad [odd rendering of Quem deus vult perdere prime dementat]. That the legal proceedings arising out of his writings and conduct have made Sir Richard Birnie the arbiter of his destiny; and that Sir Richard, in all cases within his power, is disposed to forbearance and clemency.

On 23 July, Sir Richard Birnie dutifully forwarded Ashe's petition with a covering note to Colonel Poten for the Duke of Cumberland: 'the petitioner assumes too much when he attempts to make me his friend or mediator.' On the next day, Parliament was dissolved and elections took place across the following month. Despite these and despite the revolutionary fervour sweeping Europe in the summer of 1830, the cabinet of the Duke of Wellington was preoccupied with that major potential threat to the social order in Britain, Captain Thomas Ashe. Again, George Maule, the Treasury Solicitor, was the government official whose task it was to deal with an annoyed Duke of Cumberland for whom the interests of the nation and his own personal ones were the same thing. Even in handcuffs and in Newgate, the problem of what to do with him and his manuscript had not gone away. They could not stop him writing further letters and petitions.

It was an ill-tempered royal duke who received and responded to Ashe's petition. On 25 July, the following curt missive came from St James's Palace:

The Duke of Cumberland presents his compliments to Mr Maule and requests he will have the goodness to come to his apartments tomorrow Monday 26th at 3 o'clock pm [for] a meeting between the Duke, the earl of Eldon [and] Lord Wynford concerning Ashe's business. He further requests Mr Maule [bring] all the letters and correspondence of the said Ashe as it is absolutely necessary that the earl of Eldon should see all their contents prior to his being able to give an opinion, though time presses as Ashe is to be brought up [for committal] on Thursday. But about the manuscript 'Osphia' upon which the whole turns, they were all delivered to the Duke of Wellington by Lord Wynford at the express command of his late Majesty George IV,[31]

The king had thought them safer in the 'strong closet' at Downing Street. Did Wellington want the papers the king had entrusted to him? Perhaps like his brother Ernest, the king saw Ashe as a threat to the state rather than a matter of legal opinion. Cumberland conspicuously left out the law officers he did not trust. The Treasury Solicitor immediately reported the outcome of the meeting: that not to prosecute was still thought to be the lesser of two evils. Maule had Ashe moved from the House of Correction to Newgate Prison and suggested some strategies which might ease his predicament, if he promised not to bleat in court. Nonetheless, he was evidently too dangerous for the House of Correction and merited being moved to the greater security of Newgate.

Ashe was examined in private before 'the arbiter of his destiny', Sir Richard Birnie. He was placed at the bar, charged and, gratifyingly, recognised as the author of *The Spirit of the Book*. The initial indictment at Bow Street was very cloak and dagger, the only indication of the cause of Ashe's arrest being the presence of the Treasury Solicitor Mr Maule. Ashe was described as 'an elderly man of very respectable appearance'.

Friend or not, Sir Richard Birnie transmitted Ashe's memorial to the right quarter of government and sent a letter from him to his daughter as Ashe had requested. Ashe nonetheless complained:

It appears that I am to contend with the whole power of Government. At my time of life without friends of means these are fearful odds and the difficulties which I shall have to encounter are still farther increased by withholding from me a manuscript which is absolutely necessary for my defence.[32]

Ashe was reported sent to Newgate in handcuffs 'lightly ironed' ('a precaution not usually resorted to') to await trial at the Old Bailey. Maule reported Ashe's commitment to Newgate for trial at the Old Bailey in the second week of September, 'When it will probably be necessary to trouble HRH to attend as well as Colonel Poten.'

On 9 August 1830 John Helyan Rocke, a friend of Ashe for forty years, wrote to suggest that his conduct might stem from a disordered mind, evident from his letters over the past year. Is this the Mr Rooke of Cheyne Walk mentioned in the Treasury Solicitor's papers at the time of the suppression of *The Book*? Possibly not, as he wrote from Somerton, Somerset, rather than Chelsea. Perhaps he was a connection of Ashe's curate brother. He might simply have been a well-informed philanthropist, since he appears as a petitioner in favour of other prisoners too.

The same series of Home Office papers related to legal opinion that recorded Spencer Perceval's lawyers' view of *The Claustral Palace* carry a further petition by Ashe from Newgate infirmary dated 13 August, which went close to suggesting the same thing:

> I reject the aid of counsel and interposition of the press and that in defending myself 'in forma pauperis' to palliate my offence and mitigate my punishment. I shall not name in court the unfortunate manuscript, nor shall I utter one single word or sentence, which can possibly hurt the feelings of your royal client. For 40 years I have been a distressed man, I am now 60 and covered in wounds, besides 2 fractures in the head, I have ever been misunderstood, misrepresented, misused.[33]

At this point Ashe offered, in return for the dropping of the prosecution, to be put under the surveillance of Sir Richard Birnie and sent to New South Wales. No doubt as he did in 1814, he would have missed the boat.

On 16 August an anonymous note to the Treasury Solicitor connected Ashe again with John Joseph Stockdale the publisher, 'Harriette Wilson's man ... the person who can best inform you.' How were the authorities supposed to react to anonymous notes of this kind? Had Ashe planned to publish 'Osphia' through Stockdale, presumably, he would have no copyright protection and therefore no profits were to be expected from such an 'immoral' work. Suppression money was the only likely option for Ashe to make a financial return on his labour and Stockdale, like himself, was an expert in gaining money for suppression.

The government evidently took Ashe's offer to have himself transported seriously. Ashe's enclosure asking for stay of prosecution was forwarded by Peel to Wellington. The Attorney General confirmed that prosecution was likely to be 'very unpopular if that be of any importance in the present day'. Presumably, this was a reference to the revolutionary political atmosphere. He added, not particularly helpfully, 'Sir Robert Peel and the Duke of Wellington must decide for themselves about Ashe's letter.' Wellington was still Prime Minister, governing with some reluctance until November, increasingly unpopular and disillusioned. His law officers appeared to think Ashe's fate was a political decision, the ministers that it was a legal one.

Among the lawyers, hopes of a conviction were fading. On 4 September John Conant the magistrate wrote to the Treasury Solicitor George Maule, to admit never having seen Ashe in the act of writing, so the case against him was probably dead in the water before the prosecution was brought. Four days later legal opinion confirmed that the charge could not be maintained, as the letters were not sent directly to the person threatened. This suggests that the prosecution proceeded only on political insistence. Perhaps Ashe had this opinion from his own solicitors, since, when his trial came, he seemed very relaxed.

The Attorney General, James Scarlett, was convinced of the unpopularity of the prosecution, but he was also concerned about the security of the manuscript of 'Osphia', which was in a locked desk drawer in his library at Abinger, protected only by dangerously inquisitive servants. He was asked for his legal opinion and for reassurance on the location of the manuscript:

> 'As to the MS It is locked up in the second drawer from the top facing the right hand as you sit at my bureau in my Library with your face to the window.' 'Send the key or bring it to town. [The] defendant might ask the judge to look at it. On no consideration ought it to be shewn to the jury.'[34]

Legal opinion also confirmed the late king's order in relation to the security of Ashe's papers as one of his last acts. On his death bed he feared the consequences of his legacy for the monarchy, buying, stealing, destroying and securing incriminating papers, shoring up the positions of his mistresses and his brothers against a background of revolution, when an incendiary manuscript like 'Osphia' might be a spark to tinder that could engulf The Family.

Writing on 13 September, James Scarlett was still paranoid about the security of Ashe's manuscript in the locked drawer of his library desk and the precautions that should be taken in retrieving it. He gave repeated instructions on which drawer the manuscript was in and what to do 'if the old woman in the room should look suspiciously at you'. These were undoubtedly peculiar circumstances and odd language for two senior law officers to use in the course of their duties, but the nature of Ashe's manuscript meant that nothing was quite usual or as it should be. There was something furtive about the government, as if it knew its days were numbered. The Duke of Cumberland was someone whose reputation it was obliged to try to maintain, but about whom it had its own reservations. There is something oddly noble and straightforward about Ashe's elegantly worded petitions from a position of penury and powerlessness and there is something of the language and behaviour of a conspiracy in the tired and unpopular government clinging to power.

As the date of Ashe's trial approached, the duke perhaps felt he should no longer summon the government's law officers directly. Instead, Colonel Poten, who would be called upon to give evidence, had a final meeting with the Treasury Solicitor on the following day,

The proceedings against Ashe, like so many high-profile trials before and since, combined notoriety with insufficiency in law. This acted as a deterrent to those called to give evidence. On 15 September, Charles Yardley, a clerk in the office of the police and a somewhat reluctant witness, wrote excusing himself because of a cold on the eve of the trial. While Yardley made his unavailing excuses, the accused Thomas Ashe in Newgate infirmary sent another note, rowing back somewhat from his promise not to involve the duke in the legal proceedings. 'Captain Ashe cannot protect his interests without the testimony of Colonel Poten & His Royal Highness The Duke of Cumberland. But he will put no question to either of them of a nature to wound their feelings.'

The Treasury Solicitor's file records the gaol delivery of Ashe by Colonel Poten on 16 September to stand trial, with a covering note from Poten of like date and the Crown brief, which was pretty thin. The Times of Monday 20 September 1830 reported Ashe's trial at the Old Bailey on the previous Thursday, where he stood indicted for threatening to murder the Duke of Cumberland. The report suggests Ashe kept his promise not to refer to the contents of his manuscript at his trial as there was no mention of it, so the whole point of his threatening letters was left obscure to the public.

'Thomas Ashe aged 60, author... a most respectable-looking Irishman about six feet high … was attired in a blue frock coat.' He was still living in Carlisle at this point, but his immediate address was the 'miserable lodging house' at 17 King Street Kensington. The indictment appears to suggest that the murder was to be committed at Kew (the Duke of Cumberland's house on Kew Green) on 27 May, the date of Ashe's letter. Ashe was not even in London in May, his appearance on Kew Green being on 17 July. The indictment appears to confuse the date of Ashe's threatening letter with his appearance on Kew Green, as if he were able to commit murder from three hundred miles away purely with the power of his pen.

The trial was held before Mr. Justice Bayley. Sir John Bayley was popular with barristers including Brougham, on the grounds of his competence and lack of bias, so perhaps Ashe was lucky. By convention, the judge's questions to the witnesses are attributed to 'the court' in the proceedings that follow.

'Thomas Ashe was indicted for that he, on the 27th of May, did knowingly, wilfully, and feloniously send a certain letter to His Royal Highness Ernest Augustus Duke of Cumberland, threatening to kill and murder the said Duke, which letter is as follows (the letter of 27 May read out).' There were two further, lesser, counts, charging him with sending a certain letter without stating to whom and causing and procuring the said letter to be sent to His Royal Highness the Duke of Cumberland.

Sir John Gurney conducted the prosecution. He had led the prosecution of the Cato Street conspirators in 1820 and held first place at King's Bench ahead of both the Attorney General and Lord Chancellor. He discovered to his dismay that there was a certain vagueness about the evidence of the police officers. It appeared, understandably, that no one had attached much importance to Thomas Ashe's threatening letters at the time they were sent and they struggled to remember the circumstances surrounding them, now that they had unexpectedly become the subject of an Old Bailey trial. Charles Yardley had recovered from his cold overnight. Perhaps Sir Robert Peel himself had convinced him it was in his professional interests to do so.

Charles Yardley: I am a clerk in the office of Police, Whitehall-place, Middlesex. I recollect receiving a letter by post (looking at one) – I believe this to be it, I have no doubt about it, except that

I did not mark it; I gave it to Mr. Mayne, the commissioner – it was in an envelope when I received it; I broke the seal – it was addressed, "To the commissioner of Police" on the envelope; I gave it to Mr. Mayne, with the envelope – I read it first, and have no doubt it is the same.

Court. Did you deliver to Mr. Mayne more than one letter of that description?

Charles Yardley: I did, but one other, that was to the same import as this.

Mr. Gurney. Is this letter written in blue ink, the other?

Charles Yardley: Yes.

Court: Where did you get that letter?

Charles Yardley. I received it in the same manner by post; I speak with certainty to the second letter, but not to the first – I only delivered Mr. Mayne two of this description.

Richard Mayne was first joint commissioner of the Metropolitan Police; he led the first patrol on 29 September 1829 and recruited and trained the first constables. He merited 'Esquire' after his name and spoke with greater assurance than Charles Yardley, but he could not overcome the fundamental flaw in the evidence.

Richard Mayne Esquire: I am a commissioner of the new Police. I received this letter from Mr. Yardley, it was in an envelope; I threw the envelope away after a few days – I sent the letter under seal to Colonel Poten; this other letter, written in blue ink, and signed Thomas Ashe, came a considerable time afterwards.

Court: Did you make any mark on the letter before you sent it to Colonel Poten?

Richard Mayne Esquire I did not; I had observed it sufficiently to know it is the same – I had frequent occasion to notice it; there is a mark here – I am not sure whether it was made by myself; I believe not, but I observed it shortly after.

Colonel Frederick Poten . I am aid-de-camp to His Royal Highness the Duke of Cumberland – (looking at the letter) I received this letter from Mr. Mayne, at least from the commissioners of Police, sealed in a cover; it was accompanied by a note which I have not got – I do not know what has become of it; I believe it is destroyed – I did not keep it; I do not keep notes of that kind – I read the letter; I gave the letter and note to His Royal Highness, who read it in my presence.

It was at this point that the prisoner Thomas Ashe, rather than keeping quiet and listening to the mess the prosecution was uncovering with smug satisfaction, chose to intervene in his own defence. 'I wish to ask Colonel Poten when he delivered the note and enclosure purporting to be mine, what observation did His Royal Highness, make to him, Colonel Poten?' Given that Ashe's hope of acquittal rested on the lack of proof that he had written the letter cited in the indictment, it seems a risky strategy to exhibit so much interest in its effect on its intended victim. Colonel Poten: 'I do not recollect what observation His Royal Highness made on it.' Ashe was not content with this answer and pursued his theme.

Prisoner: I wish to ask whether Colonel Poten does not recollect some gesture or passion, which indicated His Royal Highness' mind?

Colonel Poten: I do not exactly.

Mr. Gurney. Did His Royal Highness direct you to do any thing with the letter?

Colonel Poten: Yes, he directed me to send it to Lord Wynford – I am doubtful whether I sent it or took it myself; if I sent it, it was under seal.

Now Thomas Quick of 'J' Division had his moment in the spotlight.

Thomas Quick: I am an officer of the Police. On the 17th of July I was stationed at Kensington, and at seven o'clock that morning I saw the prisoner come out of a house, No. 17, King Street, Kensington Square; I followed him to Kew Green, and there saw him accost a man who had the appearance of a servant, dressed in mourning, with a white apron on; this was about two hundred yards from the

Duke of Cumberland's gate, the servant went in a direction for the Duke's gate; I did not see him enter, as a carriage drove up and hid him from view – I saw the prisoner looking very earnestly into that carriage – I afterwards saw the servant come back, and speak to him; the prisoner walked backwards and forwards in front of the Duke's house for an hour and a half, and then walked away.

Prisoner. Who instructed you to follow my steps?

Thomas Quick: My superintendent (Mr. Williams) directed me closely to observe you, and follow you wherever you went; he did not tell me for what purpose.

Prisoner: Were you informed my object was assassination?

Thomas Quick. Not directly; I had no directions whatever in that respect – I had no instructions to hinder you from committing mischief.

Prisoner: Would you have prevented me from murdering the person I addressed that day, or any other person?

Thomas Quick: Most certainly I would – it did not appear to me that you and the person you spoke to were strangers to each other by any means; I did not see him smile at you; but from the affability of manners, I thought the prisoner and him were acquainted; there was a report of a marriage taking place that morning; I observed a few people going in a direction for the chapel, but not many; there was no public assemblage – I did not know that the Rev. Mr. Jelf, the tutor to Prince George [of Cumberland] was going to be married that morning to a lady in waiting. [Emmy, Countess Schlippenbach, lady-in-waiting to Frederica, duchess of Cumberland.]

Court: You did not know that any body belonging to His Royal Highness' household was to be married that day?

Thomas Quick. No.

Prisoner. Were there not several carriages rolling by the residence of the illustrious personage in question?

Thomas Quick: I observed two, one stopped at His Royal Highness' gate; two or three people got out and entered His Royal Highness' residence; two of them were ladies; I cannot swear whether there was a third person or not; I do not know whether you were reading the motto on the carriage, nor whether the motto was "Felix in Felix" – I cannot tell whether you were armed; I saw no arms – he kept his right hand in his coat pocket; the pocket was in the pleat – I could not judge whether any arms were there, as it was a large surtout coat; I saw nobody but the servant hold any conversation with you – I had no instructions to prevent you assassinating any person, but on my own responsibility I would have done it.

John May. I am a superintendent of the New Police. On the evening of the 17th of July I went to No. 17, King Street, Kensington, and there found the prisoner; I took this letter with me – [the one written in blue ink] – I only had that letter at that time; I showed it to the prisoner, and asked if he knew the hand-writing – he hesitated a little, and answered Yes; I then asked if he had been to Kew that day – he said he had; I asked if his name was Thomas Ashe – he said Yes; I asked if he was from the north, near Carlisle – he said he was; I then took him into custody: on the 19th, at twelve o'clock in the afternoon, this other letter was shown to him at Bow-street, by Sir Richard Birnie, while he was under examination; what he said was taken in writing.

Prisoner. Was Saturday, the 17th, the first day you called at my lodging?

John May. No; I believe I first called on Thursday, the 15th, or on Friday, it might have been Wednesday – I will not be positive whether it was Wednesday or Thursday; I spoke to the landlady of the house – I was in private clothes.

Prisoner: Was the object of your visit to debauch her mind, or set her as a spy on my actions?

John May. No; I did not tell her I was an officer, or desire her to conceal from you that I had called; I know I could have apprehended you before I did; I took you exactly at a quarter before ten o'clock in the evening – I believe you were either in bed or getting in; the door was locked or bolted – you had come home about ten minutes before I arrived; I had no opportunity of taking you earlier on that night: you stated you had taken physic, but did not appear unwell; you said you were the writer of that letter: there were no arms in your room; there was nothing suspicious in your appearance or demeanour.

Whether he meant it or not there was a pleasing sense of coherence that the final evidence, or lack of it, which rescued Thomas Ashe, should come from a Conant, a family who had been rescuing him from tight places for nearly twenty years.

John Edward Conant, Esquire. I am a Police Magistrate. I know the prisoner; I have correspondence with a person of the name of Thomas Ashe, but have never seen him so as to know he was the person with whom I corresponded.

There being no proof of the letter charged in the indictment [not the one in blue ink] being in the prisoner's handwriting, the prosecution was here abandoned. There being no independent witness to confirm that the note cited in the indictment was in Ashe's handwriting, the judge instructed acquittal.

NOT GUILTY.

On 18 September 1830, two days after the trial, the Treasury Solicitor informed the Home Office in the person of Sir George Clerk, baronet, of Ashe's acquittal. On 5 August he had become under-secretary for the Home department for the few remaining months of the Wellington administration. Ashe had provided the Home Office with another unwelcome legal precedent.[35]

In November came Wellington's declaration of the perfection of the unreformed constitution and parliamentary system and his resignation as Prime Minister following defeat on the civil list bill. John Joseph Stockdale was still blackmailing him.[36]

In February 1831, J E Conant extended the grudging benevolent role of his family in the fate of Thomas Ashe, telling George Maule, 'The enclosed is from T. Ashe, I have disbursed a guinea according to his request and hope we shall hear no more of him.'[37]

It can have been no surprise to London's magistrates or the officers of the newly constituted police force that John Conant's guinea was not a large enough bribe to dispose of Thomas Ashe permanently. Despite his determination to resume his 'savage' life in Cumberland, Ashe had not finished with the duke or with the manuscript of 'Osphia'. The bill easing the penalties against Catholics may have passed into law, but there was still reason to attack the Duke of Cumberland, and further mileage and potential reward in seeking to recover 'Osphia' in person.

In 1835, Ashe was back again in the House of Correction in Cold Bath Fields for breach of the peace in relation to the manuscript of 'Osphia'. He was now aged nearly 65. He evidently looked older as his petition to the Home Office recorded his age as 70. Perhaps he lied about it in an attempt to emphasise his vulnerability.. He was still petitioning, believing he could write his way out of trouble at the very last. His crime was to have caused a breach of the peace in dispute over a manuscript with Duke of Cumberland and failure to find bail of £400 or two sureties of £200 each. His sentence was to be bound to keep the peace for two years.

In Ashe's characteristic hand, the petition is addressed 'To the right honourable Secretary of the Home Department' and then at the bottom annotated, presumably in description of himself, not the Home Secretary 'A Hard Case'. Despite this literary background, he admitted that in seeking to recover his manuscript from HRH the Duke of Cumberland 'he unfortunately made use of language not considered legal in the eyes of the law'.

> That in consequence he was conducted to Whitehall, committed to the House of Correction for two years or find bail himself for £400 and two sureties of £200 each!!!
>
> That being 70 years of age he has outlived his relatives and early connections – is a solitary and destitute individual of the world, without a patron to importune or a friend to invoke. Hence, he cannot find bail. He cannot!
>
> That thus circumstanced and seeing his broken constitution and considering his fractured head and body wounded in the King's service, an imprisonment of two years in the House of Correction must be considered a life sentence. [Then in slightly smaller writing, evidently added as an afterthought for dramatic effect] Already has he one foot in the grave.

Ashe might have been accused of melodrama again at this point, he was after all only 65, but his estimation of the weakness of his constitution was in fact accurate, as he would not survive the year.

He complained of the harshness of the regime, since his only offence was not finding bail. He suggests he would likely have received a lighter sentence if put before a judge and jury for actual assault.

He held out, even in these circumstances, the prospect of his pen being wielded in another quarter with an air of menace. 'The memorialist entertained the ambition of petitioning Parliament, but yielding to the kind advice of Governor Chesterton and the recommendation of the Visiting Justices, he relies solely on the humanity of the Right Honourable the Home Secretary.' At least for the next three weeks this source of humanity was Henry Goulburn in Robert Peel's Tory government. From 18 April, it was Lord John Russell in Lord Melbourne's Whig administration.

> That the memorialist never intended to injure or insult the Royal Duke, that he now abandons all claim upon him, and pledges his faith and honour as a soldier and a gentleman, that he will never again write of, or about, the Duke of Cumberland – no never again and he entreats the illustrious Duke may see this pledge.

This was signed 'Tho: Ashe, underneath 'Commonly called Captain Ashe', as if his fame was still a factor, despite his loneliness and destitution.

Ashe still felt it was worth complimenting the Home Secretary on his facility before adding a final reminder of his own unsuitability to be housed in it. In a postscript written in the margin, he added: 'The House of Correction is admirably suited for correction and that of Cold Bath Fields is admirably conducted, but it was never intended for a poor, infirm old officer, gentleman and author, merely in want of bail.'[38]

He had of course given similar solemn promises before. Nonetheless, Ashe's petition was evidently successful, for within months he was in Oxford and then finally back in Bath, where *The Claustral Palace* had been written in the summer of 1811. Bath, 'the paradise of women' as he had called it in *The Charms of Dandyism* was presumably the best and final place in Britain to win further confidences from the ageing beauties of the Regency, coming to take the waters to treat the ailments they had acquired in their stylish youth. They, alongside Ashe, had become relics of a more dashing and disreputable age. There is a rather Ashe-like figure among Dickens's creations, an adventurer and raconteur of an earlier age. Mr Jingle amazes the Pickwick Club with anecdotes of his travels, a storyteller you cannot quite believe, but want to because of the vividness of his story telling. Like Ashe, he is redeemed from debtors' prison and promises to live a reformed life if sent abroad. Ashe had become a Pickwickian leftover, a piece of very shabby gentility, on his uppers in Bath on the cusp of the railway age, which made everyone a traveller and no one an adventurer. Dickens reported on the passage of the Reform Bill in *The Mirror of Parliament*, a rival to Hansard, Did he and Thomas Ashe cross paths? John Barrow the editor and Dickens's maternal uncle, was known to Ashe on the Isle of Man. Ashe was a journalist who had been everywhere and known everyone but whose day had now passed. *The Pickwick Papers* in 1836-7 look back to the age just gone in another way, back to an era of incriminating love letters and the absurdity of the law in interpreting them. Instead of Henry, Duke of Cumberland's cloying missives to Lady Grosvenor or the stolen and purchased letters produced in evidence by the Milan Commission for the 'trial' of Queen Caroline, we have notes about chops and tomato sauce constructed into a promise of marriage by Mr Pickwick to Mrs Bardell, thanks to the enterprising legal mind of Mr. Serjeant Buzzfuzz. The blackmailing potential of those many royal and aristocratic indiscretions had become purely comical.

His obituary in *The Gentleman's Magazine* gave some background to Ashe's last days before his arrival in Bath. 'Mr Ashe was in Oxford a few weeks since, in a very distressed state, and received alms from the Anti-Mendicity Society.' The Oxford Charity Organisation and Anti-Mendicity Society provided small sums 'for the relief of distressed travellers' attending to a variety of clients including mad failed dons and disaffected undergraduates who had taken to roaming the countryside like The Scholar Gipsy. No doubt if there was a written application. Ashe's would have been beautifully worded.

From Oxford to Bath was a short walk for a man who had managed Carlisle to London and a few shillings in his pocket no doubt restored his spirits and his independence of mind. Bath was a fitting last refuge of the trader on aristocratic connection when the royal court itself has become less open to the trade in secrets. For all the panic he had caused, Ashe was dependent on royalty in his own way. The 'ghost' needed the personal angle and the ability to understand and predict the reaction of his subjects to his writing in order to succeed. He could not negotiate directly and single-handedly with the state.

By the time of his death Ashe was perceived as very old, perhaps a function of his destitution. *The Gentleman's Magazine* recorded the death on December 17 1835 at Bath 'at an advanced age' of 'Thomas (the well-known Captain) Ashe. Author of Travels in America 3 vols. 1806, The Spirit of the Book a novel 1808, The Liberal Critic or Henry Percy a novel 1812, Commercial View of the Brazils and Madeira 1812, Ashe's Confessions &c.'[39]

How many works, what panic, drama, suffering, greed and hilarity is represented and silently overlooked by that '&c.' How many volumes published and unpublished, confessed, retracted, circulated, bought, stolen and suppressed? Some – lovingly described, pored over and securely locked up – seem to have been lost to us. 'Osphia or the Victim of Unnatural Affections' bound in Royal Octavo with the name of Colonel Hoffmann on it may still be in the study drawer at Abinger beyond the reach of the Attorney General's cleaners. Perhaps it was returned to the Duke of Wellington and even now is to be found in the Prime Minister's 'strong closet' in Downing Street, beneath other volumes relating to scandals of much more recent vintage. Against all the odds, many of his works, which so many powerful people at various times would rather have seen destroyed, survive. There is Ashe's correspondence with the agents of Viscount Perceval, accessioned by the Bodleian Library as recently as 2008, the manuscript of *The Patriot Princess* with Ashe's sworn confession of its origins and purpose at The National Library of Scotland, and most remarkably of all, *The Claustral Palace* in the papers of the Treasury Solicitor at The National Archives.

The Claustral Palace manuscript found its way into a series of the Treasury Solicitor's Bona Vacantia case files, concerning the estates of those who had died intestate where funds might be due to the Crown. It is, somewhat improbably, dated 1850, fifteen years after Ashe's death, though there is no evidence of posthumous proceedings which might justify such a date. In Ashe's case, there are no case papers at all, only the novel, classified complacently as public record, as if it were a government administrative file. This is based on custodial history rather than creation, since the government acquired it but clearly did not write it or cause it to be written. On the other hand, could it be argued that somehow they did? It was after all a direct response to legislation devised by the king himself. More practically, it seems likely that this is a posthumous piece of classification, conferring administrative respectability on a disreputable episode. I expect the Treasury Solicitor had a cupboard of embarrassing suppressed literature in his library, of which *The Claustral Palace* was a part, rather than it being preserved according to some administrative concern for Ashe's estate. Oddly enough, the case papers of a 'bastard and bachelor' Brent Spenser is filed next to his, as if the Treasury Solicitor kept files on men who knew too much about the princesses at Frogmore, and as if the state needed to supervise and control them and their papers even after they were dead. Of course, the spelling is slightly different and it is not the case file of Princess Augusta's dashing soldier.

Context suggests this was a logical enough final resting place for *The Claustral Palace* since the events surrounding sudden death and insolvency are often embarrassing, the papers are essentially private rather than official and the Treasury Solicitor's role in the case and title to the material is not necessarily always clear. How it got into his cupboard of Embarrassing Literature is much clearer since we are given an account of it in Ashe's *Memoirs and Confessions*; it was stolen or perhaps negotiated away from his house near Bath by hired hands in the pay of the Prince Regent.

It has remained catalogued, preserved and in plain sight, but invisible because no one looked for it there, *The Claustral Palace* is lasting testimony to the tendency of the state to panic when dealing with seditious literature and then to lie about it afterwards. Throughout his life. Ashe provoked unlikely amounts of indulgence and forgiveness from a range of prominent people whose lives he made difficult. There were his looks, his charm, his clear-eyed acknowledgement of the faults of his character, but most of all his words. It was as if, unlike Queen Caroline and her own memoirs, even those he campaigned against could not quite bring themselves to consign his manuscripts to the flames, or bury their correspondence about him. He deserved literary notice even when dying in obscurity, and through his writing, his adventures live on.

What would we think *The Claustral Palace* was like, if the manuscript had been destroyed and all we had left to us were the clues it has left behind? It would be something like the standard satirical cartoons, an outsider's view of The Family, grotesque suitors, the Regent as a bloated wastrel. In fact for all its melodrama, it is something more subtle and sympathetic, with a lot of detail based on inside information, gentler but more damaging because better informed and more difficult to dismiss. The form and tone of Ashe's blackmailing literature sets him apart. He enjoys the melodrama and gothic horror suggested so irresistibly by the princesses' accounts of their own experiences, but it is not the same grotesque as contemporary cartoons or Cobbett's well-constructed, reasoned, outsider's attacks on The Thing – the establishment machine of patronage and preferment. Ashe's power comes from the fact that his fictional letters are phrased much as they might have been told to him by Caroline or the princesses themselves; and perhaps they were.

Ashe drew parallels between himself and Queen Caroline. She was constrained by the enforcement of dynastic political marriage, he, in turn, needed to be a Major in order to marry her lady in waiting and his adventures stem from his desperate attempts to become one. The repeated confidences of mother and daughter vested in him, his good humour and self-knowledge suggest Ashe was not a parasite but a sought-after, powerful and successful writer.

There are repeated patterns within The Family. George III's children were raised to be good having no other reason to exist and kept in perpetual fear that bad behaviour would undermine the institution of monarchy and the frail constitution of the monarch himself. *The Claustral Palace* showed gently and sympathetically how the constraints on the lives of the royal children corrupted their characters and this cycle was doomed to continue. Queen Victoria's determination to bring up her own children to be good, as George III had tried and failed to do, seemed to provoke some of that natural rebellion in young Bertie that was seen in George III's eldest son.

Ashe needed Caroline and the Frogmore princesses as sources and causes but he also needed Spencer Perceval and the Prince of Wales as bribers of writers and suppressors of literature. No one needed Ernest, Duke of Cumberland. Queen Victoria was brought up on Princess Mary's tales of her brothers, Victoria's Wicked Uncles, not to mention her Wicked Father if he was indeed her father. She had no need to read 'Osphia'. Victoria said of Ernest, 'He liked to hurt in everything he said. He was of an extraordinary unflinching courage for which we must admire him, but there were many dark stories connected with his name, which I will not touch upon but which make me shudder.' [40] Providence, or at least Hanover, had enacted a Salic law, which excluded Victoria from that inheritance and ensured Ernest's succession in Hanover when Victoria became Queen in Britain. Ernest believed 'the Old Royal Family' became rather overlooked by Victoria in favour of the Coburg upstarts represented by Prince Albert. Ashe was rendered obsolete by the Reform Act, the new police and by new and more efficient means of controlling the press, which was no longer a matter of bribery and threats. There were no such reforms in Hanover where Ernest could continue to create 'Stupid German Tragedies' unhindered by the restraints and intrusions of British newspapers.

What happened to the Frogmore princesses and their brothers? What outcome did the Royal Marriages Act have? Only one of the sisters had a child and that the illegitimate offspring of an equerry or even incest, despite their sole role being to produce children in carefully contrived and controlled dynastic marriages. Ernest's imprudent marriage to Frederica, which he was able to blackmail the Prince Regent into sanctioning, devastated Queen Charlotte.

Mary, the princess barely featured in the annals of *The Claustral Palace*, who attracted no scandal despite her beauty, married her cousin Prince William Frederick, second Duke of Gloucester. They had no children. Her husband's political opposition to her beloved brother the Prince Regent made her position difficult. Gloucester proved to be something of a liability to the opposition except in stirring things up and annoying the Regent.

Ashe's contemporary and narrator Princess Elizabeth married Prince Friedrich of Hesse-Homburg in 1818. The marriage was happy but came too late for a realistic hope of producing an heir. The death of Queen Charlotte in that year saw the final release of the restrictions of the Nunnery for the remaining sisters, Augusta and Sophia, but neither married. On the death of George III, Augusta inherited Frogmore House.

Princess Sophia lived in Kensington Palace after Queen Charlotte's death, her weakness for equerries, or perhaps an upbringing which gave unlikely men a fascination, continued with Sir John Conroy, who controlled and appropriated much of her money. The Duke of Wurttemberg died in 1816, stories of domestic violence gradually filtering back to The Family, bearing out the revelations of The Claustral Palace five years earlier. Charlotte and Elizabeth comfortably outlived their German husbands but returned to England only briefly and for medical purposes. The 'senior recluse', now bloated by dropsy, came in search of treatment for her condition, the always pleasantly plump Elizabeth to visit spas. Did Ashe have a last glimpse of Elizabeth or she of him at Bath in 1835? It is possible since Elizabeth was in England from January 1835 to July 1836. The 'Programma' setting out the contents of the *The Claustral Palace*, which was found in Elizabeth's papers is usually taken to be a direct attempt at blackmail. That seems unlikely since she is the sympathetic narrator; I think it more likely he sent it to her for approval.

'Playing the Perceval game'

The period of Thomas Ashe's literary life, roughly 1792 to 1830, was a very peculiar and interesting one with regards to writers and the state. An explosion of satirical literature and cartoons took on a new edge and menace in the eyes of the authorities after the French Revolution, but in Britain the means at the government's disposal to suppress seditious material, though they could be exemplary and brutal, were haphazard and often ineffective, even counter-productive. The sums expended by the government on bribing authors and editors can seem extraordinary to us; the amounts laid out by Spencer Perceval and the Treasury Solicitor for the recovery of individual stray copies of *The Book*, almost unbelievable. Were the authorities justified in devoting so much time, energy and money to suppressing seditious, or even just embarrassing, literature? What would have happened if they had not? What alternatives were available? When and why did the practice end?

The perception of the importance of royalty was key to Perceval's tactics in gaining power and to the literary career of Thomas Ashe in copying his 'game'. Both knew that the monarchy felt it was in its interests to exaggerate its own importance, both for the stability of the state and the rights and freedoms of British subjects. For without this role, what was its position in society and political purpose? The Hanoverian kings had neither an indisputable claim to the throne, nor the theoretical powers of the absolute monarchy recently overthrown in France, so they fell back on being pillars of the constitution, which married comfortably with a very natural instinctive tendency to equate their own well-being with the well-being of the state. Law officers, treasury officials and concerned citizens could all legitimately claim that the enormous government expenditure on bribes to writers, loyal and seditious ones alike, was part of a necessary attempt to preserve the status quo in dangerous times. Naturally, the writers themselves, the recipients of this largesse, of all shades of opinion, agreed with them. It suited everyone to believe that the revelation of the peccadilloes of the ruling family could precipitate revolution, even if the sheer number of peccadilloes, not least those of George IV himself, made the suppression of revelations about them a continuous and expensive business. Thomas Ashe, as we have seen, took as his model and justification the tactics of the Prime Minister himself, building his own phenomenal literary success in *The Spirit of the Book* on Perceval's decision to print, circulate and then supress *The Book*. He then followed up by offering *The Claustral Palace* for suppression both in novel and then poetical form.

Modern readers are likely to be puzzled by the panic caused in the corridors of power by writers like Thomas Ashe. Most of the time, we tell ourselves, the innate conservatism of the British people would surely have made it likely that a guffaw and a shrug rather than the storming of the Tower of London by an enraged mob would have followed the publication of works like *The Claustral Palace* or 'Osphia'. There was a lack of respect among the British for their rulers, which foreign visitors could find remarkable, but it rarely hid true revolutionary fervour, except in the minds of the king and a few shire Tories. Once or twice perhaps there was a more grounded and widely felt fear of disorder, during Queen Caroline's trial and at her funeral for example, when the Duke of Wellington doubted the loyalty of his troops. Then there was the revolutionary summer of 1830, when Europe was convulsed and Thomas Ashe and the Duke of Cumberland, in their war with one another, competed to disturb the Iron Duke's peace of mind and his efforts to preserve the status quo.

This agreed tendency to exaggerate both the power and vulnerability of the Crown did not mean there was unanimity about how to deal with threats to it like Captain Ashe. Correspondence between the Home Office and the Treasury Solicitor clearly shows the fear and tension around this issue. There were generally logical, legal, voices saying that there were no ill effects to be anticipated from the revelations threatened in the publication, or at least nothing to be gained in suppressing them, since they could simply re-emerge in a slightly altered form. Then there are powerful, sometimes political, voices, which counsel caution and persuasion. Often members of The

Family itself urged bribery or threats to defeat or turn the gentleman blackmailer. Despite the apparent power of those ranged against them, writers and cartoonists often came out on top, publishing with apparent impunity or being handsomely rewarded for suppression.

To us it seems incredible that the state could be drawn repeatedly into debating the same issues posed by a single gentleman blackmailer, and we might not believe the system of government bribery which Ashe describes in his *Memoirs and Confessions* existed at all, if the evidence for it was not so copious and overwhelming. The files of the Treasury Solicitor bulge with warrants and receipts that show Ashe was part of an industry made up of writers and cartoonists who could make more money being bribed or bought out by the government than by publishing their work. If there was a danger that the work would be considered criminal or immoral and therefore not protected by copyright, publication could be financially hazardous, as Stockdale found in publishing Harriette Wilson's *Memoirs*. A great publishing success could leave you to face the libel suits while the pirates took the profits. If you were confident of avoiding prosecution, paid suppression was easy money by comparison.

Thomas Ashe represented a particularly difficult case for the government to deal with. He was so well informed by the royal and aristocratic women who confided in him that prosecuting him risked divulging in court precisely the information those in power wished to suppress and they also knew that, true or not, the 'libel' would be widely believed.

The authorities' power to control literature seemed to rest on exemplary punishments and bribes rather than any consistent executive power to deal with it systematically. Even Lord Sidmouth's attack on seditious literature as part of 'The Six Acts' in 1819 seemed to fuel rather than stem the flow of satirical writing and prints, since the legislation added to the sense of popular grievance against the government without strengthening the practical ability of the authorities to deal with it. The libel laws often proved unworkable, since popular sentiment in the satirist's favour made finding a jury who would convict difficult. The authorities dared not risk another series of high-profile acquittals like William Hone's blasphemy trials in 1817. Hone opposed the 1832 reform bill and eventually renounced politics for religion. Like Ashe, Hone was exhausted and made bitter by labour and harsh treatment, the passion for the cause beaten out of him by poverty and illness. Perhaps the government hoped that like Hone, Ashe would just go away in the end. His petition from the Middlesex House of Correction of 1835 suggests they succeeded only in part. He may have been reduced to beggary and powerlessness in the face of state autrhority, but he pursued his campaign and his manuscript to the end regardless. It was characteristic of Ashe that he felt, even at the last, he could write his way out of trouble with a well-worded petition, and that he seems to have succeeded in escaping his two-year sentence, being sent, yet again, on his way.

The system of government by aristocratic factions held together by personal loyalty, strengthened by the endorsement and patronage of the king, offered spaces for a man like Ashe to operate in. Spencer Perceval's power over the Commons and over The Family appeared daunting but Ashe felt it rested on Perceval's literary blackmail and his ability to bribe and intimidate the press. Ashe believed that he could play the Prime Minister at his own game and govern him with the power of his pen. Gradually this personal politics dependent on royal favour was replaced by a more controlling and impersonal system of party politics. The role of the monarchy as the head of this system and a broker of governments was diminishing, so the political implications of a monarch or Regent's personal failings became less far-reaching.

The Royal Marriages Act, by enforcing 'political' marriage and politicising love, opened the floodgates for writers like Ashe who could 'blow the lid off the Nunnery' with an air of moral indignation as if he and his readers, rather than the royal family itself, were the party injured by what he found there. Looked at retrospectively The Royal Marriages Act came at the expense of the happiness of generations and formed the miserable legislative structure behind the sufferings of *The Claustral Palace*, but in fact it had little political significance, there was little to be gained by the alliances the princesses eventually made. These often came too late for the couple to have children and ensure the succession, which was the primary function of such dynastic unions. The tentacles of the Act stretched down to our own age, before it was eventually replaced by the milder legislation of the Succession to the Crown Act in 2015. Its practical consequence in terms of the succession seems at a distance to have been very slight, but its implications and the misery it inflicted are amplified and preserved in the works of Thomas Ashe. In particular, we can point to the importance and strangeness of *The Claustral Palace* as a literary survival. It is the core of this book and its greatest single discovery.

The Claustral Palace is an epistolary novel for a reason. It was composed of fictional letters but letters very like them were genuinely written, or recorded verbal confidences. These in turn were reasonably likely to fall into the hands of a trusted biographer or a blackmailing enemy. In the case of 'The Persecuted (or Perjured) Peeress', Ashe himself took both roles. Even in his campaigning, he changed sides opportunistically and wrote subtly. *The Spirit of the Book* is mistaken by some modern critics as an attack on Caroline. Even at the time of her 'trial', Ashe himself had to remind Caroline's solicitor and perhaps himself, that he was still of her party. *The Claustral Palace* was essentially an insider's view of the misery wrought on the royal family by the Act, the victims of their own father's legislation.

I came to Ashe's novel with two clear images of worlds of literature in this period in my mind. There was the upper world of gentlemen poets seeking natural inspiration; aristocratic satirists leaving their wives and debts behind in favour of a dissolute Grand Tour. Then there was a radical underworld of seditious hacks cowed by ad hoc legislation, bullied, bribed and discarded by the men in power and in opposition. I am increasingly convinced there is only one literature, not two, no underworld and over world, for Ashe wrote with equal facility in both, so to which 'world' does he belong? Despite his powerful position in society, the Prime Minister Spencer Perceval had produced, circulated and suppressed his own work, expending huge sums of public money, and promoted and suppressed partisan works by others on a routine basis. One of the provocations for the Royal Marriages Act had been the indignity of the Crown being asked to pay the costs of Prince Henry, Duke of Cumberland's adultery case, evidenced by his awful letters, but it did not prevent George III's eldest son from expending large sums of money on recovering or suppressing the letters of his many mistresses. Who was the more morally reprehensible? Ashe for writing *The Claustral Palace* of the Regent for ordering it to be stolen? Ashe for imitating Queen Caroline's letters or those of Princess Elizabeth in their causes, or the agents of the Milan Commission for buying Lady Charlotte Lindsay's letters from her own brother? Ashe was offering quality writing for money, at a time when the prejudice against earning money through talent, though still profound, was no longer so great even in England. Ashe just survived into an era of great literary change too; books of royal scandal gradually being replaced by the great reforming novel of systems and bureaucracy. Ashe needed the informal state and a panicking ad hoc executive to provide him with an environment in which to thrive as a writer. Real reform was not in his interest; there was no real place for him in a well-policed democratic society. As Ashe faded in importance so did the monarchy he plagued. Gradually, Kew faded as a sequestered royal pleasure ground to become a national botanical resource.

When looking at the career of an individual blackmailer of the period, whether Thomas Ashe or Harriette Wilson, it is tempting to think they had come up with a literary modus operandi which was particular to them and which scandalised and put them outside society. However, there were many others prepared to buy and steal letters and manuscripts to control and blackmail their opponents, not least the government and agents of the king himself. Spencer Perceval was perhaps remarkable for gaining political advantage from suppressing his own work, but it was not in itself the act of an underworld figure, simply standard practice, which in no way impinged on Perceval's sense of his own moral rectitude. It also looks an oddly fragile business model as it depended on a threat to reputation, which to modern eyes seems to offer very little lasting damage and could be readily laughed off.

There are two strikingly different official views of Captain Thomas Ashe by 1830. The Duke of Cumberland saw him as a great threat, a well-informed gentleman blackmailer, whose allegations, true or not, would certainly be believed by a disaffected reading public eager for scandal. The duke's view of his own personal importance led him to identify the preservation of his own personal reputation with the preservation of the state; a world where satire might precipitate a revolution that could only be stopped by personal action in the courts to defend the honour of the monarchy. To Sir Robert Peel he is a small nuisance to be swept away with a bureaucratic click of the 'New Police' fingers, a man to be followed and arrested as a vagrant before he could do any serious harm. Sir William Knighton as Privy Purse suppressed the practice of subsidising literature, and the writers and caricaturists who fed on such subsidy largely stopped producing it.

The love lives of the royal princesses were an ideal subject for the kind of literature Wordsworth abhorred, being sickly, stupid, tragic, not to mention German. Their predicament was not just a one-off personal issue brought about by the peculiarities of the Royal Marriages Act, it fed into a much longer lived question in life and in literature: can princes, and aristocrats in general, be made to behave like gentlemen? One can say there are two very different views of fashionable society written at about the same time in Jane Austen's *Pride and Prejudice* and *The Claustral Palace* but with a common theme, that aristocrats and royalty are not really noble without humility. The royal princesses have less freedom in marriage than Elizabeth Bennett does. The first version of *Pride & Prejudice* was titled 'First Impressions'. This phrase was taken from Fanny Burney but also recalls the Earl of Malmesbury's famous description of Caroline in his diary entry of Sunday 28 December 1794 summing up her character: 'caught by the first impression, led by the first impulse not one to make a considered choice, and in the question of marriage had no considered choice to make'.[1]

In literature, the peculiar place in society which the Royal Marriages Act gives to The Family lends itself to the fashionable epistolary form of the aristocratic novel. This is a tradition of publication set by the Prince of Wales himself, 'the publisher of my letters' as his father called him, but the events themselves savour more of the gothic horror of Matthew 'Monk' Lewis. They have lost their place at the head of the society they are supposed to represent and spend their days, stricken by madness, imprisoned by their own families, prey to ferocious guard dogs and pantomime villain German princes, some of them inside The Family itself. The royal family with some justice then is represented as being outside, even beneath, normal aristocratic society, because of the constraints set upon it, of which the Royal Marriages Act was the most concrete and conspicuous example.

Although the Royal Marriages Act was finally done away with, perhaps Harry and Meghan still have a point. The constraints of being a 'senior royal' still seemed to be disproportionate to the usefulness of the role they were asked to perform. This strange afterlife and the continuing effects of the Royal Marriages Act lend an odd retrospective legitimacy to Ashe's scandalous career, since it was his one genuine and consistent target. It was the legislation which fuelled his prose by making the love lives of the princesses at Frogmore seem politically significant.

Historians have debated the significance of the trial of Queen Caroline and its political effect. Most have noted the powerful if fleeting popularity of the queen as a wronged woman and how quickly after her husband's coronation she became a figure of fun, dying suddenly, as if in acknowledgment of her irrelevance. Ashe carried on his campaign on behalf of the princesses after her death, but to some extent was still trading on events from his prime and on his close connection with The Family from the Frogmore era. Sophia's 'dropsical malady' and the birth of Thomas Garth around 1800 were still being exploited by him in 1829, rather than any new revelations, though the reasons were topical enough and the scandal still fresh and powerful enough to trouble the Cabinet. This may partly be a reflection of Ashe's loss of place and contacts, but perhaps also of a time and a society less prone to deal with him on his own terms or commit indiscretions in a form he can use.

Is Thomas Ashe, who has occupied me for so long and now you too, any good as a writer or as man? What does he tell us about the society in which he lived or about our own? There is a lot of moral objection to his milieu, not least from Ashe himself, But as Byron said of 'Don Juan', is it not good English – is it not the thing? Byron saw in Ashe someone, like himself, who was not afraid to criticise legislation which was 'a disgrace to a civilised country' and who did not mind getting dirty to satirise the dirty world around him. Ashe was not an upright god-fearing man like Perceval, but he could see the ruthlessness in Perceval's pursuit of his principles, a ruthlessness he was far too feckless to possess himself. Almost universally, critics who have deigned to take notice of Ashe at all think his literary mire was as low as one could go even in a wicked age and that he must therefore have been a bad writer and bad man. He is called a 'vile insect' by Dorothy Stuart, though only as a prelude to quoting his prose and praising its insight into the character of Princess Elizabeth. He is otherwise thought to be dull and according to Rowland Prothero writing in the naughty 1890s, not dirty enough to be interesting. I think he writes beautifully. He was by no means a good man. His *Memoirs and Confessions,* though not entirely truthful and certainly not scrupulously accurate, are candid in the sense that they make no attempt to conceal his motivations and failings. They also make clear, in a way that is corroborated by official documents, that the government controlled a machine which bribed and threatened writers, stole letters and blackmailed opponents. The moral atmosphere in which Ashe wrote was not the preserve of a grubby underworld. It came from the top. There is genuine sympathy for the plight of the princesses in *The Claustral Palace,* for Caroline in *The Spirit of the Book* and for her daughter Charlotte in *The Patriot Princess.* We cannot be sure of the structure and tone of lost works like 'Osphia, or the Victim of Unnatural Affections' but the title gives a strong clue. It would have taken the form of letters from Sophia to one of her sisters and the focus of the book would be her feelings and not those of her wicked brother. For all their partiality, there is a reasonable amount of sympathy for the Prince Regent too, certainly more than in most opposition satire. In Ashe's books, these apparently powerful individuals are victims of forces beyond their control; legislation or social norms that they cannot escape. Most obviously, the Royal Marriages Act and the enforcement of cold political marriage on royal women with their own passions and inclinations is a recurrent theme. Ashe draws a parallel with his own experience in the *Memoirs and Confessions* where rank is a bar to his happiness. He can only marry the lovely Angelica Brunswick-Oels if he achieves the rank of major and his subsequent adventures chart his increasingly desperate attempts to do so, including bribing Mary Anne Clarke. He was not a social reformer but he was supported by those that were. The thought that government ministers would conceal the true state of the country, its indebtedness and poverty from *The Patriot Princess* seemed genuine enough, as were the many years of his own destitution. The trapdoor to poverty and imprisonment that creaked beneath the feet of the trusted royal confidant of *The Spirit of the Book* and *The Claustral Palace* was always present.

The narrative that identifies Ashe as vile tends to suggest there was a high and important plateau of public life with great men doing elevated and noble deeds. This is punctured by periodic distasteful 'sordid episodes'. These turn out to be a kind of code for occasions when women dare to appear in the story. Soon it becomes apparent that the 'sordid episodes' are not simply odd isolated descents into a regrettable underworld, but rather the sustained struggle of women attempting to free themselves from the straitjacket that society had placed them in, the struggle impinging itself for a shocking but brilliant moment on the national consciousness. The Royal Marriages Act imposed a peculiar straitjacket on the women of the royal family (princes had the freedom to evade its strictures much more easily) so that these occasions are especially frequent and prominent in the period of Thomas Ashe's career and very often he was the one to turn their private confidences into their public justification. Princesses, generally speaking, could not write and publish justifications of their own conduct. Even Caroline, who had the temerity to write her own memoir, could not in the end allow it to come to light. If it were truthful, it would certainly have undermined the popular attempts to turn her into a saint around the time of her death. In her life, she was reliant on Perceval, Brougham, Cobbett and Ashe to tell her story. Only Ashe did so at length and with genuine sympathy and relish.

Perhaps the most remarkable, if peculiar, example of Ashe's feminine voice is *The Charms of Dandyism or Living in Style*, a three volume courtesan's memoir almost entirely devoid of sexual content. There is a strong element of Ashe autobiography in 'Olivia Moreland's' vicissitudes, her residences in Pangbourne and Park Place Baker Street, her fatal inability to give up the high life, though it drives her, as it drove Ashe into the clutches of the Hydra, into the arms of men of progressively lower rank. Her prostitution mirrors what Ashe himself referred to as his literary prostitution. There is understandably a certain amount of awkwardness in this transposition of gender, not least because Ashe's poverty was much more absolute, grinding and longer-lived than Olivia's was, so that, to mirror his experience, she has to live in places she would have been far too glamorous to go near. Sometimes she sounds too much like Ashe, quoting his beloved poet Horace at points in her story when it would seem an unlikely thing for her to have done. Perhaps the most remarkable thing overall is the ease and enjoyment with which Ashe writes as a woman for three volumes. I think he won the confidences of women because he liked them, liked listening to them and took genuine pleasure in telling their stories in circumstances where they could not.

Ashe has given us the names and tantalising details of the princesses' lovers at Frogmore before they are banished by the unforgiving Family to heartbreak and sudden death. There are other forgotten names he can help us put faces to. Caroline's true love Captain Browne was a recognisable name alongside royalty and aristocracy to the readers of the *Dublin Gazette* in 1793 and perhaps still to the purchasers of the 'The Coronation of the Empress of the Nairs' in 1812 or 'The Royal Bruiser' in 1820. As a ghostly memory in the public mind, he could be brought out when needed, portrayed as perpetually young and handsome, a useful reminder of the real love that Caroline had been compelled to give up to enter into her cold political marriage with the Prince of Wales. With Caroline's death, Captain Browne was lost to the caricaturists and to the public gaze, but he stays with us as the hero of *The Spirit of the Book*. The gift of Thomas Ashe to us was not only his fictionalised account of Captain Browne, but also the view he gives us of himself, his life and writing. Those who had followed his adventures through his memoirs, his journalism, his novels and his court appearances, would have given a wry smile of recognition as they read his potted obituary in *The Gentleman's Magazine*. Alone and destitute though he might have been at the end, he was and deserves still to be 'the well-known Captain Ashe'.

Notes

Prologue

1. 'Osphia'. There is some discrepancy in the sources as to the title of Ashe's blackmailing book. The catalogue of the Wellington Papers at Southampton University Library refers to it as 'Orphia' consistently and this has been adopted by some modern writers. Ashe's own manuscript notes including the covering note to the book when it was sent to the Duke of Cumberland (in Rex v. Ashe TNA TS 11/469 (1604) 'Important Revelation' (undated)) clearly call it 'Osphia'. This follows his standard practice of using barely disguised anagrams of names (Sophia in this case) in works of blackmail. For consistency, I have stuck to 'Osphia' even in referring to the Wellington papers.

1 The Making of *The Claustral Palace*

1. 'Great State puppets only to be employed for the amusement of the public' – *The Claustral Palace by Captain Thomas Ashe Letter 26 – Princess Elizabeth on the 'genius and character of her seven illustrious brothers'*
2. Wardroper 'Kings Lords and Wicked Libellers' p.71 quoting Royal Archives GEO/15938
3. 'Lyrical Ballads' Wordsworth's Preface p.25 ll. 2-32
4. 'The model of a high-minded' Denis Gray, 'Spencer Perceval: The Evangelical Prime Minister' p.464
5. Robert Huish 'Memoirs of Caroline' p.257, Denis Gray p.83
6. Linklater 'Why Spencer Perceval Had to Die' p.80.
7. *The Book* p.204
8. Gray 'Spencer Perceval: The Evangelical Prime Minister' p.85 *The Book* p.205-43
9. Medd 'Romilly: A Life of Samuel Romilly, Lawyer and Reformer' p.267
10. See *The Book* and *The Spirit of the Book* chapter below

2 *Memoirs and Confessions*

1. 'She has a ready conception' (E A Smith 'Queen's Trial' p.7)
2. '...out of her bedroom window at night.' Fraser 'Unruly Queen' p.20

3. 'Caroline explained her continued spinsterhood' Nightingale 'Memoirs of Caroline' i 35-8, Fraser 'Unruly Queen' p.27)
4. 'He thought the character of the Princess' Huish 'Memoirs of Caroline' I 18, Aspinall Correspondence of George Prince of Wales ii 407
5. 'It remains however to be seen' 16 October 1796, Bickley 'Lord Glenbervie Diaries' I 88
6. 'The report contained four hundred folio pages, all in my own hand-writing, 'Memoirs & Confessions' vol. i p.122
7. 'The best horsewoman in Ireland' Bickley 'Lord Glenbervie Diaries' vol. I p.38, p.39 note January 1794.
8. 'To the town of Lausanne I took an invincible dislike.' 'Memoirs & Confessions' vol. i p.165)
9. 'Yesterday morning arrived the Princess Royal' Tillyard 'Citizen Lord' p.154 Dublin Gazette 26 Jan 1793 '
10. 'By such means' 'Memoirs & Confessions' vol. i p.264
11. Ashe's Home Office Memorials mitigating his offences with reference to his military service and war wounds: (see evidence of these in Chapter 7 TNA HO 48/28 13 Aug 1830).
12. Henry Maunde Clive Caplan 'Jane Austen's Banker Brother' Persuasions Jane Austen Society of North America No 20 (1998) – One of their profitable lines was the trade in military commissions TNA PMG 2/62-121
13. 'At Arklow it was my lot' 'Memoirs & Confessions' vol. ii p.32
14. Army lists joins 83rd regiment in 1784 leaves 1804 regiment disbanded Muster lists of 83rd 1st Bttn 1804 TNA WO 12/8675, 2nd bttn 1804-5 TNA WO 12/8735, on half pay 1787-1804. Canadian Fencibles 1804-6 TNA WO 12/10523 travelling in America 1806 Captain Hays Co June-Sep 1806 Ashe is recorded as being 'absent without leave'
15. 'During my researches' 'Memoirs & Confessions' vol. ii. pp.120-121
16. 'The great Megalonyx' 'Memoirs of Mammoth' p.31
17. The bill of sale for Bullock's Napoleonic material, Grosvenor Prints stock number 11320
18. The British Library's copy 'Memoirs of Mammoth' (1806) BL 728 c 26
19. Initial application British Library MS Loan 96 RLF 1/206/1 letter from Sir Richard Phillips MS Loan 96 RLF 1/206/2
20. 'Messrs. Cadell and Davies preferred works on divinity' 'Memoirs & Confessions' vol. ii. pp. 235-236

3 *The Book* and *The Spirit of the Book*

1. Treasury Solicitor file with evidence submitted to the Delicate Investigation and Milan Commission TNA TS 11/111
2. Lady Douglas's evidence TNA TS 11/111 item 22
3. Colonel McMahon as interviewer Fraser 'Unruly Queen' p 155
4. Monitoring reports TNA TS 11/111 item 10
5. *Memoirs and Confessions* vol. iii pp. 51-64
6. Memoirs and Confessions vol. iii p. 74
7. Memoirs and Confessions vol. iii p. 78
8. Memoirs and Confessions vol. iii pp. 80-1
9. Ingrams 'Life and Adventures of William Cobbett' p.205

10. Attorney General v. Blagdon TNA TS 11/462 (1565)
11. Francis Blagdon's (Royal) Literary Fund file British Library MS Loan 96 RLF 1/280
12. TNA TS 11/106 f. 40a 6 Aug 1808, William Playfair was reported to have a copy.
13. TNA TS 11/106 f.4 14 Nov 1808 Playfair's defence
14. Another Treasury Solicitor file TNA TS 11/594
15. Another slim file (undertakings) TNA TS 23/33
16. Richard Edwards to Spencer Perceval 27 January 1809 TNA TS 11/106 f.42a
17. Lady Milbanke to William Adam 6 March 1809. TNA TS 11/106 f.50a
18. Simon Le Blanc to Treasury Solicitor 9 Mar 1809 TNA TS 11/106 f.43a
19. TS 11/106 f.9 and f.167 10 March 1809
20. File copy of the advertisement. TNA TS 11/106 f. 23
21. JC Herries to Treasury Solicitor 5 Apr 1809 TNA TS 11/106 f. 14
22. Playfair to Perceval TS 11/106 f. 11a 10 April 1809 and 4 May 1809 f. 39a
23. William Playfair's (Royal) Literary Fund file British Library MS Loan 96 RLF 1/121
24. William Lindsell TNA TS 11/106 5-7 May 1809 f 98 (his name is rendered as 'Maxwell' in index to the file though his signature and identity are clear)
25. JC Herries to Treasury Solicitor 29 June 1809 TNA TS 11/106 f. 15
26. Aspinall 'Correspondence of George Prince of Wales' vi 488 letter 2663n 8 Nov 1809
27. TNA TS 11/594 9 Jan 1810
28. Thomas Ashe (Royal) Literary Fund file British Library MS Loan 96 RLF 1/206/4-6
29. Davenport Sedley to Perceval 18 April 1810 TS 11/106 f 4a
30. Davenport Sedley, 21 May 1810 TNA TS 11/594
31. *Memoirs and Confessions* vol.iii p.84
32. All these documents by date within TNA TS 11/594
33. All these documents by date within TNA TS 11/594
34. 27 Nov 1810 TS 11/106 f 49a
35. 'Fiction for want of fact' TNA TS 11/106 f.161
36. Thomas Ashe (Royal) Literary Fund British Library MS Loan 96 RLF 1/206 3, 7-9
37. 'If the narrative of what passed' TNA TS 11/106 f.22a
38. Undertakings of John Turnbull TNA TS 23/33
39. William Bays TNA TS 11/106 f. 27 and f. 34
40. Fraser 'Unruly Queen' p. 266 Mary Hill Marchioness of Downshire .her copy of Ashe's *Memoirs and Confessions* was offered by Bernard Quaritch (London Book Fair 2020 lot 5 along with two volumes by Olivia Serres 'Duchess of Cumberland' her 'historical romance on Caroline's first love 'Memoirs of a Princess' and her 'Flights of Fancy' also from Lady Downshire's library)
    'A mediocre and fantastic work' [Fraser ibid. p.257) quoting Baron Ramdohr Hanoverian minister in Rome Royal Archives Geo Box 8/6 5 November 1814]
41. The Coronation of the Empress of the Nairs. Plate from the 'Scourge', iv. 173 1 September 1812
42. 'The Spirit of the Book or Anticipation of the year 1813' January 1813 BM number 1868,0808.8044. Described M. Dorothy George, 'Catalogue of Political and Personal Satires in the British Museum', IX, 1949

4 *The Claustral Palace*

1. Fraser 'Princesses' p. 215
2. 'Thus provided I sat down' Memoirs and Confessions vol. iii.148
3. He was driven to commit suicide, 7 February 1830, by luridly publicized allegations of his wife's adultery with the infamous Duke of Cumberland. Aspinall 'Letters of George IV' iii 1577 Appendix 'Lady Graves Scandal' p.505
4. Wicked Ernest p citing the synopsis Royal Archives Geo Add 11/213-5 Claustral Palace poems unsold at Sotheby's in 1999 [previously Simon Finch 1994] Unsold at £700-900 lot 102 15 July 1999. Possibly subsequently offered LOT 5: Thomas Ashe ms 'Claustral Palace' poems Duke of York's copy, 1811 - 1814 Estimate: £2250 Bernard Quaritch Ltd, 09-Dec-2015 Treasury Solicitor file on both *The Claustral Palace* and 'Osphia '(TS 11/462 (1604))
5. 'We do not see any steps' TNA HO 48/15 law officers' opinion on the suppression of the Claustral Palace May 1812
6. *The Claustral Palace* TNA TS 17/1388
7. 'Tiresome and confined life' Aspinall 'Correspondence of George, Prince of Wales' ii 162, no. 591)
8. 'She was afterwards very grateful' Flora Fraser in 'Princesses' p.213
9. Other candidates. Flora Fraser 'Princesses' p. 171 also notes that Sophia was the only sister to take Caroline's side in the marital war. Caroline was the go between with Sophia and Colonel Garth, Miss Garth his niece was Sophia's confidante and in Caroline's household at Blackheath. p. 206 Sophia and Caroline were brought together by the King's alarming affection in his madness –. Sophia refers to the Queen as 'The Old Lady' as Ashe does in *The Claustral Palace*. She also (p. 235) adds evidence of Caroline at Frogmore seeing the defiance of the Princesses and their attempts to maintain their secret relationships at first hand. Walking the grounds with the Duke of York, she found one of Princess Amelia's love notes to Colonel Fitzroy left in a hedge by one of her ladies in waiting. Perhaps uncharacteristically Caroline then kept Amelia talking so she could not keep the assignation. Fraser also identifies Caroline as reproducing (p. 218) the sisters' unflattering remarks about their brothers

5 *The Patriot Princess*

1. 'Sinks her so low' Fraser 'Princesses' p. 274
2. 'Enjoy yourself' Fraser 'Princesses' p. 288
3. 'She is quite equal' Thea Holme 'Prinny's Daughter' p.78
4. Memoirs and Confessions vol. III Chapter 13
5. Walter Honeyford Yate letters and papers to Mary, Countess Berkeley 1813-4 Farahar-Dupre http://www.farahardupre.co.uk 1 April 2008 stock number 51159
6. Andrew Nicholson 'The Letters of John Murray to Lord Byron' (p31f) 'Lord Byron has lately bought a copy' TNA TS 11/106 n.d. f.303)
7. Thomas Moore 'Life Journal and Letters of Lord Byron' p.224f.
8. Prothero 'The Letters and Works of Lord Byron'. (1899) vol 3 p.4 n.1

9. National Library of Scotland MS 5751
10. Thomas Ashe letters to John, Viscount Perceval and his agents Bodleian MS Eng. 7284 ff. 31-57 the letters which follow from cited from this source appear, with a couple of exceptions, in date order
11. 'Memoirs & Confessions' vol iii XVIII pp 247 and 250
12. Bodleian MS Eng. 7284 6 March 1814 [f48-49] subsequent letters by date from this source
13. 'Memoirs & Confessions' vol. iii p.188f.
14. 'Memoirs & Confessions' vol. iii p.222
15. Lady Douglas to the Treasury Solicitor 19 May 1814 TNA TS 11/111 (item 1a)
16. Bodleian MS Eng. 7284 6 March 1814 [f55-57]
17. Jonathan Ashe letters re the Kilmainham chaplaincy Bloomsbury Auctions 12 May 2011 lot 115
18. MS of *The Patriot Princess* National Library of Scotland MS 5751
19. TNA TS 11/469 (1604) Rex v Ashe
20. As reported in *Memoirs and Confessions* vol. iii Chapter XVII
21. Egmont Papers Supplementary Vol II 1 ff. 1-64 BL Add MSS 78704 f. 76 f. 78
22. 'Memoirs & Confessions' vol. i p.6
23. 'Memoirs & Confessions' vol. i vii
24. Byron McGann ed. Complete Poetical Works, 3.91
25. Nightingale 'Memoirs of the Public and Private Life' p. 467 and p.461
26. 'Royal Correspondence' 1822 Letter XVII p. 89 Caroline to Charlotte from Athens 28 April 1816
27. Duke of York Letter to Bathurst 26 Oct 1817 HMC Bathurst MSS p. 441

6 Her Majesty's Saviour

1. 'The manifold evils of a public enquiry' (E A Smith 'Queen's Trial' p.18)
2. 'There was great ground for alarm.' (E A Smith 'Queen's Trial' p.16)
3. 'Paradise of women' Charms of Dandyism. Vol i Chap. IX p.74
4. 'In a Margate packet boat' Charms of Dandyism Vol. iii Chapter XI p.95
5. Ashe's final application to the Literary Fund BL Loan 96 RLF 1/206 (10-14).
6. Joseph Nightingale's applications to the Literary Fund. The Fund was more generous to his widow than to him directly (RLF 1/311)
7. JJ Stockdale application to the Literary Fund British Library MS Loan 96 RLF 1/589 rejected three times
8. TNA TS 11/116
9. TNA TS 11/115
10. 'We and the public have reason to doubt in the fidelity of the troops' E A Smith 'Queen's Trial' p.50ff
11. At least one observer, Lady Charlotte Lindsay, E A Smith 'Queen's Trial' p. 58
12. 'I do think the Queen's affair very formidable' E A Smith 'Queen's Trial' p.82
13. The endowment of fifty hospitals E A Smith 'Queen's Trial' p.116
14. Joseph Nightingale Last Days of Queen Caroline (1822) p.90
15. 'To describe to you her appearance and manner far is beyond my powers' E A Smith p.94.

16. Ashe's letter to William Vizard 4 Sep 1820 Royal Archives Geo IV Box 12: Aspinall 'Letters of King George IV' ii 364
17. Mary Crandon evidence about Ashe Aspinall 'Letters of King George IV' ii 375 1 Nov 1820
18. 'Anyway the queen is quite mad' E A Smith 'Queen's Trial' p 121
19. 'The most shameful thing that has appeared in the whole transaction' E A Smith 'Queen's Trial' p.161
20. 'The Duke of Gloucester [is] for her stoutly' E A Smith 'Queen's Trial' p.164-5
21. "They (the Opposition) meant it to go to the Commons to give the Queen an opportunity of recriminating' E A Smith 'Queen's Trial' p.205
22. 4 Dec 1820 Dobson v Ashe as reported in *The Times*
23. 'This book she always said contained the whole history of her life' E A Smith 'Queen's Trial' p.258
24. Funeral correspondence TNA HO 44/9/91 26 Aug 1821. Conant's resignation due to ill health TNA HO 44/1/30
25. JJ Stockdale bankruptcy file 1822 TNA B 3/4606

7 The Victim of Unnatural Affections

1. Manx Annals of Eighty Years Ago by George Goodwin Chapter 14 'Newspapers' *Peel City Guardian 21 September 1901 — March 1902*
2. TNA TS 11/469 (1604) John Wardroper draws on this in 'Wicked Ernest'
3. 'In Harriette Wilson's *Memoirs*' Frances Wilson 'The Courtesan's Revenge p.225
4. 'An atrocious libel...Shall we pay him the £100?' TNA TS 11/ 469 (1604) 5 October 1829 Copy in Southampton University Library Wellington Papers WP 1/1054/9
5. Wellington to Lyndhurst 14 October 1829 Wellington Papers WP 1/1054/26, the note to Wynford three days later WP 1/1054/38
6. Wellington to Wynford 21 October Wellington Papers WP 1/1054/56 and to Lyndhurst on the following day 22 Oct 1829 WP 1/1054/62
7. TNA TS 11/469 (1604) 26 October 1829. Copy in Wellington Papers WP 1/1054/65.
8. 'Villiers, Duke of Buckingham and Spencer Perceval had never been assassinated' also TNA TS 11/469 (1604) 26 October 1829
9. 28 Oct 1829 Wellington Papers WP 1/1054/77
10. 'As near the wind as possible' Wellington Papers WP 1/1054/78
11. TNA TS 11/469 (1604) 31 October 1829
12. 1 November 1829 WP 1/1059/1 Wellington Papers
13. 5 November 1829 WP 1/1059/16 Wellington Papers
14. TNA TS 11/469 (1604) 7, 9 and 10 November 1829
15. Earl of Ellenborough Political Diary 1828-1830 14 November 1829 (vol. II page 83)
16. 'Library pursuits' TNA TS 11/469 (1604) 16 Nov 1829
17. Earl of Ellenborough Political Diary 1828-1830 16 November 1829 (vol. II page 83)
18. British Library MS add 40399 f 383 Peel – Best (Wynford) correspondence
19. Aspinall 'Letters of King George IV' iii item 1577 William Knighton's diary 10 February 1830

20. Aspinall 'Letters of King George IV' iii p.505 Appendix 'The Lady Graves Scandal'
21. TNA TS 11/469 (1604) 27 May 1830
22. 5 June note about the surveillance of Ashe Wellington Papers WP 1/1122/13 8 June 1830 Wellington's note to Wynford, new evidence to be mulled over. Ashe's letter in will be given to law officers WP 1/1122/25
23. Earl of Ellenborough Political Diary 1828-1830 8 June 1830 vol. II p. 162
24. TNA TS 11/469 (1604) all these documents in date order
25. Peel to Wellington 15 July 1830 Wellington Papers WP 1/1122/20)
26. TNA TS 11/469 (1604) Report, Attorney General and Home Office note all 17 July 1830
27. Earl of Ellenborough's Political Diary 1828-1830 vol. II page 191 17 July 1830
28. Lord Eldon wrote to Sir Robert Peel, 18 July 1830 British Library MS Add 40315 f 324
29. Flora Fraser notes 'Princesses' p. 348 Tommy Garth was in negotiations around box of documents relating to his birth, p. 388 was in King's Bench prison for debt until £10,000 came from Sir Herbert Taylor in 1834, which naturally led to further appeals for funds from him and from his daughter. The 1830 Chancery proceedings Garth v Taylor TNA C 13/939/4.
30. TNA TS 11/469 (1604) 22 June 1830
31. TNA TS 11/469 (1604) 25 June 1830 all these documents in date order in that file.
32. TNA TS 11/469 (1604) 29 June 1830
33. TNA HO 48/28 Law officers' opinion on the suppression of 'Osphia'. Including Ashe's petition to Sir Richard Birnie from Newgate Infirmary (13 August 1830) with a covering note from the Treasury Solicitor, George Maule to Sir Robert Peel (19 August 1830)
34. TNA TS 11/469 (1604) 10 Sep 1830
35. HO 48/28 Law officers' reports and opinions. Case papers 1830-1 18 September 1830
36. Wellington Papers 6 Nov 1830 WP 1/1154/9/7
37. 'Hear no more of him' TNA TS 11/469 (1604) 6 February 1831
38. Petition 29 March 1835 TNA HO 17/18/74
39. Obituary Gentleman's Magazine 1836 vol. 5 p.213
40. 'He liked to hurt in everything he said' Fraser 'Princesses' p. 392-3

Epilogue: 'Playing the Perceval game'

1. 'Caught by the first impression' EA Smith Queen's Trial p.7.

Bibliography

Manuscripts by Thomas Ashe

'The Claustral Palace or Memoirs of the Family' The National Archives TS 17/1388
'The Patriot Princess or Political Monitor' National Library of Scotland MS 5751
Thomas Ashe, army officer and writer: copy letters to agents of Viscount Perceval and one original letter to Perceval 1813-4 Bodleian Library MS.Eng.c.7284
Royal Archives GEO Add 11/213, 214 and 215 Printed pre-notice, handwritten 'Programma' and title page and chapter headings of *The Claustral Palace* novel circulated to Princess Elizabeth
Home Office petition 1835 TNA HO 17/18/74
Applications to the (Royal) Literary Fund 1807-1820 British Library MS Loan 96 RLF 1/206

Manuscript sources about Thomas Ashe

Treasury solicitors papers TNA TS 11
Home Office legal papers Claustral Palace TNA HO 48/15 Osphia TNA HO 48/28
Southampton University Wellington papers 1829-30
Honyford Yate letters to the Countess of Berkeley and her agents 1813-1814 about the manuscript of Thomas Ashe's 'The Perjured Peeress' (Farrahar/Dupre website http://www.farahardupre.co.uk 1 April 2008 stock number 51159)
Letters of Jonathan Ashe relating to the chaplaincy of the King's Military Infirmary, Ireland c.1815 (Bloomsbury Auctions 12 May 2011 lot 155)

Printed Books

Anon *Royal Correspondence or letters between her late Royal Highness Princess Charlotte and her royal mother Queen Caroline of England* (London 1822)
T. Ashe
Memoirs of Mammoth, 1808

Bibliography

Travels in America, 1808

The Spirit of the Book, 1811

Memoirs and Confessions of Captain Ashe. London: Henry Colburn, 1815

The Charms of Dandyism or Living in Style by Olivia Moreland, 1819

The Manx Sketch Book, 1825.

A. Aspinall *The later correspondence of George III* (1962-70)

A. Aspinall *The Correspondence of George, Prince of Wales* 1770-1812 (1963-71)

A. Aspinall *Letters of George IV 1812-1830* (1938)

A. Aspinall *Letters of the Princess Charlotte 1811-1817* (1949)

A. Aspinall *Politics and the Press* (1949)

Bell, Captain *Henry Colloquia Mensalia; or, the Familiar Discourses of Dr. Martin Luther At His Table* (1791)

Francis Bickley *The Diaries of Sylvester Douglas, Lord Glenbervie*

Lesley Blanch *Harriette Wilson's Memoirs: The Greatest Courtesan of her Age* (John Murray 1957)

Catherine Curzon *The Daughters of George III: Sisters and Princesses* (Pen & Sword 2020)

Flora Fraser *Princesses* (Bloomsbury 2004)

Flora Fraser *Unruly Queen* (Knopf 1996)

M. Dorothy George *Catalogue of Political and Personal Satires in the British Museum, IX* (1949)

Denis Gray *Spencer Perceval: The Evangelical Prime Minister* (Manchester University Press 1963)

Janice Hadlow *The Strangest Family* (William Collins 2014)

Olwen Hedley *Queen Charlotte* (John Murray 1975)

Christopher Hibbert *George IV* (1976)

Historical Manuscripts Commission Bathurst Papers (HMSO 1923)

Thea Holme *Prinny's Daughter: A Life of Princess Charlotte of Wales* (London 1976)

Robert Huish *Memoirs of Caroline, Queen Consort of England* (London 1821)

Richard Ingrams *The Life and Adventures of William Cobbett* (Harper Collins 2005)

Edward Law, Earl of Ellenborough *Political Diary 1828-1830* ed. Lord Colchester (London 1881)

Andro Linklater *Why Spencer Perceval Had to Die* (A&C Black 2012)

Iain McCalman *Radical Underworld: Prophets, Revolutionaries and Pornographers in London 1795-1840* (Cambridge University Press 1988)

J. J. McGann (ed.) *Lord Byron: the complete poetical works*, 7 vols. (1980–93)

Patrick Medd Romilly: *A Life of Samuel Romilly, Lawyer and Reformer* (Collins, London 1968)

Thomas Moore (ed.) *Letters and journals of Lord Byron, with notices of his life* (1830)

Andrew Nicholson *The Letters of John Murray to Lord Byron* (Liverpool University Press 2007)

Joseph Nightingale *Memoirs Public and Private of Queen Caroline* (1820)

Joseph Nightingale *Memoirs of her late Majesty Queen Caroline* (1821-2)

Joseph Nightingale *Last Days of Queen Caroline* (1822)

Alison Plowden. *Caroline & Charlotte: the Regent's wife and daughter, 1795-1821* (London 1989).

Rowland Prothero *The Letters and Works of Lord Byron* (1898-1904)

Jane Robins *Rebel Queen, The Trial of Caroline* (Simon & Schuster 2006)

Olivia Serres *Memoirs of a Princess or First Love* (London 1812)

E A Smith *The Queen on Trial: The Affair of Queen Caroline* (Sutton Publishing 1993)

Dorothy Margaret Stuart *The Daughters of George III* (2017)

Stella Tillyard *Citizen Lord: Lord Edward Fitzgerald 1763-1798* (Chatto & Windus 1997)

John Wardroper *King's Lords and Wicked Libelers: Satire and Protest 1760-1837* (John Murray 1973)

John Wardroper *Wicked Ernest* (Shelfmark 2002)

Ben Wilson *The Laughter of Triumph: William Hone and the Fight for the Free Press* (Faber 2005)

Frances Wilson *The Courtesan's Revenge: Harriette Wilson the Woman who Blackmailed the King* (Faber 2003)

W. Wordsworth and S T Coleridge *Lyrical Ballads* ed. Derek Roper (Northcote House 1987)

Index